LAW OF THE LAND, LAWS OF THE BIBLE

The Law of the Land, Laws of The Bible

AND THEIR MODERN APPLICATION

WORLD WIDE RULED

CIVIL, CRIMINAL, DIVINE LAW IN "THE UNITED STATES OF AMERICA"

LAW OF THE LAND, LAWS OF THE BIBLE

KEVIN EARL JAMES JUNIOR

VOLUME TWO M2024

For You, My Brother and Sister, The Student

Here are the Laws, Statutes, and Commandments of our Father who art in heaven, God the Lord, the Father, The Most High of Israel and his son, the first begotten of the dead, Jesus the Christ, our Savior. It is much more than just the Ten Commandments. Although the Laws were written in us, the genocide against us brethren have most with a "cold heart" and premature "judgment", manifesting Sin. God has turned his back on us because we have turned our backs from THE LAW. There is an adversarial system against us to usurp the Land and the identities of the homeborn brethren of God, us being his holy people. It is up to the men who have been beheaded, wrongly imprisoned, left for dead, and/or removed from the household to restore the Kingdom of the Lord. No longer will we live in Civiliter Mortuus and no longer will we adhere to the sun worship but the true Sabbath day, "Saturday", as we all know it to be. There are many ways we have all failed God, but let this book of God's Laws and the Law of the Land be implanted once again so that we are forgiven. Know thyself first. Then the rest is "HIStory". God bless you and may the elusive Truth be with you.

-Kevin Earl James Junior

"A great scholar once said, "If a man-made law cannot be traced to a divine source, then not only should its effectiveness be questioned but, even more, its intent should be suspected."

The Divine Law, as revealed to Moses and taught by Christ, must be discerned spiritually and put into practice in our daily life. Wise decisions, based on obedience to the laws of the Bible - so abundant in mercy and justice, bring about the constant harmony and peace which can be ours." -Great Master Edition

"Let us pray, because we definitely have sinned." – Tupac Shakur

TABLE OF CONTENTS
TITLE PAGE...................................... 1
For You, My Brother and Sister, The Student... 3

Welcome to Volume Two

INTRODUCTION 6
CRIMINAL LAW 7
THE LAWS OF PROPERTY 33
LAWS OF INHERITANCE.................... 62
CONTRACTS 68
LAWS OF FAMILY LIFE 83
KINDS AND POWERS OF GOVERNMENTS 102
TAX LAWS 116
MILITARY LAWS 132
COURT PROCEDURE 145
LAWS OF CITIZENSHIP 162
RELIGIOUS LAWS 174
TEN COMMANDMENTS – Exodus 20:1-17 The Ten Commandments 259
SOCIAL SECURITY LAWS 274
LABOR LAWS 309
HUMANE LAWS 321
TORTS 356

Welcome to Volume Two.

In this Volume, I will be laying out the methods of prosecution and the "CODES" behind the CANON LAW today. You will finally differentiate MATTER OF RIGHT and MATTER OF FACT. The FACTS are that THE UNITED STATES OF AMERICA, the LAND, belongs to God. The Most High God of Israel, The Father, God who formed ADAM from the DUST and breathed life into his nostrils. I will reference the U.S., Federal, and specific State codes and summarize to my capability. Unfortunately, there are rules against publishing books, documents with government information but nothing says I can't reference them. I encourage you to research YOUR local, municipal laws, as this book wouldn't fit anywhere if I was to reference every jurisdiction.

CRIMINAL LAW

ADULTERY - *Exodus 20:14*- 14 Thou shalt not commit adultery.

Deuteronomy 22:22-25- 22 If a man be found lying with a woman married to a husband, then they shall both of them die, *both* the man that lay with the woman, and the woman: so shalt thou put away evil from Israel.

23 If a damsel *that is* a virgin be betrothed unto a husband, and a man find her in the city, and lie with her; 24 then ye shall bring them both out unto the gate of that city, and ye shall stone them with stones that they die; the damsel, because she cried not, *being* in the city; and the man, because he hath humbled his neighbor's wife: so, thou shalt put away evil from among you.

25 But if a man find a betrothed damsel in the field, and the man force her, and lie with her; then the man only that lay with her shall die: **26** but unto the damsel thou shalt do nothing; *there is* in the damsel no sin *worthy* of death: for as when a man riseth against his neighbor, and slayeth him, even so *is* this matter: **27** for he found her in the field, *and* the betrothed damsel cried, and *there was* none to save her.

CRIMINAL LAW: NCJ Number 136579 by *MJ Siegel* **"JOURNAL OF FAMILY LAW"** Abstract - "ADULTERY is a crime in MOST of the United States and occurs in MOST American marriages." The author stated that laws banning extramarital sex are NOT enforced and citizens do not consider themselves CRIMINALS for committing ADULTERY. Adulterers are protected through a Supreme Court decision to privatize part of the CRIMINAL LAW. As you'll see below, there's not much to prosecute in the code system. Marital infidelity is more of a financial issue in America handled in court, not a criminal case. California won't penalize you for it, just look for yourself.

CRM 1948. MARRIAGE FRAUD

8 U.S.C. §1325 (C) AND U.S.C. §1546

California Civil Code Division 1, Part 2 §43.5 (d)

ARSON - *Exodus 22:6* - *If* fire break out, and catch in thorns, so that the stacks of corn, or the standing corn, or the field, be consumed *therewith;* he that kindled the fire shall surely make restitution.

CRIMINAL LAW: The meaning of ARSON changes depending on JURISDICTION. There are differences in the charges of ARSON at STATE and FEDERAL level. **Title 18 Chapter 5 § 81 U.S. Code** designates ARSON within special MARITIME and TERRITORIAL JURISDICTION of the United States. The severity of charges and the nature of the charge is SPECULATIVE. However, the Model Penal Code labels ARSON as this in their explanatory note for **§220.1-220.3** "the principal reason for the severe punishment historically associated with this offense is the attendant risk to human life." "Although Section 220.1 reserves felony sanctions to conduct productive of that risk. Setting fire to personal property under circumstances not likely to endanger human life is relegated to the offense of criminal mischief." (Model Penal Code in quotations)

BRIBERY – *Exodus 23:8* - And thou shalt take no gift: for the gift blindeth the wise, and perverteth the words of the righteous.

Deuteronomy 16:19 - *Thou* shalt not wrest judgment; thou shalt not respect persons, neither take a gift: for a gift doth blind the eyes of the wise, and pervert the words of the righteous.

2 Chronicles 19:7 - *Wherefore* now let the fear of the LORD be upon you; take heed and do it: for *there* is no iniquity with the LORD OUR GOD, nor respect of persons, nor taking of gifts.

Job 15:34 - *For* the congregation of hypocrites *shall* be desolate, and fire shall consume the tabernacles of bribery.

Amos 5:12- For I know your manifold transgressions and your mighty sins: they afflict the just, they take a bribe, and they turn aside the poor in the gate *from their right.*

CRIMINAL LAW: BRIBERY in CIVIL LAW referencing **M.P.C. § 224.8 Commercial Bribery and Breach of Duty to Act Disinterestedly**, would be considered a MISDEMEANOR to accept any gift, money, or position having a duty of FIDELITY, to rig a contest or sport of any sort, and one who accepts remuneration.

18 U.S.C. §201, 211, 217 are in regard to ALL Government officials or employees, and charges come with fine and no more than 1 year's imprisonment and 2 years for **§ 201 Bribery of public officials and witnesses. §224 Bribery affecting sporting goods** carries up to 5 years imprisonment and **§226 Bribery affecting port security** up to 15 years due to the threat of domestic terrorism. **California Penal Code Title 15, §641** and **641.3(a)** state that commercial bribery is punishable by imprisonment in the county jail for not more than 1 year if the bribe is under 1,000 dollars, 16 months in state PRISON if bribe is over 1,000 dollars.

DEFIANCE OF AUTHORITY *Numbers 15:30,* 31 - 30 But the soul that doeth *ought* presumptuously, *whether he be* born in the land, or a stranger, the same reproacheth the LORD; and that soul shall be cut off from among his people. 31 Because he hath despised the word of the LORD, and hath broken his commandment, that soul shall utterly be cut off; his iniquity *shall* be upon him.

Deuteronomy 17:12, 13 - *And* the man that will do presumptuously, and will not hearken unto the priest that standeth to minister there before the LORD thy GOD, or unto the judge, even that man shall die: and thou shalt put away the evil from Israel. **13** And all the people shall hear, and fear, and do no more presumptuously.

CRIMINAL LAW: A person charged with DEFIANCE OF AUTHORITY would be considered an OUTLAW, or someone who FAILS TO APPEAR in courts or one who EVADES or RESISTS arrest. **Title 18 U.S. Code § 111 Assaulting, RESISTING, or IMPEDING certain officers or employees**

DID YOU KNOW: There's a COMMON LAW right to resist an UNLAWFUL ARREST? Reexamination of this right has been ongoing for more than 25 years with the impetus of this reappraisal being provided by **Uniform Arrest Act §5**. But don't go doing that without proper evidence for your cause.

CIVIL CODES referencing DEFIANCE OF AUTHORITY: **Title 18 U.S. Code § 1071** Concealing Person from Arrest **Title 18 U.S. Code Chapter 73** Obstruction of Justice **Title 18 § 1073** Flight to avoid prosecution or giving testimony.

According to **25 Code of Federal Regulations (C.F.R.) §11.434**, a RESISTING ARREST charge is only a misdemeanor, even if the pursuant harms them or anyone else.

EVADING Police is a STATE level charge, severity of charge depending on your jurisdiction and the offense occurring within that pursuit.

FRAUD - *Leviticus 6:1-5* - 1 And the LORD spake unto Moses, saying, 2 If a soul sin, and commit a trespass against the LORD, and lie unto his neighbour in that which was delivered him to keep, or in fellowship, or in a thing taken away by violence, or hath deceived his neighbour; 3 Or have found that which was lost, and lieth concerning it, and sweareth falsely; in any of all these that a man doeth, sinning therein: 4 Then it shall be, because he hath sinned, and is guilty, that he shall restore that which he took violently away, or the thing which he hath deceitfully gotten, or that which was delivered him to keep, or the lost thing which he found, 5 Or all that about which he hath sworn falsely; he shall even restore it in the principal, and shall add the fifth part more thereto, and give it unto him to whom it appertaineth, in the day of his trespass offering. *Deuteronomy 25:13-16* - 13 Thou shalt not have in thy bag divers weights, a great and a small. 14 Thou shalt not have in thine house divers measures, a great and a small. 15 *But* thou shalt have a perfect and just weight, a perfect and just measure shalt thou have: that thy days may be lengthened in the land which the LORD thy GOD giveth thee. 16 For all that do such things, *and* all that do unrighteously, *are* an abomination unto the LORD thy GOD.

CRIMINAL LAW: Title 18 U.S. Code Chapter 47 FRAUD mainly protects the United States and its 'interests' more than an individual who had been the victim of some form of a fraudulent transaction. Judgment for fraudulent activities and/or actions result in biblical "like" action such as double the repayment of dispersed funds to business, entity, or person. **California Penal Code Part 1, Title 7, Chapter 10.5 Fraud and Embezzlement: Victim Restitution § 186.11(a)(1)** is an example of how the STATE would protect the individual, synonymous to the United States protecting commerce, in respect to their interests.

CIVIL CODES IN 18 U.S.C. WORTH MENTIONING:
§1021 Title Records §1025 False pretenses on high seas and other waters §1028 Fraud and related activity in connection with identification documents, authentication features and information §1029 Fraud and related activity in connection with access devices §1030 Fraud and related activity in connection with computers §Major Fraud Against the United States §1038 False Information and hoaxes §1039 Fraud and related activity in connection with obtaining confidential phone records information of a covered entity §1040 Fraud in connection with major disaster or emergency benefits - IN OTHER WORDS, stay out of debt and resist the temptation to keep up with the times of Saturn.

INCEST - *Leviticus 20:11-21* - 11 And the man that lieth with his father's wife hath uncovered his father's nakedness: both of them shall surely be put to death; their blood shall be upon them. 12 And if a man lie with his daughter in law, both of them shall surely be put to death: they have wrought confusion; their blood *shall* be upon them. 13 If a man also lie with mankind, as he lieth with a woman, both of them have committed an abomination: they shall surely be put to death; their blood *shall* be upon them. 14 And if a man take a wife and her mother, it is wickedness: they shall be burnt with fire, both he and they; that there be no wickedness among you. 15 And if a man lie with a beast, he shall surely be put to death: and ye shall slay the beast. 16 And if a woman approach unto any beast, and lie down thereto, thou shalt kill the woman, and the beast: they shall surely be put to death; their blood *shall* be upon them. **17** And if a man shall take his sister, his father's daughter, or his mother's daughter, and see her nakedness, and she see his nakedness; it *is* a wicked thing; and they shall be cut off in the sight of their people: he hath uncovered his sister's nakedness; he shall bear his iniquity. **18** And if a man shall lie with a woman having her sickness. And shall uncover her nakedness; he hath discovered her fountain, and she hath uncovered the fountain of her blood: and both of them shall be cut off from among their people. **19** And thou shalt not uncover the nakedness of thy mother's sister, nor of thy father's sister: for he uncovereth his near kin: they shall bear their iniquity. **20** And if a man shall lie with his uncle's wife, he hath covered his uncle's nakedness: they shall bear their sin; they shall die childless. **21** And if a man shall take his brother's wife, it is an unclean thing: he hath uncovered his brother's nakedness; they shall be childless.

CRIMINAL LAW - Laws regarding INCEST differ depending on jurisdiction, age range of the parties involved, and nature of family relationship. When INCEST involves an adult and child, it is a form of child sexual abuse and/or a possible WILLFUL TORT SUIT. The charge in the eyes of the law is called "SEXUAL RELATIONS BETWEEN FAMILY MEMBERS WHO ARE NOT SPOUSES". INCEST is often charged as a FELONY, punishable from five years to life imprisonment, the people involved are separated, a child of a parent convicted of INCEST may be taken away and placed in foster care. If there is a sex crime, the offender must register as a lifetime sex offender. The **New York Penal Law, Article 130**, demonstrates how the state specifies charges within its jurisdiction.

KIDNAPPING - *Exodus 21:16* - And he that stealeth a man, and selleth him, or if found in his hand, he shall surely be put to death.

Deuteronomy 24:7 - If a man be found stealing any of his brethren of the children of Israel, and maketh merchandise of him, or selleth him; then that thief shall die; and thou shalt put evil away from among you.

In **CRIMINAL LAW**, the United States Sentencing Commission has guidelines which govern kidnapping offenses. Referencing **Title 18 U.S. Code §1201**, if the abductee is returned in a certain amount of time (24 hours), it becomes a REBUTTABLE PRESUMPTION that such person has been transported in INTERSTATE or FOREIGN COMMERCE, making the abductor's sentence up to 20 years, same sentence as abducting/kidnapping a child. The **New York Penal Law, Article 135**, gives the abductor 12 HOURS until it becomes a FIRST-DEGREE charge. The New York Penal Law recognizes TRAFFICKING inside of the KIDNAPPING charge as well, with up to 12 charges total under kidnapping. The STATES are less strict on their sentencing guidelines making the abduction of children up to 11 years. In **California Penal Code**[1] **Part 1, Title 8, Chapter 3 § 209 (a)(b)** and **209.5(a)** shows that California isn't protecting abductors with life imprisonment WITH the possibility of parole. The United States will assume jurisdiction over its employees, officers, representatives, agents, if one is a victim

---

[1] I reference the California Penal Code and New York Penal Law because California and New York have the largest number of citizens in each state. In this document, these will not be the only State laws and codes mentioned.

of such charge but again, our Father, who is in heaven, made the LAW PERFECT and there to protect YOU.

REMOVAL OF LANDMARKS - *Deuteronomy 19:14* - *Thou* shalt not remove thy neighbor's landmark, which they of old time have set in thine inheritance, which thou shalt inherit in the land that the LORD thy GOD giveth thee to possess it.

CIVIL CODE: Let us go over the CIVIL CODES in regard to REMOVAL OF LANDMARKS. There are no formal charges under the name REMOVAL OF LANDMARKS federally but we have **Title 18, Chapter 65, MALICIOUS MISCHIEF and §1361 DESTRUCTION OF GOVERNMENT PROPERTY.** At STATE level, the charges usually are in the form of CRIMINAL MISCHIEF. **Model Penal Code (M.P.C.) §220.2 Causing or Risking Catastrophe §220.3** Criminal Mischief **New York Penal Law Article 145** Criminal Mischief & Related Offenses **California Penal Code Title 13 CRIMES AGAINST PROPERTY, Title 14 MALICIOUS MISCHIEF, Title 15** MISCELLANEOUS CRIMES, §640(d)(2), §640.5 (a)(1), §640.6. Depending on the intention of the criminal (destruction, death, utter removal), one of the charges listed above, or similar depending on your jurisdiction, will be used against the perpetrator.

MANSLAUGHTER – *Exodus 21:12-14* - **12** He that smiteth a man, so that he die, shall be surely put to death, **13** And if a man lie not in wait, but God deliver him into his hand; then I will appoint thee a place whither he shall flee. **14** But if a man come presumptuously upon his neighbor, to slay him with guile; thou shalt take him from mine altar, that he may die.

Numbers 35:6-34 - **6** And among the cities which ye shall give unto the Levites *there shall be* six cities for refuge, which ye shall appoint for the manslayer, that he may flee thither: and to them ye shall add forty and two cities. **7** *So* all the cities which ye shall give to the Levites *shall be* forty and eight cities: them *shall ye give* with their suburbs. **8** And the cities which ye shall give *shall be* of the possession of the children of Israel: from *them that have* many ye shall give many; but from *them that have* few ye shall give few: every one shall give of his cities unto the Levites according to his inheritance which he inheriteth.

The Cities of Refuge

(Deuteronomy 19.1-13)

9 And the Lord spake unto Moses, saying, **10** Speak unto the children of Israel, and say unto them, When ye be come over Jordan into the land of Canaan, **11** then ye shall appoint you cities to be cities of refuge for you, that the slayer may flee thither, which killeth any person at unawares. **12** And they shall be unto you cities for refuge from the avenger; that the manslayer die not, until he stand before the congregation in judgment. **13** And of these cities which ye shall give, six cities shall ye have for refuge. **14** Ye shall give three cities on this side Jordan, and three cities shall ye give in the land of Canaan, *which* shall be cities of refuge. **15** These six cities shall be a refuge, *both* for the children of Israel, and for the stranger, and for the sojourner among them; that every one that killeth any person unawares may flee thither.

16 And if he smite him with an instrument of iron, so that he die, he *is* a murderer: the murderer shall surely be put to death. **17** And if he smite him with throwing a stone, wherewith he may die, and he die, he *is* a murderer: the murderer shall surely be put to death. **18** Or *if* he smite him with a hand weapon of wood, wherewith he may die, and he die, he *is* a murderer: the murderer shall surely be put to death. **19** The revenger of blood himself shall slay the murderer: when he meeteth him, he shall slay him. **20** But if he thrust him of hatred, or hurl at him by laying of wait, that he die; **21** or in enmity smite him with his hand, that he die: he that smote *him* shall surely be put to death; *for* he *is* a murderer: the revenger of blood shall slay the murderer, when he meeteth him.

22 But if he thrust him suddenly without enmity, or have cast upon him any thing without laying of wait, **23** or with any stone, wherewith a man may die, seeing *him* not, and cast *it* upon him, that he die, and *was* not his enemy, neither sought his harm: **24** then the congregation shall judge between the slayer and the revenger of blood according to these judgments: **25** and the congregation shall deliver the slayer out of the hand of the revenger of blood, and the congregation shall restore him to the city of his refuge, whither he was fled: and he shall abide in it unto the death of the high priest, which was anointed with the holy oil. **26** But if the slayer shall at any time come without the border of the city of his refuge, whither he was fled; **27** and the revenger of blood find him without the borders of the city of his refuge, and the revenger of blood kill the slayer; he shall not be guilty of blood: **28** because he should have remained in the city of his refuge until the death of the high priest: but after the death of the high priest the slayer shall return into the land of his possession.

The Law concerning Bloodshed

29 So these *things* shall be for a statute of judgment unto you throughout your generations in all your dwellings. **30** Whoso killeth any person, the murderer shall be put to death by the mouth of witnesses: but one witness shall not testify against any person *to cause him* to die. **31** Moreover ye shall take no satisfaction for the life of a murderer, which *is* guilty of death: but he shall be surely put to death. **32** And ye shall take no satisfaction for him that is fled to the city of his refuge, that he should come again to dwell in the land, until the death of the priest. **33** So ye shall not pollute the land wherein ye *are*: for blood it defileth the land: and the land cannot be cleansed of the blood that is shed therein, but by the blood of him that shed it. **34** Defile not therefore the land which ye shall inhabit, wherein I dwell: for I the Lord dwell among the children of Israel.

Joshua 20:4-6 - **4** And when he that doth flee unto one of those cities shall stand at the entering of the gate of the city, and shall declare his cause in the ears of the elders of that city, they shall take him into the city unto them, and give him a place, that he may dwell among them. **5** And if the avenger of blood pursue after him, then they shall not deliver the slayer up into his hand; because he smote his neighbour unwittingly, and hated him not beforetime. **6** And he shall dwell in that city, until he stand before the congregation for judgment, *and* until the death of the high priest that shall be in those days: then shall the slayer return, and come his own city, and unto his own house, unto the city from whence he fled.

CRIMINAL LAW: According to **M.P.C. §210.1**, CRIMINAL HOMICIDE is murder, MANSLAUGHTER or negligent homicide. **§210.3** defines of

MANSLAUGHTER to include both reckless homicide and homicide that would otherwise be murder but for the presence of "extreme emotional disturbance for which there is a reasonable explanation or excuse." **New York Penal Law, Article 125,** categorizes MANSLAUGHTER into the following groups: VEHICULAR MANSLAUGHTER 1 & 2, 1 being the more serious charge, MANSLAUGHTER 1 & 2, again MANSLAUGHTER 1 being the greater charge, AGGRAVATED MANSLAUGHTER 1 & 2, both serious offenses. **Texas Penal Code, Title 5, Chapter 19, §19.04** summarizes a MANSLAUGHTER charge into two sentences, simply saying if a person recklessly causes the death of an individual, it is a felony of the 2nd degree. **California Penal Code, Part 1, Title 8, Chapter 1, § §191.5, 192, 192.5, 193, 193.5, 193.7, and 194** covers all bases of MANSLAUGHTER, not clearly defined prima facie in its own chapter but inside of the Chapter of Homicide. In **Title 18, U.S. Code, Chapter 51, §1113,** an ATTEMPTED MANSLAUGHTER charge will land a criminal in prison for no more than seven years.

MURDER – *Genesis 9:5, 6* - 5 And surely your blood of your lives will I require; at the hand of man; at the hand of every man's brother will I require the life of man. 6 Who so sheddeth man's blood, by man shall his blood be shed: for in the image of God made he man.

Exodus 20:13, 21:12-14 - Thou shalt not kill. (*21:12-14*) 12 He that smiteth a man, so that he die, shall be surely put to death. 13 And if a man lie not in wait, but God deliver *him* into his hand; then I will appoint thee a place whither he shall flee. 14 But if a man come presumptuously upon his neighbor, to slay him with guile; thou shalt take him from mine altar, that he may die.

Numbers 35:6-34 - **6** And among the cities which ye shall give unto the Levites *there shall be* six cities for refuge, which ye shall appoint for the manslayer, that he may flee thither: and to them ye shall add forty and two c cities. **7** *So* all the cities which ye shall give to the Levites *shall be* forty and eight cities: them *shall ye give* with their suburbs. **8** And the cities which ye shall give *shall be* of the possession of the children of Israel: from *them that have* many ye shall give many; but from *them that have* few ye shall give few: every one shall give of his cities unto the Levites according to his inheritance which he inheriteth.

The Cities of Refuge

(Deuteronomy 19.1-13)

9 And the Lord spake unto Moses, saying, **10** Speak unto the children of Israel, and say unto them, When ye be come over Jordan into the land of Canaan, **11** then ye shall appoint you cities to be cities of refuge for you, that the slayer may flee thither, which killeth any person at unawares. **12** And they shall be unto you cities for refuge from the avenger; that the manslayer die not, until he stand before the congregation in judgment. **13** And of these cities which ye shall give, six cities shall ye have for refuge. **14** Ye shall give three cities on this side Jordan, and three cities shall ye give in the land of Canaan, *which* shall be cities of refuge. **15** These six cities shall be a refuge, *both* for the children of Israel, and for the stranger, and for the sojourner among them; that every one that killeth any person unawares may flee thither.

16 And if he smite him with an instrument of iron, so that he die, he *is* a murderer: the murderer shall surely be put to death. **17** And if he smite him with throwing a stone, wherewith he may die, and he die, he *is* a murderer: the murderer shall surely be put to death. **18** Or *if* he smite him with a hand weapon of wood, wherewith he may die, and he die, he *is* a murderer: the murderer shall surely be put to death. **19** The revenger of blood himself shall slay the murderer: when he meeteth him, he shall slay him. **20** But if he thrust him of hatred, or hurl at him by laying of wait, that he die; **21** or in enmity smite him with his hand, that he die: he that smote *him* shall surely be put to death; *for* he *is* a murderer: the revenger of blood shall slay the murderer, when he meeteth him.

22 But if he thrust him suddenly without enmity, or have cast upon him any thing without laying of wait, **23** or with any stone, wherewith a man may die, seeing *him* not, and cast *it* upon him, that he die, and *was* not his enemy, neither sought his harm: **24** then the congregation shall judge between the slayer and the revenger of blood according to these judgments: **25** and the congregation shall deliver the slayer out of the hand of the revenger of blood, and the congregation shall restore him to the city of his refuge, whither he was fled: and he shall abide in it unto the death of the high priest, which was anointed with the holy oil. **26** But if the slayer shall at any time come without the border of the city of his refuge, whither he was fled; **27** and the revenger of blood find him without the borders of the city of his refuge, and the revenger of blood kill the slayer; he shall not be guilty of blood: **28** because he should have remained in the city of his refuge until the death of the high priest: but after the death of the high priest the slayer shall return into the land of his possession.

The Law concerning Bloodshed

29 So these *things* shall be for a statute of judgment unto you throughout your generations in all your dwellings. **30** Whoso killeth any person, the murderer shall be put to death by the mouth of witnesses: but one witness shall not testify against any person *to cause him* to die. **31** Moreover ye shall take no satisfaction for the life of a murderer, which *is* guilty of death: but he shall be surely put to death. **32** And ye shall take no satisfaction for him that is fled to the city of his refuge, that he should come again to dwell in the land, until the death of the priest. **33** So ye shall not pollute the land wherein ye *are*: for blood it defileth the land: and the land cannot be cleansed of the blood that is shed therein, but by the blood of him that shed it. **34** Defile not therefore the land which ye shall inhabit, wherein I dwell: for I the Lord dwell among the children of Israel.

CRIMINAL LAW: Title 18, U.S. Code, Chapter 51, HOMICIDE § 1111 (18 U.S.C. §1111), makes MURDER of all kind a life sentence, a true CIVIL death. An ATTEMPTED MURDER will place you in prison up to 20 years, under **U.S. Code.**

§1117 Conspiracy to murder under U.S. Code states person(s) can go to prison for any amount of time had they done any overt act to affect the object of the conspiracy.

However, the **M.P.C. §210.2(2)** states that MURDER is a felony of the 1st degree, but a person may be sentenced to DEATH, as provided in **§210.6** of the M.P.C., which is a more BIBLICAL approach to MURDER. Not all systems work the same, using **Texas Penal Code** as an example. The **Texas Penal Code, §12.32** groups the offense of MURDER in with any other 1st degree felony charge. Which doesn't truly give the offender the proper punishment. It's similar to due process in codes.

PERJURY – *Exodus 20:16* - Thou shalt not bear false witness against thy neighbour.

Leviticus 19:12 - And ye shall not swear by my name falsely, neither shalt thou profane the name of thy God: I *am* the LORD.

Deuteronomy 19:16-20 - **16** If a false witness rise up against any man to testify against him *that which* is wrong; **17** Then both the men, between whom the controversy is, shall stand before the LORD, before the priests and the judges, which shall be in those days; **18** And the judges shall make diligent inquisition: and , behold, if the witness be a false witness, *and* hath testified falsely against his brother; **19** Then shall ye do unto him, as he had thought to have done unto his brother: so shalt thou put the evil away from among you. **20** And those which remain shall hear, and fear, and shall henceforth commit no more any such evil among you.

CIVIL CODE: In Title 18 U.S. Code, Chapter 79 PERJURY §1621, §1623 the perpetrator is given a maximum of five years, for procuring false statements under oath before and/or ancillary to a court proceeding. Also, an important note from **28 U.S. Code, Chapter 116, §1746**, ALL rules, orders, regulations, or requirements have to be proved by a sworn declaration under PENALTY OF PERJURY.

I will use the M.P.C. as a broadened, lengthened example of the framework of a perjurious charge. **M.P.C. Part II, Article 241, §241.1(1)** A person is guilty of perjury, **a felony of the**

3rd **degree,** if in any official proceeding, he makes a false statement under the oath or equivalent affirmation, or SWEARS or affirms the truth of a statement previously made, when the statement is material and he does not believe it to be true. Retraction of a statement made in the course of an official proceeding is also an offense.

PERVERTING JUSTICE – *Exodus 23:1,2,6,7* - 1 Thou shalt not raise a false report: put not thine hand with the wicked to be an unrighteous witness. 2 Thou shalt not follow a multitude to *do* evil; neither shalt thou speak in a cause (case) to decline after many to wrest *judgment.* 6 Thou shalt not wrest the judgment of thy poor in his cause (case). 7 Keep thee far from a false matter; and the innocent and righteous slay thou not: for I will not justify the wicked.

Deuteronomy 16:19, 20 - 19 Thou shalt not wrest judgment; thou shalt not respect persons, neither take a gift: for a gift doth blind the eyes of the wise, and pervert the words of the righteous. 20 That which is altogether just shalt thou follow, that thou mayest live, and inherit the land which the LORD thy God giveth thee.

CIVIL CODE: Named similarly to the charge in England and Wales, or COMMON LAW jurisdictions (where our law derives from), **PERVERTING THE COURSE OF JUSTICE** is an offense committed when a person prevents justice from being brought upon themselves or another. In the U.S. we'd call it OBSTRUCTION OF JUSTICE, which is an umbrella term for various crimes like white collar, process, and public-order crimes. PERJURY would also fall under an OBSTRUCTION OF JUSTICE, so charges may be similar depending on the jurisdiction. Any "tampering" whether it be jury tampering, witness tampering, destruction of evidence, or lying, that'll be considered an obstruction.

If we were to expand on PERVERTING JUSTICE, it would be a fascinating read. The *jus commune* legal system in England and America (Great Britain), perverts the justice of God's law in its make. E.g., think about the statutes such as Praemunire, Statute of Mortmain, Statute of Merton, and Statute of Provisors created to denounce certain Clauses in the Magna Carta to benefit others.

40th CLAUSE OF THE MAGNA CARTA: To no one will we sell, to no one will we refuse or delay, right or justice.

POLYGAMY – *1 Corinthians 7:2* - Nevertheless, *to avoid* fornication, let every man have his own wife, and let every woman have her own husband.

1 Timothy 3:2 - A bishop then must be blameless, the husband of one wife, vigilant, sober, of good behaviour, given to hospitality, apt to teach;

CRIMINAL LAW: The Supreme Court in 1878 upheld the law forbidding the practice of POLYGAMY when challenged by FREEDOM OF RELIGION, after the 1862 federal law forbidding POLYGAMY. This goes against *Exodus 12:49.* Made popular by MORMONIST Joseph Smith and the Church of Jesus Christ of Latter-day Saints, when he wrote in 1831 the **Doctrine of Covenants**, this odious practice has spilled into mainstream broadcasts of worship. A case worth studying on this charge is ***Reynolds v U.S.,*** 98 U.S. 145, 164 (1878). EVERY JURISDICTION and STATE under the **Edmunds Anti-Polygamy Act** has made the practice of POLYGAMY illegal. One more important note is that BIGAMY, marrying someone else while already married, is a charge brought up in proceedings related to POLYGAMY.

PROSTITUTION – *Leviticus 21:9* - And the daughter of any priest, if she profane herself by playing the whore, she profaneth her father: she shall be burnt with fire.

Deuteronomy 23:17 - There shall be no whore of the daughters of Israel, nor a sodomite of the sons of Israel.

CRIMINAL LAW: The charge of prostitution according to **Title 18 U.S. Code, Chapter 117, § 2421(a), 2422, 2423, 2425, 2427, and 3509** comes in many forms and covers almost every base stating that, the entire business, the way that prostitution is ran, how the players locate and coerce their victims, and the payment for sexual purposes is against the law. The **California Penal Code** hides in **§647(b)(1)** what they define a prostitute as, along with no chapter or section outlining the nature of the crime in itself, while the New York Penal Law gives PROSTITUTION a section in its entirety **New York Penal Law, Article 230, §230.00.** We all know that Nevada is notorious for prostitution, but what are their laws regarding this charge? **Title 15, Nevada Code, Chapter 201, NRS 201.354** says that, "1. It is unlawful for any person to engage in prostitution or solicitation therefore, except in a LICENSED HOUSE OF PROSTITUTION." So, in some areas of our great nation, people are allowed to participate in lewd, blasphemous acts in the eyes of CIVIL LAW.

RAPE – *Deuteronomy 22:25, 26* - 25 But if a man find a betrothed damsel in the field, and the man force her, and lie with her: then the man only that lay with her shall die: **26** But unto the damsel thou shalt do nothing; *there is* in the damsel no sin *worthy* of death: for as when a man riseth against his neighbor, and slayeth him, even so is this matter:

CRIMINAL LAW: Interestingly, RAPE is covered in the U.S. Code under **10 U.S.C. ARMED FORCES §920 Art.**

120(a). RAPE used to have in 1946 have its own chapter in **18 U.S.C. Chapter 99 RAPE (NOW REPEALED by PUBLIC LAW 99-646)**, covering the special maritime and territorial jurisdiction of the United States. An offender would be sentenced to DEATH or any number of years imprisoned, up to the judge. Also, if one has CARNAL KNOWLEDGE of whether a female was under the age of 16 and chooses to make her his wife, he shall receive no more than 15 years maximum in prison. Along with a repeal, the name of the charge RAPE was changed into AGGRAVATED SEXUAL ABUSE and SEX OFFENSES with the penalties being of a lesser degree than before.

SEDUCTION – *Exodus 22:16, 17* - **16** And if a man entice a maid that is not betrothed, and lie with her, he shall surely endow her to be his wife. **17** If her father utterly refuse to give her unto him, he shall pay money according to the DOWRY OF VIRGINS.

CRIMINAL LAW: While there aren't any current civil laws criminalizing SEDUCTION in itself as a charge, in the late 20th century, men were persecuted for attempting intercourse with a woman and had no plans of marrying the woman. There is no uniform rule of law on the act of seduction, and there are states that will prosecute a man for seduction or universally, depending on the age of the targeted individual.

In the United States at one point, THE TORT OF SEDUCTION allowed a father to collect damages from a man whom seduced his daughter, ultimately slowing down the production of the family business. The TORT OF SEDUCTION has been abolished in most states due to the fear of fraudulent lawsuits and a disinterest in the general public's outlook of the matter, citing it as property interests in humans. This outlook led to the enactment of the HEART BALM statutes, abolishing causes of action for seduction, breach of promise, ALIENATION of affection, criminal conversation in most states.

SLANDER – *Leviticus 19:16* - Thou shalt not go up and down as a talebearer among thy people: neither shalt thou stand against the blood of thy neighbor: I am the LORD.

CRIMINAL LAW: SLANDER in CIVIL LAW has the power to remove immunity from jurisdiction of the courts. The term SLANDER is mainly used for **DEFAMATION**, any action or other proceeding for defamation, libel, slander, or similar claim alleging that forms of speech are false, have caused damage to reputation or emotional distress, have presented any person in a false light, or resulted in criticism, dishonor, or condemnation of any person. **(28 U.S.C., Chapter 181 FOREIGN JUDGMENTS, §4101 Definitions)** The charge of SLANDER, depending on the severity of the charge could also be a CIVIL TORT case.

SODOMY – *Leviticus 18:22, 20:13* - **18:22** Thou shalt not lie with mankind, as with womankind: it *is* abomination. **20:13** If a man also lie with mankind, as he lieth with a woman both of them have committed an abomination: they shall surely be put to death; their blood *shall* be upon them.

Deuteronomy 23:17 - There shall be no whore of the daughters of Israel, nor a sodomite of the sons of Israel.

1 Kings 14:24, 15:12, 22:46 - **14:24** And there were also sodomites in the land: *and* they did according to all the abominations of the nations which the LORD cast out before the children of Israel. **15:12** And he took away the sodomites out of the land, and removed all the idols that his fathers had made. **22:46** And the remnant of the sodomites, which remained in the days of his father Asa, he took out of the land.

2 Kings 23:7 - And he brake down the houses of the sodomites, that *were* by the house of the LORD, where the women wove hangings for the grove.

CRIMINAL LAW: A 2013 amendment to the **U.S. Code, PUBLIC LAW 113-66 (a) FORCIBLE SODOMY** - Any person subject to this chapter who engages in unnatural carnal copulation with another person of the same or opposite sex or with an animal is guilty of SODOMY. (b) Any person found guilty of SODOMY shall be punished as a COURT MARTIAL may direct. Prior to 1962, SODOMY was a FELONY in every state, punished by a lengthy term of imprisonment and hard labor. In 1962, the Model Penal Code (M.P.C.) removed CONSENSUAL SODOMY from its criminal code and replaced it with the crime to solicit for SODOMY. **Michigan Comp. Laws § 750.158** Crimes against nature or SODOMY gives an offender 15 years, repeat offenders, life, while **Idaho** has the harshest penalty, life imprisonment.

THEFT – *Exodus 20:15, 22:1-5* - 20:15 Thou shalt not steal. (*22:1-5*) 1 If a man shall steal an ox, or a sheep, and kill it, or sell it; he shall restore five oxen for an ox, and four sheep for a sheep.

2 If a thief be found breaking up, and be smitten that he die, *there shall* no blood *be shed* for him. 3 If the sun be risen upon him, *there shall be* blood *shed* for him; *for* he should make full restitution: if he have nothing, then he shall be sold for his theft. 4 If the theft be certainly found in his hand alive, whether it be ox, or ass, or sheep; he shall restore double.

5 If a man shall cause a field or vineyard to be eaten, and shall put in his beast, and shall feed in another man's field; of the best of his own field, and of the best of his own vineyard, shall he make restitution.

CRIMINAL LAW: Let's discuss **18 U.S.C. Chapter 31 – EMBEZZLEMENT AND THEFT.** We all know what happens to the child or teenager that pockets a pair of earrings. They're usually scolded by security and scared enough from booking not to do it again. Over $500 dollars it is then considered a felonious crime. Most of the sections are going over ways that one can steal blatantly or craftily from the government. Once again, what about the "mom and pop" businesses or the guy who had his bike stolen? Federally you're protected in **Title 10 § 929 Art. 129 Burglary; unlawful entry**, with the burglar being punished by COURT MARTIAL. **§ 662 Receiving stolen property within special maritime and territorial jurisdiction** restitutes NOT the victim of its stolen property. How about **18 U.S. Code Chapter 103 Robberies and burglaries involving controlled substances?** If you have CONTROLLED SUBSTANCES. Docs IDENTITY THEFT count? Yes. Title 18 U.S. Code § 1028 **Aggravated identity theft**, imprisons the perpetrator for up to two years, five years repeated offense. A few fun facts, Nebraska classifies a burglary as a Class IIA FELONY with no minimum punishment, but a maximum penalty of 20 years imprisonment. GRAND THEFT is a crime that involves the seizure of property worth more than $300, in California Penal Code **§487**, it states $950. **Florida Statutes** have a set of strict GRAND THEFT laws, landing a thief up to five years in prison.

ABOUT CRIMIMAL LAW IN THE UNITED STATES OF AMERICA: CRIMINAL LAW has been covered in this section for the **most part**, considering the charges that weren't mentioned are mostly financial encumbrances or are related to the crimes above. The excessive coding is an example of how at every chance, the "True American's" rights and general outlook of the LAW becomes shrouded in mystery as to what is right and what is wrong in the eyes of the LAW.

THE LAWS OF PROPERTY

RIGHTS OF ALIENS – *Exodus 12:49* - One law shall be to him that is homeborn, and unto the stranger that sojourneth among you.

Leviticus 24:22 - Ye shall have one manner of law, as well for the stranger, as for one of your own country: for I am the LORD your God.

CIVIL CODE: Definition of ALIENATION – A transfer of TITLE; or a legal conveyance of property to another.

THEIR RIGHTS: U.S. Constitution Amendment 14 Section 1 of 1868

DAMAGES BY OR TO ANIMALS – *Exodus 21:35, 36* - **35** And if one man's ox hurt another's that he die; then they shall sell the live ox, and divide the money of it; and the dead ox also they shall divide. **36** Or if it be known that the ox hath used to push in time past, and his owner hath not kept him in; he shall surely pay ox for ox; and the dead shall be his own.

Leviticus 24:18-21 - **18** And he that killeth a beast shall make it good; beast for beast. **19** And if a man cause a blemish in his neighbor; as he hath done, so shall it be done to him; **20** Breach for breach, eye for eye, tooth for tooth: as he hath caused a blemish in a man, so hall it be done to him *again*. **21** And he that killeth a beast, he shall restore it: and he that killeth a man, he shall be put to death.

CIVIL CODE: In the **Texas Penal Code, Title 10 HEALTH AND SAFETY OF ANIMALS, Chapter 822 REGULATION OF ANIMALS**, not only follows the FOUNDATIONAL LAW, they have in detail described the way that a person may be responsible for an animal and the detention of animals that have the potential to cause danger in their local area. The **ANIMAL DAMAGE CONTROL ACT,** created by the **U.S. Fish and Wildlife Service** in 1931, provided broad authority for investigation, demonstration, and control of MAMMALIAN PREDATORS, rodents and birds. Federally, it appears to be no immediate charges for the regulation of damages by animals or to animals. According to the **C.F.R, Title 9 ANIMALS AND ANIMAL PRODUCTS**, they'll inspect the products of the animals you plan to sell for you.

WAR BOOTY – *Numbers 31:9, 25-54* - **31:9** And the children of Israel took *all* the women of Mid´i-an captives, and their little ones, and took the spoil of all their cattle, and all their flocks, and all their goods. *25-54* **25** And the Lord spake unto Moses, saying, **26** Take the sum of the prey that was taken, *both* of man and of beast, thou, and Ele-a´zar the priest, and the chief fathers of the congregation: **27** and divide the prey into two parts; between them that took the war upon them, who went out to battle, and between all the congregation. **28** And levy a tribute unto the Lord of the men of war which went out to battle: one soul of five hundred, *both* of the persons, and of the beeves, and of the asses, and of the sheep: **29** take *it* of their half, and give *it* unto Ele-a´zar the priest, *for* a heave offering of the Lord. **30** And of the children of Israel's half, thou shalt take one portion of fifty, of the persons, of the beeves, of the asses, and of the flocks, of all manner of beasts, and give them unto the Levites, which keep the charge of the tabernacle of the Lord. **31** And Moses and Ele-a´zar the priest did as the Lord commanded Moses.

32 And the booty, *being* the rest of the prey which the men of war had caught, was six hundred thousand and seventy thousand and five thousand sheep, **33** and threescore and twelve thousand beeves, **34** and threescore and one thousand asses, **35** and thirty and two thousand persons in all, of women that had not known man by lying with him. **36** And the half, *which was* the portion of them that went out to war, was in number three hundred thousand and seven and thirty thousand and five hundred sheep: **37** and the Lord's tribute of the sheep was six hundred and threescore and fifteen. **38** And the beeves *were* thirty and six thousand; of which the Lord's tribute *was* threescore and twelve. **39** And the asses *were* thirty thousand and five hundred; of which the Lord's tribute *was* threescore and one. **40** And the persons *were* sixteen thousand; of which the Lord's tribute *was* thirty and two persons. **41** And Moses gave the tribute, *which was* the Lord's heave offering, unto Ele-a´zar the priest, as the Lord commanded Moses.

42 And of the children of Israel's half, which Moses divided from the men that warred, **43** (now the half *that pertained unto* the congregation was three hundred thousand and thirty thousand *and* seven thousand and five hundred sheep, **44** and thirty and six thousand beeves, **45** and thirty thousand asses and five hundred, **46** and sixteen thousand persons,) **47** even of the children of Israel's half, Moses took one portion of fifty, *both* of man and of beast, and gave them unto the Levites, which kept the charge of the tabernacle of the Lord; as the Lord commanded Moses.

48 And the officers which *were* over thousands of the host, the captains of thousands, and captains of hundreds, came near unto Moses: **49** and they said unto Moses, Thy servants have taken the sum of the men of war which *are* under our charge, and there lacketh not one man of us. **50** We have therefore brought an oblation for the Lord, what every man hath gotten, of jewels of gold, chains, and bracelets, rings, earrings, and tablets, to make an atonement for our souls before the Lord. **51** And Moses and Ele-a´zar the priest took the gold of them, *even* all wrought jewels. **52** And all the gold of the offering that they offered up to the Lord, of the captains of thousands, and of the captains of hundreds, was sixteen thousand seven hundred and fifty shekels. **53** (*For* the men of war had taken spoil, every man for himself.) **54** And Moses and Ele-a´zar the priest took the gold of the captains of thousands and of hundreds, and brought it into the tabernacle of the congregation, *for* a memorial for the children of Israel before the Lord.

Deuteronomy 20:13-16 - **13** and when the Lord thy God hath delivered it into thine hands, thou shalt smite every male thereof with the edge of the sword: **14** but the women, and the little ones, and the cattle, and all that is in the city, *even* all the spoil thereof, shalt thou take unto thyself; and thou shalt eat the spoil of thine enemies, which the Lord thy God hath given thee. **15** Thus shalt thou do unto all the cities *which are* very far off from thee, which *are* not of the cities of these nations. **16** But of the cities of these people, which the Lord thy God doth give thee *for* an inheritance, thou shalt save alive nothing that breatheth:

1 Samuel 30:21-25 - **21** And David came to the two hundred men, which were so faint that they could not follow David, whom they had made also to abide at the brook Besor: and they went forth to meet David, and to meet the people that *were* with him: and when David came near to the people, he saluted them. **22** Then answered all the wicked men, and *men* of Be´li-al, of those that went with David, and said, Because they went not with us, we will not give them *aught* of the spoil that we have recovered, save to every man his wife and his children, that they may lead *them* away, and depart. **23** Then said David, Ye shall not do so, my brethren, with that which the Lord hath given us, who hath preserved us, and delivered the company that came against us into our hand. **24** For who will hearken unto you in this matter? but as his part *is* that goeth down to the battle, so *shall* his part *be* that tarrieth by the stuff: they shall part alike. **25** And it was *so* from that day forward, that he made it a statute and an ordinance for Israel unto this day.

CIVIL CODE: In Title 10 U.S. Code § 2579 WAR BOOTY (b)(1) it gives the Secretary of Defense the authority to regulate all battlefield objects that doesn't blemish the conduct of combat operations or result in the mistreatment of enemy personnel. **(2)** When forces of the United States are operating in **THEATER OF OPERATIONS**, enemy material captured or found abandoned shall be turned over to appropriate United States or allied military personnel. A member of the armed forces may not take from a theater of operations as a souvenir an object formerly in the possession of the enemy. Kevin Gillespie points out that wars that involve the United States are THEATER OF WAR. Let's point out one more treasure received from enemy forces through God's Land. The Land itself and the women.

FAST FORWARD TO 2023: The U.S. left behind (gave) $7.12 billion worth of military equipment, including aircraft, air to ground munitions, military vehicles, weapons, communications equipment, and other materials, after the

US withdrawal from Afghanistan was concluded on August 30, 2021.

BORROWED PROPERTY – *Exodus 22:14* - And if a man borrow *ought* of his neighbor, and it be hurt, or die, the owner thereof *being* not with it, he shall surely make *it* good.

Nehemiah 5:11 - Restore, I pray you, to them, even this day, their lands, their vineyards, their oliveyards, and their houses, also the hundredth part of the money, and of the corn, the wine, and the oil, that ye exact of them.

CIVIL CODE: It would be correct to bring up the **HOMESTEAD ACT (1862)** as a reminder to the families inhabiting God's kingdom through ALLODIAL TITLES or ALLODIUM. You are granted a LEASE; we are prohibited from selling our land in FEE SIMPLE. The Land belongs to God and every 50 years by JUBILEE, you MUST RETURN THE LAND BACK TO ITS ORIGINAL OWNER if they come back for it. Or AB INITIO, according to Bouvier pg. 5, when a man enters upon lands or into the house of another by AUTHORITY OF LAW, and afterwards abuses that authority, he becomes a trespasser.

RIGHTS OF CITIZENS – *Exodus 12:49* - One law shall be to him that is homeborn, and unto the stranger that sojourneth among you.

Leviticus 24:22 - Ye shall have one manner of law, as well for the stranger, as for one of your own country: for I am the LORD your God.

CIVIL CODE: California Civil Code Division 2. **PROPERTY, Part 1. PROPERTY IN GENERAL Title 2**

OWNERSHIP section (§) 671 states "Any person, regardless of their citizenship status, may take, hold, and dispose of property, real or personal, within this state". In **Article 2. Conditions of Ownership §711,** it says "Conditions restraining ALIENATION, when repugnant to the interest created, ARE VOID". Californians are living in a dream world.

Let's talk about citizens. The DUE PROCESS CLAUSE is found in both the 5th and 14th Amendments to the U.S. Constitution, which "prohibit" the deprivation of "life, liberty, or property" by the federal and state governments respectively without DUE PROCESS OF LAW. *Lochner v. New York* 198 U.S. 45 (1905)

DAMAGES FOR THEFT – *Exodus 22:4, 5* - **4** If the theft be certainly found in his hand alive, whether it be ox, or ass, or sheep; he shall restore double. **5** If a man shall cause a field or vineyard to be eaten, and shall put in his beast, and shall feed in another man's field; of the best of his own field, and of the best of his own vineyard, shall he make restitution.

CIVIL CODE: Since we're here in the topic of theft, let's discuss what some of the punishments are for GRAND LARCENY THEFT, federally. A form of restitution for the victim perhaps can be that Grand Larceny theft imprisonment and fine both depend upon the value of the item stolen as well as other aggravating factors. From Federal Charges, most STATE LAWS recognize the difference between larceny theft at a misdemeanor level and larceny theft that rises to the level of a felony. The specific level at which this happens is defined by STATES. In New York Penal Code, their CLAIM OF RIGHT defense §155.15 is an affirmative defense that the property was taken in good faith, the defendant believes that they have a right to possess it.

DEEDS - *Jeremiah 32:9-14* -

9 And I bought the field of Hanameel my uncle's son, that *was* in Anathoth, and weighed him the money, *even* seventeen shekels of silver. **10** And I subscribed the evidence, and sealed it, and took witnesses, and weighed *him* the money in the balances. **11** So I took the evidence of the purchase, *both* that which was sealed *according* to the **law** and custom, and that which was open: **12** And I gave the evidence of the purchase unto Baruch the son of Neriah, the son of Maaseiah, in the sight of Hanameel mine uncle's *son,* and in the presence of the witnesses that subscribed the book of the purchase, before all the Jews that sat in the court of the prison. **13** And I charged Baruch before them saying, **14** Thus saith the LORD of hosts, the God of Israel; Take these evidences, this evidence of the purchase, both which is sealed, and this evidence which is open' and put them in an earthen vessel, that they may continue many days.

CIVIL LAW: TITLE DEEDS are considered as part of the inheritance and pass to the heir as real estate. A TENANT IN TAIL is, therefore, entitled to them; and **chancery** will, enable him to get possession of them. Only some jurisdictions seal the DEED but all attest, sign, and/or deliver it. ENFORCING DEED AT COMMON LAW: 1) It must state on its face that it is a deed, using wording like "This Deed..." or "executed as a deed". 2) It must indicate that the instrument itself conveys some privilege or thing to someone. 3) The grantor must have the legal ability to grant the thing or privilege, and the grantee must have the legal capacity to receive it. 4) It must be executed by the GRANTOR in presence of the prescribed number of witnesses, known as instrumentary witnesses (solemn form). 5) In some jurisdictions, a SEAL must be affixed to it. 6) It must be delivered to and in some jurisdictions, accepted by the grantee (acceptance). Conditions attached to the acceptance of a deed, in the back of the scroll in our case, are known as COVENANTS.

DAMAGE BY FIRE - *Exodus 22:6* - If fire break out, and catch in thorns, so that the stacks of corn, or the standing corn, or the field, be consumed *therewith;* he that kindled the fire shall surely make restitution.

COMMON LAW: If a family, business, or individual in the modern times doesn't have ACCIDENTAL DAMAGE INSURANCE to cover the damages of what was lost, then the person responsible should restore what was lost, EVEN IF THERE IS INSURANCE. If the person doesn't want to pay or take responsibility, it becomes an ARSON charge under the **CRIMINAL DAMAGE ACT of 1971**. The **CRIMINAL DAMAGE ACT of 1971** states that a person commits criminal damage if they destroy or damage property owned by a third party, and/or are RECKLESS as to whether such property would be destroyed or damaged.

PAYMENT OF INDEMNITY – *2 Kings 3:4* - And Mesha king of Moab was a sheepmaster, and rendered unto the king of Israel an hundred thousand lambs, and an hundred thousand rams, with the wool.

CIVIL PROCEDURES: A common form of INDEMNITY in connection to this document is the REPARATIONS a winning country seeks from a losing country after a war. The indemnity that GERMANY paid after WORLD WAR 1 was completed in 2010. Now in contrast, ACTS OF

INDEMNITY protect individuals who have acted illegally from being subject to penalties, applying to police officers or government officials, who are compelled to do ILLEGAL ACTS in order to carry out the duties of their job. Look at indemnity as a form of insurance without State Farm acting as a third party.

INHERITANCE – See **LAWS OF INHERITANCE**

INTEREST – *Exodus 22:25* - If thou lend money to *any* of my people *that is* poor by thee, thou shalt not be to him as an usurer, neither shalt thou lay upon him usury.

Deuteronomy 23:19, 20 - 19 Thou shalt not lend upon usury to thy brother; usury of money, usury of victuals, usury of any thing that is lent upon usury: 20 unto a stranger thou mayest lend upon usury; but unto thy brother thou shalt not lend upon usury: that the Lord thy God may bless thee in all that thou settest thine hand to in the land whither thou goest to possess it.

Nehemiah 5:11 - Restore, I pray you, to them, even this day, their lands, their vineyards, their oliveyards, and their houses, also the hundredth part of the money, and of the corn, the wine, and the oil, that ye exact of them.

CIVIL CODE: ANY BUSINESS, PERSON, INDIVIDUAL, MAN or WOMAN operating on loans, fees, interest, or the monetary gain through the desperation of another living in the makings of an inflated, debt-based system, is guilty of USURY and guilty of going against God's word. **California Constitution Article XV – USURY – Section 1** says that "The rate of interest upon the loan or forbearance of any money, goods, or things in action, or on accounts after demand, shall be 7 percent per annum but it shall be competent for the parties to any loan or forbearance of any money, goods, or things in action to **CONTRACT IN WRITING** for a rate of interest:" Then in Section 2, it waives the maximum 10 percent interest away from pawnbrokers, real estate brokers, or personal property brokers. **12 U.S. Code §86 - USURIOUS INTEREST; PENALTY FOR TAKING; LIMITATIONS** penalizes for taking more than what was deemed acceptable from **12 U.S. Code §85 - RATE OF INTEREST ON LOANS, DISCOUNTS, AND PURCHASES**, which says, "Any association may take, receive, reserve, and charge on any loan or discount made, or upon any notes, bills of exchange, or other evidences of debt, interest at the rate allowed by the **LAWS OF THE STATE, TERRITORY, OR DISTRICT** where the bank is located, or at a rate of **1 PER CENTUM** in excess of the discount rate on ninety-day commercial in effect at the Federal reserve bank in the Federal reserve district where the bank is located, whichever may be the greater, and no more, except that where by the laws of any **STATE** a different rate is limited for banks organized under State laws, the rate so limited shall be allowed for associations organized or existing in any such State under title 62 of the Revised Statutes." So, as you can see, corporations and banks have taken this to the extreme and find loopholes in the form of FEES to compensate their organizations.

CLAUSE 10 OF THE MAGNA CARTA CONSTITUTION: If one who has borrowed from the Jews any sum, great or small, die before that loan be repaid, the debt shall not bear interest while the heir is under age, of whomsoever he may hold; and if the debt fall into our hands, we will not take anything except the principal sum contained in the bond.

ALLOTMENT OF LAND – *Numbers 26:52-56* - 52 And the Lord spake unto Moses, saying, **53** Unto these the land shall be divided for an inheritance according to the number of names. **54** To many thou shalt give the more inheritance, and to few thou shalt give the less inheritance: to every one shall his inheritance be given according to those that were numbered of him. **55** Notwithstanding the land shall be divided by lot: according to the names of the tribes of their fathers they shall inherit. **56** According to the lot shall the possession thereof be divided between many and few.

CIVIL CODE: 48 U.S. Code Chp.11 – ALIEN OWNERS OF LAND §1502 Previously acquired lands; mining or incorporated village lands "This chapter shall not apply to land owned in any of the Territories of the United States by aliens, which was acquired on March 3, 1887, so long as it held by then owners, their heirs or legal representatives, nor to any alien who shall become a bona fide resident of the United States," So what happened March 3, 1887?
The **Tucker Act** (March 3, 1887, Ch. 359, 24 Stat. 505, 28 U.S.C. § 1491) is a federal statute of the United States by which the United States government has waived its sovereign immunity with respect to certain lawsuits.

The Tucker Act may be divided into the "Big" Tucker Act, which applies to claims above $10,000 and gives jurisdiction to the United States Court of Federal Claims, and the "Little" Tucker Act (28 U.S.C. § 1346), the current version of which gives concurrent jurisdiction to the Court of Federal Claims and the District Courts "for the recovery of any internal-revenue tax alleged to have been erroneously or illegally assessed or collected, or any penalty claimed to have been collected without authority or any sum alleged to have been excessive or in any manner wrongfully collected under the internal-revenue laws", and for claims below $10,000.[1]

Explicitly excluded are suits in which a claim is based on a tort by the government.

MISSOURI REVISED STATUTES, TITLE XXIX, Ch. 442.025 (1) Conveyance to SELF and others to create joint estate – Any person or persons owning real estate, or any interest therein, which he or they have power to convey, may effectively convey such -real estate by a conveyance naming himself or themselves and another person or persons, or one or more of themselves and another person or persons, as grantees, and the conveyance has the same effect as to whether it creates a joint tenancy in partnership, as if it were a conveyance from a stranger who owned the real estate to the persons named as grantees in the conveyance.

Noah Webster 1828 Dictionary Definition Time: (ALLODIAL) – Pertaining to allodium; FREEHOLD; FREE OF RENT or SERVICE; held independence of a lord paramount; OPPOSED TO FEUDAL. What's PARAMOUNT? Superior to all others; possessing the highest title or jurisdiction. You know, like the Father, God?

RELEASE OF LAND - *Leviticus 25:8-34* - 8
And thou shalt number seven sabbaths of years unto thee, seven times seven years; and the space of the seven sabbaths of years shall be unto thee forty and nine years. **9** Then shalt thou cause the trumpet of the jubilee to sound on the tenth day of the seventh month, in the day of atonement shall ye make the trumpet sound throughout all your land. **10** And ye shall hallow the fiftieth year, and proclaim

liberty throughout all the land unto all the inhabitants thereof: it shall be a jubilee unto you; and ye shall return every man unto his possession, and ye shall return every man unto his family. **11** A jubilee shall that fiftieth year be unto you: ye shall not sow, neither reap that which groweth of itself in it, nor gather the grapes in it of thy vine undressed. **12** For it is the jubilee; it shall be holy unto you: ye shall eat the increase thereof out of the field.

13 In the year of this jubilee ye shall return every man unto his possession. **14** And if thou sell aught unto thy neighbor, or buyest aught of thy neighbor's hand, ye shall not oppress one another: **15** according to the number of years after the jubilee thou shalt buy of thy neighbor, and according unto the number of years of the fruits he shall sell unto thee: **16** according to the multitude of years thou shalt increase the price thereof, and according to the fewness of years thou shalt diminish the price of it: for according to the number of the years of the fruits doth he sell unto thee. **17** Ye shall not therefore oppress one another; but thou shalt fear thy God: for I am the Lord your God.

18 Wherefore ye shall do my statutes, and keep my judgments, and do them; and ye shall dwell in the land in safety. **19** And the land shall yield her fruit, and ye shall eat your fill, and dwell therein in safety. **20** And if ye shall say, What shall we eat the seventh year? behold, we shall not sow, nor gather in our increase: **21** then I will command my blessing upon you in the sixth year, and it shall bring forth fruit for three years. **22** And ye shall sow the eighth year, and eat yet of old fruit until the ninth year; until her fruits come in ye shall eat of the old store. **23** The land shall not be sold for ever: for the land is mine; for ye are strangers and sojourners with me. **24** And in all the land of your possession ye shall grant a redemption for the land.

25 If thy brother be waxen poor, and hath sold away some of his possession, and if any of his kin come to redeem it, then shall he redeem that which his brother sold. **26** And if the man have none to redeem it, and himself be able to redeem it; **27** then let him count the years of the sale thereof, and restore the overplus unto the man to whom he sold it; that he may return unto his possession. **28** But if he be not able to restore it to him, then that which is sold shall remain in the hand of him that hath bought it until the year of jubilee: and in the jubilee it shall go out, and he shall return unto his possession.

29 And if a man sell a dwelling house in a walled city, then he may redeem it within a whole year after it is sold; within a full year may he redeem it. **30** And if it be not redeemed within the space of a full year, then the house that is in the walled city shall be established for ever to him that bought it throughout his generations: it shall not go out in the jubilee. **31** But the houses of the villages which have no wall round about them shall be counted as the fields of the country: they may be redeemed, and they shall go out in the jubilee. **32** Notwithstanding the cities of the Levites, and the houses of the cities of their possession, may the Levites redeem at any time. **33** And if a man purchase of the Levites, then the house that was sold, and the city of his possession, shall go out in the year of jubilee: for the houses of the cities of the Levites are their possession among the children of Israel. **34** But the field of the suburbs of their cities may not be sold; for it is their perpetual possession.

TRUST LAW: In most jurisdictions, a PROBATE COURT would prove the validity of a WILL and TESTAMENT of the deceased (TESTATOR) and what happens to the testator's estate who died INTESTATE (without a will). The EXECUTOR, which is named in the will, has the legal power to dispose of the testator's assets but only as the testator described in the will. If a person dies without a will, the **ADMINISTRATOR** would take the place of the deceased and that can include the next of kin, closest relative, etc. If the value of the estate is small, depending on the jurisdiction, the probate process may be avoided. In California, it's not necessary to go through with probate proceedings if the value of the property is under $184,500 through the Small Estate Summary Procedure.

48 U.S. Code Ch. 11 §1504. Conveyance of lands in Territories by aliens before escheat proceedings Here's the United States defense against improperly held lands: **§ 1505 Proceedings for escheat of improperly held lands and § 1506 Condemnation and sale of lands in escheat proceedings.** The Federal Courts are waiting for cases of this type, with these types of cases being just one of the few within their jurisdiction.

SALE OF LAND – *Leviticus 25:23-28* - **23** The land shall not be sold for ever: for the land *is* mine; for ye *are* strangers and sojourners with me. **24** And in all the land of your possession ye shall grant a redemption for the land.

25 If thy brother be waxen poor, and hath sold away *some* of his possession, and if any of his kin come to redeem it, then shall he redeem that which his brother sold. **26** And if the man have none to redeem it, and himself be able to redeem it; **27** then let him count the years of the sale thereof, and restore the overplus unto the man to whom he sold it; that he may return unto his possession. **28** But if he be not able to restore *it* to him, then that which is sold shall remain in the hand of him that hath bought it until the year of jubilee: and in the jubilee it shall go out, and he shall return unto his possession.

CIVIL CODE: 48 U.S. Code Ch. 11 §1501. Lands in Territories says "No alien or person who is not a CITIZEN of the United States, or who has not declared his intention to become a citizen of the United States in the manner provided by law shall acquire title to or own any land in any of the Territories of the United States except as hereinafter provided." Can you receive "DUAL CITIZENSHIP" anywhere else? So in regard to the Code, **§1505** states, "It shall be the duty of the Attorney General of the United States, when he shall be informed or have reason to believe that lands in ANY of the Territories of the United States are being held contrary to the provisions of this chapter, to institute or cause to be instituted suit in behalf of the United States in the district court of the Territory in the district where such land or a part thereof may be situated, praying for the escheat of the same on behalf of the United States to the United States."

Without the success of ESCHEAT in the hand of the Federal government, Adam, the man labeled black unwillingly, can claim what's his through research and dedication to the Word of God.

TRANSFER OF LAND – *Ruth 4:3-11* - 3 And he said unto the kinsman, Na-o´mi, that is come again out of the country of Moab, selleth a parcel of land, which *was* our brother Elim´elech's**: 4** and I thought to advertise thee, saying, Buy *it* before the inhabitants, and before the elders of my people. If thou wilt redeem *it*, redeem *it*: but if thou wilt not redeem *it, then* tell me, that I may know: for *there is* none to redeem *it* besides thee; and I *am* after thee. And he said, I will redeem *it*. **5** Then said Boaz, What day thou buyest the field of the hand of Na-o´mi, thou must buy *it* also of Ruth the Moabitess, the wife of the dead, to raise up the name of the dead upon his inheritance. **6** And the kinsman said, I cannot redeem *it* for myself, lest I mar mine own inheritance: redeem thou my right to thyself; for I cannot redeem *it.*

7 Now this *was the manner* in former time in Israel concerning redeeming and concerning changing, for to confirm all things; a man plucked off his shoe, and gave *it* to his neighbor: and this *was* a testimony in Israel. **8** Therefore the kinsman said unto Boaz, Buy *it* for thee. So he drew off his shoe. **9** And Boaz said unto the elders, and *unto* all the people, Ye *are* witnesses this day, that I have bought all that *was* Elim´elech's, and all that *was* Chil´i-on's and Mahlon's, of the hand of Na-o´mi. **10** Moreover Ruth the Moabitess, the wife of Mahlon, have I purchased to be my wife, to raise up the name of the dead upon his inheritance, that the name of the dead be not cut off from among his brethren, and from the gate of his place: ye *are* witnesses this day. **11** And all the people that *were* in the gate, and the elders, said, *We are* witnesses. The Lord make the woman that is come into thine house like Rachel and like Le´ah, which two did build the house of Israel: and do thou worthily in Eph´ratah, and be famous in Bethlehem:

<u>Jeremiah 32:9-14</u> - **9** And I bought the field of Hanameel my uncle's son, that *was* in Anathoth, and weighed him the money, *even* seventeen shekels of silver. **10** And I subscribed the evidence, and sealed it, and took witnesses, and weighed *him* the money in the balances. **11** So I took the evidence of the purchase, *both* that which was sealed *according* to the **law** and custom, and that which was open: **12** And I gave the evidence of the purchase unto Baruch the son of Neriah, the son of Maaseiah, in the sight of Hanameel mine uncle's *son,* and in the presence of the

witnesses that subscribed the book of the purchase, before all the Jews that sat in the court of the prison. **13** And I charged Baruch before them saying, **14** Thus saith the LORD of hosts, the God of Israel; Take these evidences, this evidence of the purchase, both which is sealed, and this evidence which is open' and put them in an earthen vessel, that they may continue many days.

CIVIL CODE: We lease our land and not in FEE SIMPLE do we sell or release ownership of something that belongs to God. You may ask, if it's not owned by some family overseas, who has the property right now? **40 U.S. Code §1301 Charge of Property transferred to the Federal Government** and then they'll presume the role by **§1302. Lease of buildings** or by **§1303 Disposition of surplus real property**

REMOVAL OF LANDMARKS - *Deuteronomy 19:14* - Thou shalt not remove thy neighbor's landmark, which they of old time have set in thine inheritance, which thou shalt inherit in the land that the LORD thy God giveth thee to possess it.

THE 43RD CLAUSE OF THE MAGNA CARTA: If anyone holding of some escheat (such as the honor of Wallingford, Nottingham, Boulogne, Lancaster, or of other escheats which are in our hands and are baronies) shall die, his heir shall give no other relief, and perform no other service to us than he would have done to the baron if that barony had been in the baron's hand; and we shall hold it in the same manner in which the baron held it.

MORTGAGES - *Nehemiah 5:2-5* - **2** For there were that said, We, our sons, and our daughters, *are* many: therefore we take up corn *for them*, that we may eat, and live. **3** *Some* also there were that said, We have mortgaged our lands, vineyards, and houses, that we might buy corn, because of the dearth. **4** There were also that said, We have borrowed money for the king's tribute, *and that upon* our lands and vineyards. **5** Yet now our flesh *is* as the flesh of our brethren, our children as their children: and, lo, we bring into bondage our sons and our daughters to be servants, and *some* of our daughters are brought into bondage *already*: neither *is it* in our power to *redeem them*; for other men have our lands and vineyards.

REAL ESTATE NIGHTMARE: In CODE, what is a MORTGAGE? Well, it's security for a loan that a LENDER makes to the BORROWER. You never own it and never will own the mineral rights or the land under the home. The transfer of wealth in REAL ESTATE is in foreclosure.

Defining MORTGAGE in the 1828 Noah Webster's Dictionary yields terrifying results. It defines **MORTGAGE** as, "1. A DEAD PLEDGE; the grant of an estate in fee as security for the payment of money, and on the condition that if the money shall be paid according to the contract, the grant shall be void. And the mortgagee shall re-convey the estate to the MORTGAGER (LENDER)(BANK).

Ever heard of the **EQUITY OF REDEMPTION**? The *equity of redemption* is a defaulting mortgagor's right to prevent foreclosure proceedings on the property and redeem the mortgaged property by discharging the debt secured by the mortgage within a REASONABLE AMOUNT OF TIME, according to Wex.

SALE OF PERSONAL PROPERTY – *Leviticus 25:14* - And if thou sell ought unto thy neighbor, or buyest *ought* of thy neighbor's hand, ye shall not oppress one another:

CIVIL CODE: Under **Title 12 Chapter 4 Subchapter III— NATIONAL BANK SHARES § 548.** State taxation, **SAVINGS PROVISION** Public Law 91-156, §3, December 24, 1969, 83 Stat. 435,** as amended by **Public Law 92-213, §4(a), December 22, 1971, 85 Stat. 775,** provided that: "(a) Except as provided in subsection (b) of this section, prior to January 1, 1973, no tax may be imposed on any class of banks by or under authority of any State legislation in effect prior to the enactment of this Act [Dec. 24, 1969] (b) The prohibition of subsection (a) of this section does not apply to "(1) any sales tax or use tax complementary thereto, (2) ANY TAX (including a documentary stamp tax) on the execution, delivery, or recordation of documents, or (3) any tax on TANGIBLE PERSONAL PROPERTY (not including cash or currency), or for any license, registration, transfer, excise or other fee or tax imposed on the ownership, use or transfer of tangible personal property.

So, the government gets involved over personal property sales over $500 dollars and there is a tax imposed on you, the seller. In 2023, the government has found a way to tax "decentralized" currency and money sharing applications with payments over $600 dollars that you may have on your mobile phones, computers, and/or tablets. "Doing business" anywhere is subject to state tax, local tax, and fees imposed on buyer from seller.

LET'S NOT FORGET THE LANGUAGE, PERSONAL PROPERTY can also be defined in COMMON LAW as chattels or personalty, a name used in the plantation days for the working class.

PLEDGES - *Exodus 22:26, 27* - 26 If thou at all take thy neighbor's raiment to pledge, thou shalt deliver it unto him by that the sun goeth down: **27** For that *is* his covering only, it *is* his raiment for his skin: wherein shall he sleep? And it shall come to pass, when he crieth unto me, that I will hear; for I am gracious.

Deuteronomy 24:6, 10, 11, 13 - 24:6 No man shall take the nether or the upper millstone to pledge: for he taketh *a man's* life to pledge. 10 When thou dost lend thy brother any thing, thou shalt not go into his house to fetch his pledge. 11 Thou shalt stand abroad, and the man to whom thou dost lend shall bring out the pledge abroad unto thee. 13 In any case thou shalt deliver him the pledge again when the sun goeth down, that he may sleep in his own raiment, and bless thee: and it shall be righteousness unto thee before the LORD thy God.

2 Kings 4:1-7 - 1 Now there cried a certain woman of the wives of the sons of the prophets unto Eli´sha, saying, Thy servant my husband is dead; and thou knowest that thy servant did fear the Lord: and the creditor is come to take unto him my two sons to be bondmen. 2 And Eli´sha said unto her, What shall I do for thee? tell me, what hast thou in the house? And she said, Thine handmaid hath not any thing in the house, save a pot of oil. 3 Then he said, Go, borrow thee vessels abroad of all thy neighbors, *even* empty vessels; borrow not a few. 4 And when thou art come in, thou shalt shut the door upon thee and upon thy sons, and shalt pour out into all those vessels, and thou shalt set aside that which is full. 5 So she went from him, and shut the door upon her and upon her sons, who brought *the vessels* to her; and she poured out. 6 And it came to pass, when the vessels were full, that she said unto her son, Bring me yet a vessel. And he said unto her, *There is* not a vessel more. And the oil stayed. 7 Then she came and told the man of God. And he said, Go, sell the oil, and pay thy debt, and live thou and thy children of the rest.

TRUST LAW: Now in LAW, what's a PLEDGE that you may be familiar with again? A MORTGAGE, a DEAD PLEDGE. You will pay the bank for the house that they own.

THEFT - *Exodus 20:15, 22:1-4* - **20:15** Thou shalt not steal. **(22:1-4) 1** If a man shall steal an ox, or a sheep, and kill it, or sell it; he shall restore five oxen for an ox, and four sheep for a sheep.

2 If a thief be found breaking up, and be smitten that he die, *there shall* no blood *be shed* for him. **3** If the sun be risen upon him, *there shall be* blood *shed* for him; *for* he should make full restitution: if he have nothing, then he shall be sold for his theft. **4** If the theft be certainly found in his hand alive, whether it be ox, or ass, or sheep; he shall restore double.

CRIMINAL LAW: There are a few things you may not think is THEFT but in actuality, it is. Such as **NY Penal Law Title J §165.35 Fortune Telling.** Yes, that is a form of thievery but in the law, THEFT can be disguised under many names. For instance, we've discussed ARSON, a form of theft by destruction if you can see it that way, BURGLARY, defined in the **Missouri Revised Statutes Title XXXVIII Chapter 569 §569.160** as a person knowingly entering or remaining in a building or uninhabitable structure for the purpose of committing an offense therein with explosives or deadly weapon or causing any immediate physical injury to any person that isn't a participant in the crime. ROBBERY, another name for THEFT, under **§570.023 of Missouri Revised Statutes,** a follower of COMMON LAW) is the act of forcibly stealing property causing serious physical injury, armed with a deadly weapon, or stealing any controlled substances from a pharmacy.

I'd like to point out, I see FRAUD a great deal in matters of THEFT in the code civil. The distinction in charges found in **California Penal Code** between **Title 8. CRIMES AGAINST THE PERSON** and **Title 13. CRIMES AGAINST PROPERTY** will be distinguished, like the U.S. Code, but not AS distinguished. ROBBERY is what happens to the *person*, BURGLARY is what happens to the *property*. In **18 U.S.C. Pt. 1 CRIMES**, the following chapters are all focused on various forms of theft such as **Chapter 25 – Counterfeiting and forgery, Chapter 31 – Embezzlement and theft, Chapter 43 – False personation, Chapter 47 – Fraud and false statements, Chapter 55 – Kidnapping, Chapter 77 – Peonage, slavery, and trafficking in persons, Chapter 95 – Racketeering, Chapter 96 – Racketeer influenced and corrupt organizations, Chapter 103 – Robbery and burglary, Chapter 113 – Stolen property**, to name a few.

BREACH OF TRUST- *Leviticus 6:1-5* - 1 And the Lord spake unto Moses, saying, **2** If a soul sin, and commit a trespass against the Lord, and lie unto his neighbor in that which was delivered him to keep, or in fellowship, or in a thing taken away by violence, or hath deceived his neighbor; **3** or have found that which was lost, and lieth concerning it, and sweareth falsely; in any of all these that a man doeth, sinning therein: **4** then it shall be, because he hath sinned, and is guilty, that he shall restore that which he took violently away, or the thing which he hath deceitfully gotten, or that which was delivered him to keep, or the lost thing which he found, **5** or all that about which he hath sworn falsely; he shall even restore it in the principal, and shall add the fifth part more thereto, *and* give it unto him to whom it appertaineth, in the day of his trespass offering.

If there's a *conflict of interest* with a trustee, there are restrictions that the Courts can enforce. If the trustee FAILS in their duties, it would be considered a CIVIL BREACH OF TRUST and the trustee can be left with severe liabilities.

CIVIL CODE: California Probate Code Div. 9 Part 4 Chapter 4 Article 1. Liability for Breach of Trust §16400 a BREACH OF TRUST is defined as a violation by the trustee of any duty that the trustee owes the beneficiary. Of the states observed thus far, TRUST LAW in those states seem to be modeled after the **Uniform Trust Code**, which was approved by the Uniform Law Commissioners in 2000. The **Laws of New York, Consolidated Laws of New York, Chapter 17-B. Estates, Powers, and Trusts Article 7 §7-2.4** calls a "BREACH OF TRUST" a CONTRAVENTION.

TRUSTEES – *Matthew 25:14-30* - **14** For *the kingdom of heaven is* as a man traveling into a far country, *who* called his own servants, and delivered unto them his goods. **15** And unto one he gave five talents, to another two, and to another one; to every man according to his several ability; and straightway took his journey. **16** Then he that had received the five talents went and traded with the same, and made *them* other five talents. **17** And likewise he that *had received* two, he also gained other two. **18** But he that had received one went and digged in the earth, and hid his lord's money. **19** After a long time the lord of those servants cometh, and reckoneth with them. **20** And so he that had received five talents came and brought other five talents, saying, Lord, thou deliveredst unto me five talents: behold, I have gained beside them five talents more. **21** His lord said unto him, Well done, *thou* good and faithful servant: thou hast been faithful over a few things, I will make thee ruler over many things: enter thou into the joy of thy lord. **22** He also that had received two talents came and said, Lord, thou deliveredst unto me two talents: behold, I have gained two other talents beside them. **23** His lord said unto him, Well done, good and faithful servant; thou hast been faithful over a few things, I will make thee ruler over many things: enter thou into the joy of thy lord. **24** Then he which had received the one talent came and said, Lord, I knew thee that thou art a hard man, reaping where thou hast not sown, and gathering where thou hast not strewed: **25** and I was afraid, and went and hid thy talent in the earth: lo, *there* thou hast *that is* thine. **26** His lord answered and said unto him, *Thou* wicked and slothful servant, thou knewest that I reap where I sowed not, and gather where I have not strewed: **27** thou oughtest therefore to have put my money to the exchangers, and *then* at my coming I should have received mine own with usury. **28** Take therefore the talent from him, and give *it* unto him which hath ten talents. **29** For unto every one that hath shall be given, and he shall have abundance: but from him that hath not shall be taken away even that which he hath. **30** And cast ye the unprofitable servant into outer darkness: there shall be weeping and gnashing of teeth.

<u>*Luke 19:11-27*</u>

The Parable of the Ten Pounds

11 And as they heard these things, he added and spake a parable, because he was nigh to Jerusalem, and because they thought that the kingdom of God should immediately appear. **12** He said therefore, A certain nobleman went into a far country to receive for himself a kingdom, and to return. **13** And he called his ten servants, and delivered them ten pounds, and said unto them, Occupy till I come. **14** But his citizens hated him, and sent a message after him, saying, We will not have this *man* to reign over us. **15** And it came to pass, that when he was returned, having received the kingdom, then he commanded these servants to be called unto him, to whom he had given the money, that he might know how much every man had gained by trading. **16** Then came the first, saying, Lord, thy pound hath gained ten pounds. **17** And he said unto him, Well, thou good servant: because thou hast been faithful in a very little, have thou authority over ten cities. **18** And the second came, saying, Lord, thy pound hath gained five pounds. **19** And he said likewise to him, Be thou also over five cities. **20** And another came, saying, Lord, behold, *here is* thy pound, which I have kept laid up in a napkin: **21** for I feared thee, because thou art an austere man: thou takest up that thou layedst not down, and reapest that thou didst not sow. **22** And he saith unto him, Out of thine own mouth will I judge thee, *thou* wicked servant. Thou knewest that I was an austere man, taking up that I laid not down, and reaping that I did not sow: **23** wherefore then gavest not thou my money into the bank, that at my coming I might have required mine own with usury? **24** And he said unto them that stood by, Take from him the pound, and give *it* to him that hath ten pounds. **25** (And they said unto him, Lord, he hath ten pounds.) **26** For I say unto you, That unto every one which hath shall be given; and from him that hath not, even that he hath shall be taken away from him. **27** But those mine enemies, which would not that I should reign over them, bring hither, and slay *them* before me.

CIVIL CODE: Missouri Revised Statutes Title XXXI, Chapter 456 – Trusts and Trustees – Uniform Trust Code § 456.7-702 – Trustee's bond. 1. A trustee shall give bond to secure performance of the trustee's duties only if the court finds that a bond is needed to protect the interests of the beneficiaries or is required by the terms of the trust and the court has not dispensed with the requirement. In **California Probate Code Division 9 Part 3 Chapter 1 Trustees** gives the general scope of the duties of the trustee and what they may or may not do. Albeit, the TRUSTEE is granted a great deal of power throughout the **California Trust Law**, in which it lists the administrative duties of the trustee in **Part 4. Trust Administration Chapter 1. Duties of Trustees, Chapter 2. Powers of Trustees, and Chapter 4. Liability of Trustees to Beneficiaries** and in **Part 6 RIGHTS OF THIRD PERSONS Chapter 1. Liability of Trustee to Third Persons.**

FOR YOUR RECORD: There is an OFFICE OF TRUST RECORDS under the Bureau of Trust Funds Administration, which manages the records and information that upholds the legal obligation of the trust relationship between the Federal government AMERICAN INDIANS and ALASKA NATIVES. The AMERICAN INDIAN RECORDS REPOSITORY (AIRR) office holds and protects in an underground facility located in Lenexa, Kansas, millions of original, historic documents describing the Federal government's treaty obligations to Native Americans. Knowing what happened with the Afro-Americans name and their identity change in the Dawes Rolls from 1898-1914, its worth checking on the records of the time period of 1898-1914 at this facility, although it's not open to the public.

LAW OF THE LAND, LAWS OF THE BIBLE

LAWS OF INHERITANCE

DAUGHTERS – *Numbers 27:7, 8* **- 7** The daughters of Zelophehad speak right: thou shalt surely give them a possession of an inheritance among their father's brethren; and thou shalt cause the inheritance of their father to pass unto them. **8** And thou shalt speak unto the children of Israel, saying, If a man die, and have no son, then ye shall cause his inheritance to pass unto his daughter.

CIVIL MATTERS: Now would be a good time to bring up **The Rule in Shelley's Case,** which is a RULE OF LAW that may apply to certain future interests in REAL PROPERTY and TRUSTS created in COMMON LAW jurisdictions. The ancestor by any GIFT or CONVEYANCE takes an ALLODIAL TITLE and limited to HEIRS in FEE SIMPLE. (Remember, we LEASE under the STATUTES of God)

California Probate Code Division 9 TRUST LAW Part 5 JUDICIAL PROCEEDINGS CONCERNING TRUSTS
§17400 (b) This chapter does not prevent the transfer of the place of administration of a trust or of trust property to another jurisdiction by any other available means. §17401(a) The court may make an order for the transfer of the place of administration of a trust or the transfer of some or all of the

trust property to a jurisdiction outside this state as provided in this chapter.

FIRSTBORN – *Deuteronomy 21:15-17* - **15** If a man have two wives, one beloved, and another hated, and they have born him children, *both* the beloved and the hated; and if the firstborn son be hers that was hated: **16** Then it shall be, when he maketh his sons to inherit *that* which he hath, *that* he may not make the son of the beloved firstborn before the son of the hated, *which is indeed* the firstborn: **17** But he shall acknowledge the son of the hated *for* the firstborn, by giving him a double portion of all that he hath: for he is the beginning of his strength; the right of the firstborn *is* his.

LESSON: In 1917, Pope Pius XII, I meant Woodrow Wilson, relied heavily on a state-mandated enlistment of soldiers by way of CONSCRIPTION in World War I, famously known as the DRAFT. The **HARLEM HELLFIGHTERS of the 369th INFANTRY REGIMENT**, originally formed as the 15th NEW YORK NATIONAL GUARD REGIMENT, was one of the first Afro-American regiments to serve with the American Expeditionary Forces during WWI. The men of this regiment were FIRSTBORN sons, who lost their names and heirship to the French in 1919. The **Selective Service System**, an independent agency of the U.S. government, drafts a contingent plan and prepares two types of drafts, a **general draft** consisting of able bodied 18-25-year aged men and a **special skills draft,** based on particular professional licensing in specified health care occupations. ALL MALE U.S. CITIZENS and IMMIGRANT NON-CITIZENS are required by law to register to the Selective Service System within 30 days of turning 18 years of age. That's how you get men to war and the chance to prove themselves to white soldiers that they're "civilized" and capable of being productive members of the Society.

ORDERS OF – *Numbers 27:7-11* - **7** The daughters of Zelo´phehad speak right: thou shalt surely give them a possession of an inheritance among their father's brethren; and thou shalt cause the inheritance of their father to pass unto them. **8** And thou shalt speak unto the children of Israel, saying, If a man die, and have no son, then ye shall cause his inheritance to pass unto his daughter. **9** And if he have no daughter, then ye shall give his inheritance unto his brethren. **10** And if he have no brethren, then ye shall give his inheritance unto his father's brethren. **11** And if his father have no brethren, then ye shall give his inheritance unto his kinsman that is next to him of his family, and he shall possess it: and it shall be unto the children of Israel a statute of judgment, as the Lord commanded Moses.

CIVIL CODE: In the **California Probate Code Division 9, Part 3, Chapter 1 Article 4 Appointment of Trustees** §15660(a) If the trust has no trustee or if the trust instrument requires a vacancy in the office of a co-trustee to be filled, the vacancy shall be filled as provided in this section. **(c)** If the vacancy in the office of trustee is not filled as provided in subdivision (b), the vacancy may be filled by a TRUST COMPANY that has agreed to accept the trust on agreement of all adult beneficiaries who are receiving or are entitled to receive income under the trust or to receive a distribution of principal if the trust were terminated at the time the agreement is made. **(d)** If the vacancy in the office of trustee is not filled as provided in subdivision (b) or (c), on petition of any interested person of any person named as trustee in the trust instrument, THE COURT MAY, in its discretion, appoint a trustee to fill the vacancy.

You see how easy it is to acquire land but the sport of competition is a common trait amongst the countrymen?

SLAVES – *Leviticus 25:46* - **46** And ye shall take them as an inheritance for your children after you, to inherit *them for* a possession; they shall be your bondmen for ever: but over your brethren the children of Israel ye shall not rule one over another with rigour.

SONS – *Genesis 21:10-13* - **10** Wherefore she said unto Abraham, Cast out this bondwoman and her son: for the son of this bondwoman shall not be heir with my son, *even* with Isaac. **11** And the thing was very grievous in Abraham's sight because of his son. **12** And God said unto Abraham, Let it not be grievous in thy sight because of the lad, and because of thy bondwoman; in all that Sarah hath said unto thee, hearken unto her voice; for in Isaac shall thy seed be called. **13** And also of the son of the bondwoman will I make a nation, because he *is* thy seed.

Deuteronomy 21:15-17 - **15** If a man have two wives, one beloved, and another hated, and they have borne him children, *both* the beloved and the hated; and *if* the firstborn son be hers that was hated: **16** then it shall be, when he maketh his sons to inherit *that* which he hath, *that* he may not make the son of the beloved firstborn before the son of the hated, *which is indeed* the firstborn: **17** but he shall acknowledge the son of the hated *for* the firstborn, by giving him a double portion of all that he hath: for he *is* the beginning of his strength; the right of the firstborn *is* his.

I Chronicles 5:1 - Now the sons of Reuben the firstborn of Israel, (for he *was* the firstborn; but forasmuch as he defiled his father's bed, his birthright was given unto the sons of Joseph the son of Israel: and the genealogy is not to be reckoned after the birthright.

WHEN A MAN DIES CHILDLESS – *Deuteronomy 25:5-10* - **5** If brethren dwell together, and one of them die, and have no child, the wife of the dead shall not marry without unto a stranger: her husband's brother shall go in unto her, and take her to him to wife, and perform the duty of a husband's brother unto her. **6** And it shall be, *that* the firstborn which she beareth shall succeed in the name of his brother *which is* dead, that his name be not put out of Israel. **7** And if the man like not to take his brother's wife, then let his brother's wife go up to the gate unto the elders, and say, My husband's brother refuseth to raise up unto his brother a name in Israel, he will not perform the duty of my husband's brother. **8** Then the elders of his city shall call him, and speak unto him: and *if* he stand *to it*, and say, I like not to take her; **9** then shall his brother's wife come unto him in the presence of the elders, and loose his shoe from off his foot, and spit in his face, and shall answer and say, So shall it be done unto that man that will not build up his brother's house. **10** And his name shall be called in Israel, The house of him that hath his shoe loosed.

WIVES – *Ruth 4:1-12* - **1** Then went Boaz up to the gate, and sat him down there: and, behold, the kinsman of whom Boaz spake came by; unto whom he said, Ho, such a one! turn aside, sit down here. And he turned aside, and sat down. **2** And he took ten men of the elders of the city, and said, Sit ye down here. And they sat down. **3** And he said unto the kinsman, Na-o´mi, that is come again out of the country of Moab, selleth a parcel of land, which *was* our brother Elim´elech's: **4** and I thought to advertise thee, saying, Buy *it* before the inhabitants, and before the elders of my people. If thou wilt redeem *it*, redeem *it*: but if thou wilt not redeem *it, then* tell me, that I may know: for *there is* none to redeem *it* besides thee; and I *am* after thee. And he said, I will redeem *it*. **5** Then said Boaz, What day thou buyest the field of the hand of Na-o´mi, thou must buy *it* also of Ruth the Moabitess, the wife of the dead, to raise up the name of the dead upon his inheritance. **6** And the kinsman said, I cannot redeem *it* for myself, lest I mar mine own inheritance: redeem thou my right to thyself; for I cannot redeem *it.*

7 Now this *was the manner* in former time in Israel concerning redeeming and concerning changing, for to confirm all things; a man plucked off his shoe, and gave *it* to his neighbor: and this *was* a testimony in Israel. **8** Therefore the kinsman said unto Boaz, Buy *it* for thee. So he drew off his shoe. **9** And Boaz said unto the elders, and *unto* all the people, Ye *are* witnesses this day, that I have bought all that *was* Elim´elech's, and all that *was* Chil´i-on's and Mahlon's, of the hand of Na-o´mi. **10** Moreover Ruth the Moabitess, the wife of Mahlon, have I purchased to be my wife, to raise up the name of the dead upon his inheritance, that the name of the dead be not cut off from among his brethren, and from the gate of his place: ye *are* witnesses this day. **11** And all the people that *were* in the gate, and the elders, said, *We are* witnesses. The Lord make the woman that is come into thine house like Rachel and like Le´ah, which two did build the house of Israel: and do thou worthily in Eph´ratah, and be famous in Bethlehem: **12** and let thy house be like the house of Pharez, whom Tamar bare unto Judah, of the seed which the Lord shall give thee of this young woman.

CIVIL CODE: Laws of New York, **Consolidated Laws of New York**, Chapter 50, Article 6, **§ 190 Dower**, states "no inchoate (commenced) right of dower shall be possessed by a wife during coveture, and no widow shall be endowed, in any lands whereof her husband became seized of an estate of inheritance.

CONTRACTS

DEBTS - *Exodus 22:25* If thou lend money to *any of* my people *that is* poor by thee, thou shalt not be to him as an usurer, neither shalt thou lay upon him usury.

Deuteronomy 15:1-3, 23:19, 20 **1** At the end of *every* seven years thou shalt make a release. **2** And this *is* the manner of the release: Every creditor that lendeth *aught* unto his neighbor shall release *it*; he shall not exact *it* of his neighbor, or of his brother; because it is called the Lord's release. **3** Of a foreigner thou mayest exact *it again*: but *that* which is thine with thy brother thine hand shall release; *23:19, 20* **19** Thou shalt not lend upon usury to thy brother; usury of money, usury of victuals, usury of any thing that is lent upon usury: **20** unto a stranger thou mayest lend upon usury; but unto thy brother thou shalt not lend upon usury: that the Lord thy God may bless thee in all that thou settest thine hand to in the land whither thou goest to possess it.

Nehemiah 5:11 Restore, I pray you, to them, even this day, their lands, their vineyards, their oliveyards, and their houses, also the hundredth part of the money, and of the corn, the wine, and the oil, that ye exact of them.

CIVIL CODE: 11 U.S. Code - BANKRUPTCY - Chapter 1 **§101. Definitions** (28) The term "indenture" means mortgage, deed of trust, or indenture, under which there is outstanding a security, other than a voting-trust certificate, constituting a claim against the debtor, a claim secured by a lien on any of the debtor's property, or an equity security of the debtor. **§102. Rules of construction (2)** "claim against the debtor" includes claim against property of the debtor.

WITH FELLOW CITIZENS – *Deuteronomy 15:1-3, 23:19, 20* 1 At the end of *every* seven years thou shalt make a release. 2 And this *is* the manner of the release: Every creditor that lendeth *aught* unto his neighbor shall release *it*; he shall not exact *it* of his neighbor, or of his brother; because it is called the Lord's release. 3 Of a foreigner thou mayest exact *it again*: but *that* which is thine with thy brother thine hand shall release; *23:19, 20* 19 Thou shalt not lend upon usury to thy brother; usury of money, usury of victuals, usury of any thing that is lent upon usury: 20 unto a stranger thou mayest lend upon usury; but unto thy brother thou shalt not lend upon usury: that the Lord thy God may bless thee in all that thou settest thine hand to in the land whither thou goest to possess it.

WITH FOREIGNERS – *Deuteronomy 15:1-3, 23:19, 20* 1 At the end of *every* seven years thou shalt make a release. 2 And this *is* the manner of the release: Every creditor that lendeth *aught* unto his neighbor shall release *it*; he shall not exact *it* of his neighbor, or of his brother; because it is called the Lord's release. 3 Of a foreigner thou mayest exact *it again*: but *that* which is thine with thy brother thine hand shall release; *23:19, 20* 19 Thou shalt not lend upon usury to thy brother; usury of money, usury of victuals, usury of any thing that is lent upon usury: 20 unto a stranger thou mayest lend upon usury; but unto thy brother thou shalt not lend upon usury: that the Lord thy God may bless thee in all that thou settest thine hand to in the land whither thou goest to possess it.

INTEREST - *Exodus 22:25* If thou lend money to *any of* my people *that is* poor by thee, thou shalt not be to him as an usurer, neither shalt thou lay upon him usury.

Leviticus 25:36 Take thou no usury of him, or increase: but fear thy God; that thy brother may live with thee.

Deuteronomy 23:19, 20 **19** Thou shalt not lend upon usury to thy brother; usury of money, usury of victuals, usury of any thing that is lent upon usury: **20** unto a stranger thou mayest lend upon usury; but unto thy brother thou shalt not lend upon usury: that the Lord thy God may bless thee in all that thou settest thine hand to in the land whither thou goest to possess it.

Ezekiel 18:10-13 **10** If he beget a son *that is* a robber, a shedder of blood, and *that* doeth the like to *any* one of these *things*, **11** and that doeth not any of those *duties*, but even hath eaten upon the mountains, and defiled his neighbor's wife, **12** hath oppressed the poor and needy, hath spoiled by violence, hath not restored the pledge, and hath lifted up his eyes to the idols, hath committed abomination, **13** hath given forth upon usury, and hath taken increase: shall he then live? he shall not live: he hath done all these abominations; he shall surely die; his blood shall be upon him.

Unfortunately, in the United States, we'll run into interest at every turn, which is advantageous to lenders. An Annual Percentage Rate (APR) is the yearly interest generated by a total charged to borrowers. What do we borrow that'll generate interest? A sum of money to purchase or place interest in a home, vehicle, or major purchase that the average American couldn't typically afford out of pocket. **The Truth in Lending Act (1968)** "mandated" that lenders disclose the Annual Percentage Rate charged to borrowers.

LOANS - *Exodus 22:25* If thou lend money to *any of* my people *that is* poor by thee, thou shalt not be to him as an usurer, neither shalt thou lay upon him usury.

Deuteronomy 23:19, 20 **19** Thou shalt not lend upon usury to thy brother; usury of money, usury of victuals, usury of any thing that is lent upon usury: **20** unto a stranger thou mayest lend upon usury; but unto thy brother thou shalt not lend upon usury: that the Lord thy God may bless thee in all that thou settest thine hand to in the land whither thou goest to possess it.

2 Kings 4:1-7 **1** Now there cried a certain woman of the wives of the sons of the prophets unto Eli´sha, saying, Thy servant my husband is dead; and thou knowest that thy servant did fear the Lord: and the creditor is come to take unto him my two sons to be bondmen. **2** And Eli´sha said unto her, What shall I do for thee? tell me, what hast thou in the house? And she said, Thine handmaid hath not any thing in the house, save a pot of oil. **3** Then he said, Go, borrow thee vessels abroad of all thy neighbors, *even* empty vessels; borrow not a few. **4** And when thou art come in, thou shalt shut the door upon thee and upon thy sons, and shalt pour out into all those vessels, and thou shalt set aside that which is full.

Nehemiah 5:2-5 **2** For there were that said, We, our sons, and our daughters, *are* many: therefore we take up corn *for them*, that we may eat, and live. **3** *Some* also there were that said, We have mortgaged our lands, vineyards, and houses, that we might buy corn, because of the dearth. **4** There were also that said, We have borrowed money for the king's tribute, *and that upon* our lands and vineyards. **5** Yet now our flesh *is* as the flesh of our brethren, our children as their children: and, lo, we bring into bondage our sons and our daughters to be servants, and *some* of our daughters are brought into bondage *already*: neither *is it* in our power to *redeem them*, for other men have our lands and vineyards.

MORTGAGES - *Nehemiah 5:2-5* 2 For there were that said, We, our sons, and our daughters, *are* many: therefore we take up corn *for them*, that we may eat, and live. 3 *Some* also there were that said, We have mortgaged our lands, vineyards, and houses, that we might buy corn, because of the dearth. 4 There were also that said, We have borrowed money for the king's tribute, *and that upon* our lands and vineyards. 5 Yet now our flesh *is* as the flesh of our brethren, our children as their children: and, lo, we bring into bondage our sons and our daughters to be servants, and *some* of our daughters are brought into bondage *already*: neither *is it* in our power to *redeem them*, for other men have our lands and vineyards.

CIVIL CODE: In New York, there's a corporation in charge of mortgages. New York Public Law, Private Housing Finance Law Article 7 MORTGAGE FACILITIES CORPORATION § 304 Purposes, Powers and Operation 1. The purpose of the corporation shall be to assist, promote, encourage and stimulate the development and rehabilitation of blighted areas by rendering financial assistance in the construction, rehabilitation or purchase of housing accommodations in blighted or deteriorating urban areas in this state by making first mortgage loans in areas designated by the corporation, such loans to be made on a sound economic basis by the application of sound mortgage lending principles. This is **MORTMAIN**, an inalienable ownership of real estate by a CORPORATION or legal institution, the homes are in DEAD HANDS.

PLEDGES - *Exodus 22:26, 27* **26** If thou at all take thy neighbor's raiment to pledge, thou shalt deliver it unto him by that the sun goeth down: **27** For that *is* his covering only, it *is* his raiment for his skin: wherein shall he sleep? And it shall come to pass, when he crieth unto me, that I will hear; for I am gracious.

Deuteronomy 24:6, 10, 11, 13 **6** No man shall take the nether or the upper millstone to pledge: for he taketh *a man's* life to pledge. **10** When thou dost lend thy brother any thing, thou shalt not go into his house to fetch his pledge. **11** Thou shalt stand abroad, and the man to whom thou dost lend shall bring out the pledge abroad unto thee. **13** In any case thou shalt deliver him the pledge again when the sun goeth down, that he may sleep in his own raiment, and bless thee: and it shall be righteousness unto thee before the LORD thy God.

2 Kings 4:1-7 **1** Now there cried a certain woman of the wives of the sons of the prophets unto Eli´sha, saying, Thy servant my husband is dead; and thou knowest that thy servant did fear the Lord: and the creditor is come to take unto him my two sons to be bondmen. **2** And Eli´sha said unto her, What shall I do for thee? tell me, what hast thou in the house? And she said, Thine handmaid hath not any thing in the house, save a pot of oil. **3** Then he said, Go, borrow thee vessels abroad of all thy neighbors, *even* empty vessels; borrow not a few. **4** And when thou art come in, thou shalt shut the door upon thee and upon thy sons, and shalt pour out into all those vessels, and thou shalt set aside that which is full. **5** So she went from him, and shut the door upon her and upon her sons, who brought *the vessels* to her;

and she poured out. **6** And it came to pass, when the vessels were full, that she said unto her son, Bring me yet a vessel. And he said unto her, *There is* not a vessel more. And the oil stayed. **7** Then she came and told the man of God. And he said, Go, sell the oil, and pay thy debt, and live thou and thy children of the rest.

Ezekiel 18:10-13 **10** If he beget a son *that is* a robber, a shedder of blood, and *that* doeth the like to *any* one of these *things*, **11** and that doeth not any of those *duties*, but even hath eaten upon the mountains, and defiled his neighbor's wife, **12** hath oppressed the poor and needy, hath spoiled by violence, hath not restored the pledge, and hath lifted up his eyes to the idols, hath committed abomination, **13** hath given forth upon usury, and hath taken increase: shall he then live? he shall not live: he hath done all these abominations; he shall surely die; his blood shall be upon him.

SALES – *Leviticus 25:14* And if thou sell ought unto thy neighbor, or buyest *ought* of thy neighbor's hand, ye shall not oppress one another:

LAISSEZ-FAIRE, an ideological, competitive economic system based on letting activities run their course, free from economic interventionism. The Federal government after Reconstruction, restored power to the white supremacists and adopted a **LAISSEZ-FAIRE** policy to the Negro. The policy resulted in disfranchisement, social, educational, and employment discrimination, and peonage according to Robert A. Gibson from the Yale-New Haven Teachers Institute. How could something like laissez-faire have such an adverse impact on the people who built the country of America up already? Through laissez-faire capitalism,

capitalism FREE of regulations, with minimal governance, operating on competition and profits. DIRECT GOVERNMENT INVOLVEMENT was in the mind and hearts of the Founding Fathers due to the radical policies of the Articles of Confederation. **(PSALM 83:5** For they have consulted together with one consent: they are confederate against thee:)

SALES OF LAND - *Leviticus 25:23-28* **23** The land shall not be sold for ever: for the land *is* mine; for ye *are* strangers and sojourners with me. **24** And in all the land of your possession ye shall grant a redemption for the land.

25 If thy brother be waxen poor, and hath sold away *some* of his possession, and if any of his kin come to redeem it, then shall he redeem that which his brother sold. **26** And if the man have none to redeem it, and himself be able to redeem it; **27** then let him count the years of the sale thereof, and restore the overplus unto the man to whom he sold it; that he may return unto his possession. **28** But if he be not able to restore *it* to him, then that which is sold shall remain in the hand of him that hath bought it until the year of jubilee: and in the jubilee it shall go out, and he shall return unto his possession.

Ruth 4:3-11 **3** And he said unto the kinsman, Na-o´mi, that is come again out of the country of Moab, selleth a parcel of land, which *was* our brother Elim´elech's: **4** and I thought to advertise thee, saying, Buy *it* before the inhabitants, and before the elders of my people. If thou wilt redeem *it,* redeem *it:* but if thou wilt not redeem *it, then* tell me, that I may know: for *there is* none to redeem *it* besides thee; and I *am* after thee. And he said, I will redeem *it.* **5** Then said Boaz, What day thou buyest the field of the hand of Na-o´mi, thou must buy *it* also of Ruth the Moabitess, the wife of the dead, to raise up the name of the dead upon his inheritance. **6** And the kinsman said, I cannot redeem *it* for myself, lest I mar mine own inheritance: redeem thou my right to thyself; for I cannot redeem *it.*

7 Now this *was the manner* in former time in Israel concerning redeeming and concerning changing, for to confirm all things; a man plucked off his shoe, and gave *it* to his neighbor: and this *was* a testimony in Israel. **8** Therefore the kinsman said unto Boaz, Buy *it* for thee. So he drew off his shoe. **9** And Boaz said unto the elders, and *unto* all the people, Ye *are* witnesses this day, that I have bought all that *was* Elim´elech's, and all that *was* Chil´i-on's and Mahlon's, of the hand of Na-o´mi. **10** Moreover Ruth the Moabitess, the wife of Mahlon, have I purchased to be my wife, to raise up the name of the dead upon his inheritance, that the name of the dead be not cut off from among his brethren, and from the gate of his place: ye *are* witnesses this day. **11** And all the people that *were* in the gate, and the elders, said, *We are* witnesses. The Lord make the woman that is come into thine house like Rachel and like Le´ah, which two did build the house of Israel: and do thou worthily in Eph´ratah, and be famous in Bethlehem:

Jeremiah 32:9-14 **9** And I bought the field of Hanameel my uncle's son, that *was* in Anathoth, and weighed him the money, *even* seventeen shekels of silver. **10** And I subscribed the evidence, and sealed it, and took witnesses, and weighed *him* the money in the balances. **11** So I took the evidence of the purchase, *both* that which was sealed *according* to the **law** and custom, and that which was open: **12** And I gave the evidence of the purchase unto Baruch the son of Neriah, the son of Maaseiah, in the sight of Hanameel mine uncle's *son,* and in the presence of the witnesses that subscribed the book of the purchase, before all the Jews that sat in the court of the prison. **13** And I charged Baruch before them saying, **14** Thus saith the LORD of hosts, the God of Israel; Take these evidences, this evidence of the purchase, both which is sealed, and this evidence which is open' and put them in an earthen vessel, that they may continue many days.

CIVIL CODE: In most of our cases, we'd have to go to court to determine the succession of the property. The following codes will verify just how states determine our eligibility to reclaim or claim the Land back from the water.

California Probate Code Division 8, Part 1. § 13151. Exclusive of the property described in section 13050, if a decedent dies leaving real property in this state and the gross value of the decedent's real and personal property in this state does not exceed one hundred sixty-six thousand two hundred fifty dollars ($166,250), as adjusted periodically in accordance with **§890,** and 40 days have elapsed since the death of the decedent, the successor of the decedent to an interest in a particular item of property that is real property, without procuring letters of administration or awaiting the probate of the will, may file a petition in the superior court of the county in which the estate of the decedent may be administered requesting a court order determining that the petitioner has succeeded to that real property. **§13206(a)** If property is transferred to a transferee under this chapter, and the decedent's personal representative later determines that another person has a superior right to the property by testate or intestate succession from decedent, the personal representative may request that the transferred property be restored to the estate.

Finding a place to live in America becomes ambiguous when your records have been destroyed, you had name changes in the Dawes Roll and land destroyed by national spread flooding, etc. You'll come to find looking up your land, name, heritage, and/or origins to see that you have so many relatives and people with the same name as yours and that you've been presumed dead or mentally incapacitated, unable to redeem what's properly yours. Here's what I mean. In Missouri Revised Statutes, Title XXIX, Chapter 443, §443.330. **Trustee failing to execute trust, parties interested may proceed, how** - If any trustee in any deed of trust to secure the payment of a debt or other liability shall die, or has died, shall become or has become mentally incapacitated, shall remove or has removed out of this state, shall neglect or refuse or has neglected or refused to act as such trustee, or shall or has become unable by sickness or other disability, to perform or execute his trust, **any person** interested in the debt or other liability secured by such deed of trust, may present his or their affidavit, stating the fact of the case, specifically, to the circuit court of the county in which the property or estate conveyed by such deed of trust, or any part thereof, is situated.

OF SERVITUDE- *Exodus 21:2-4* 2 If thou buy a Hebrew servant, six years he shall serve: and in the seventh he shall go out free for nothing. 3 If he came in by himself, he shall go out by himself: if he were married, then his wife shall go out with him. 4 If his master have given him a wife, and she have borne him sons or daughters; the wife and her children shall be her master's, and he shall go out by himself.

Leviticus 25:39 And if thy brother *that dwelleth* by thee be waxen poor, and be sold unto thee; thou shalt not compel him to serve as a bondservant:

Deuteronomy 15:12 And if thy brother, an Hebrew man, or an Hebrew woman, be sold unto thee, and serve thee six years; then in the seventh year thou shalt let him go free from thee.

SURETIES - *Proverbs 6:1-2, 11:15, 17:18, 22:26* **1** My son, if thou be surety for thy friend, *if* thou hast stricken thy hand with a stranger, **2** Thou are snared with the words of thy mouth, thou art taken with the words of thy mouth. **11:15** He that is surety for a stranger shall smart *for it:* and he that hateth suretiship is sure. **17:18** A man void of understanding striketh hands, *and* becometh surety in the presence of his friend. **22:26** Be not thou *one* of them that strike hands, *or* of them that are sureties for debts.

STATUTES: In LAW, one who enters into a bond or recognizance to answer for another's appearance in court, or for his payment of a debt or for the performance of some act, and who in case of the principal debtor's failure, is compellable to pay the debt or damages. You want to pay for another man's mistake? In Missouri Revised Statutes Title XXVIII, Chapter 433 Suretyship, the principal debtor and other parties liable may be sued, there's interest due, entitlement of judgment on the principal debtor, even attainment after death from the co-suretor's estate.

TRUSTEES - *Exodus 22:12, 14, 15* **12** And if it be stolen from him, he shall make restitution unto the owner thereof. **14** And if a man borrow *ought* of his neighbor, and it be hurt, or die, the owner thereof *being* not with it, he shall surely make *it* good. **15** But if the owner thereof *be* with it, he shall not make *it* good: if it *be* an hired *thing,* it came for his hire.

Leviticus 6:1-5 **1** And the Lord spake unto Moses, saying, **2** If a soul sin, and commit a trespass against the Lord, and lie unto his neighbor in that which was delivered him to keep, or in fellowship, or in a thing taken away by violence, or hath deceived his neighbor; **3** or have found that which was lost, and lieth concerning it, and sweareth falsely; in any of all these that a man doeth, sinning therein: **4** then it shall be, because he hath sinned, and is guilty, that he shall restore that which he took violently away, or the thing which he hath deceitfully gotten, or that which was delivered him to keep, or the lost thing which he found, **5** or all that about which he hath sworn falsely; he shall even restore it in the principal, and shall add the fifth part more thereto, *and* give it unto him to whom it appertaineth, in the day of his trespass offering.

CIVIL CODE: In relation to contractual relations and trust, **§431.040** of the Missouri Revised Statutes, **Fraud in sale of nursery stock—damages recoverable**, Any person, firm or corporation doing business in this state as nurserymen or tree dealers, who shall falsely represent the grade or variety of any fruit trees, vines, shrubs, plants or bulbs which they sell, shall be guilty of a misdemeanor, and responsible for double the purchase price of such fruit trees, vines, shrubs, plants or bulbs as damage, to be recovered by the purchaser of same.

In the Consolidated Laws of New York, Chapter 50 REAL PROPERTY ARTICLE 4-A **§126**, a trustee can be identified as a corporation, firm, or trust indenture or other similar instruments or any successor of such trustee, along with restrictions identified in **§127 Restrictions on trustees.**

USURY - *Exodus 22:25* If thou lend money to *any of* my people *that is* poor by thee, thou shalt not be to him as an usurer, neither shalt thou lay upon him usury.

Leviticus 25:36 Take thou no usury of him, or increase: but fear thy God; that thy brother may live with thee.

Deuteronomy 23:19, 20 **19** Thou shalt not lend upon usury to thy brother; usury of money, usury of victuals, usury of any thing that is lent upon usury: **20** unto a stranger thou mayest lend upon usury; but unto thy brother thou shalt not lend upon usury: that the Lord thy God may bless thee in all that thou settest thine hand to in the land whither thou goest to possess it.

Ezekiel 18:10-13 **10** If he beget a son *that is* a robber, a shedder of blood, and *that* doeth the like to *any* one of these *things*, **11** and that doeth not any of those *duties*, but even hath eaten upon the mountains, and defiled his neighbor's wife, **12** hath oppressed the poor and needy, hath spoiled by violence, hath not restored the pledge, and hath lifted up his eyes to the idols, hath committed abomination, **13** hath given forth upon usury, and hath taken increase: shall he then live? he shall not live: he hath done all these abominations; he shall surely die; his blood shall be upon him.

CIVIL CODE: California Civil Code Division 3, Part 4, Title 1.5 Consumers Legal Remedies Act, Chapter 3 Deceptive Practices **§1770(a)** Gives a comprehensive list of offenses in relation to usury without actually using the term USURY. All of the States are guilty of USURY so ambiguously, you're protected from SOME deceptive practices. **§1770(a)** protects a consumer from deceptive acts or practices undertaken by any person in a transaction intended to result or that results in the sale or lease of goods or services to any consumer deemed unlawful.

WAGES – *Leviticus 19:13* Thou shalt not defraud thy neighbour, neither rob *him*: the wages of him that is hired shall not abide with thee all night until the morning.

Deuteronomy 24:15 At his day thou shalt give *him* his hire, neither shall the sun go down upon it; for he is poor, and setteth his heart upon it: lest he cry against thee unto the LORD, and it be sin unto thee.

CIVIL CODE: The Fair Labor Standards Act of 1938, amended 29 U.S. Code **§201**, is the most "important" piece of **NEW DEAL LEGISLATION** according to Franklin Delano Roosevelt, a wolf of Wall St. Described applies to employees engaged in **INTERSTATE COMMERCE** or in the production of goods for commerce, or who are employed by an enterprise engaged in commerce or in the production of goods. The FLSA (1938) is a law creating the right to a minimum wage and time and a half overtime pay when an employee works over 40 hours per week. This "act" has been aggressively amended over 15 times.

LAWS OF FAMILY LIFE

CONCUBINES – *Genesis 21:10-14* **10** Wherefore she said unto Abraham, Cast out this bondwoman and her son: for the son of this bondwoman shall not be heir with my son, *even* with Isaac. **11** And the thing was very grievous in Abraham's sight because of his son. **12** And God said unto Abraham, Let it not be grievous in thy sight because of the lad, and because of thy bondwoman; in all that Sarah hath said unto thee, hearken unto her voice; for in Isaac shall thy seed be called. **13** And also of the son of the bondwoman will I make a nation, because he *is* thy seed. **14** And Abraham rose up early in the morning, and took bread, and a bottle of water, and gave *it* unto Hagar, putting *it* on her shoulder, and the child, and sent her away: and she departed, and wandered in the wilderness of Beer-sheba.

Exodus 21:7-11 **7** And if a man sell his daughter to be a maidservant, she shall not go out as the menservants do. **8** If she please not her master, who hath betrothed her to himself, then shall he let her be redeemed: to sell her unto a strange nation he shall have no power, seeing he hath dealt deceitfully with her. **9** And if he have betrothed her unto his son, he shall deal with her after the manner of daughters. **10** If he take him another *wife*, her food, her raiment, and her duty of marriage, shall he not diminish. **11** And if he do not these three unto her, then shall she go out free without money.

1 Kings 11:3 And he had seven hundred wives, princesses, and three hundred concubines: and his wives turned away his heart.

In the U.S., having **CONCUBINES** isn't a common trait and is deemed a crime by the name of **BIGAMY**. **BIGAMY** in most penal codes is defined as cohabitating, purporting to marry another, or entering any domestic partnership with one who is or believed to be married already. It is punishable as a misdemeanor or a felony, depending on your jurisdiction and/or state.

DIVORCE – *Leviticus 21:7, 14, 22:13* **7** They shall not take a wife *that is* a whore, or profane; neither shall they take a woman put away from her husband: for he *is* holy unto his God. **14** A widow, or a divorced woman, or profane, *or* a harlot, these shall he not take: but he shall take a virgin of his own people to wife. **22:13** But if the priest's daughter be a widow, or divorced, and have no child, and is returned unto her father's house, as in her youth, she shall eat of her father's meat: but there shall no stranger eat thereof.

Numbers 30:9 But every vow of a widow, and of her that is divorced, wherewith they have bound their souls, shall stand against her.

Deuteronomy 24:1-4 **1** When a man hath taken a wife, and married her, and it come to pass that she find no favor in his eyes, because he hath found some uncleanness in her: then let him write her a bill of divorcement, and give *it* in her hand, and send her out of his house. **2** And when she is departed out of his house, she may go and be another man's *wife*. **3** And *if* the latter husband hate her, and write her a bill of divorcement, and giveth *it* in her hand, and sendeth her out of his house; or if the latter husband die, which took her *to be* his wife; **4** her former husband, which sent her away, may not take her again to be his wife, after that she is defiled; for that *is* abomination before the Lord: and thou shalt not cause the land to sin, which the Lord thy God giveth thee *for* an inheritance.

Isaiah 50:1 Thus saith the Lord, Where *is* the bill of your mother's divorcement, whom I have put away? or which of my creditors *is it* to whom I have sold you? Behold, for your iniquities have ye sold yourselves, and for your transgressions is your mother put away.

Jeremiah 3:8 And I saw, when for all the causes whereby backsliding Israel committed adultery, I had put her away, and given her a bill of divorce; yet her treacherous sister Judah feared not, but went and played the harlot also.

Matthew 5:32, 19:3-9 **5:32** but I say unto you, That whosoever shall put away his wife, saving for the cause of fornication, causeth her to commit adultery: and whosoever shall marry her that is divorced committeth adultery. ***19:3-9*** **3** The Pharisees also came unto him, tempting him, and saying unto him, Is it lawful for a man to put away his wife for every cause? **4** And he answered and said unto them, Have ye not read, that he which made *them* at the beginning made them male and female, **5** and said,

> For this cause shall a man leave father and mother,
>
> and shall cleave to his wife:
>
> and they twain shall be one flesh?

6 Wherefore they are no more twain, but one flesh. What therefore God hath joined together, let not man put asunder. **7** They say unto him, Why did Moses then command to give a writing of divorcement, and to put her away? **8** He saith unto them, Moses because of the hardness of your hearts suffered you to put away your wives: but from the beginning it was not so. **9** And I say unto you, Whosoever shall put away his wife, except *it be* for fornication, and shall marry another, committeth adultery: and whoso marrieth her which is put away doth commit adultery.

Mark 10:2-12 **2** And the Pharisees came to him, and asked him, Is it lawful for a man to put away *his* wife? tempting him. **3** And he answered and said unto them, What did Moses command you? **4** And they said, Moses suffered to write a bill of divorcement, and to put *her* away. **5** And Jesus answered and said unto them, For the hardness of your heart he wrote you this precept. **6** But from the beginning of the creation God made them male and female. **7** For this cause shall a man leave his father and mother, and cleave to his wife; **8** and they twain shall be one flesh: so then they are no more twain, but one flesh. **9** What therefore God hath joined together, let not man put asunder.

10 And in the house his disciples asked him again of the same *matter*. **11** And he saith unto them, Whosoever shall put away his wife, and marry another, committeth adultery against her. **12** And if a woman shall put away her husband, and be married to another, she committeth adultery.

Luke 16:18 Whosoever putteth away his wife, and marrieth another, committeth adultery: and whosoever marrieth her that is put away from *her* husband committeth adultery.

1 Corinthians 7:10, 39 10 And unto the married I command, *yet* not I, but the Lord, Let not the wife depart from *her* husband: 39 The wife is bound by the law as long as her husband liveth; but if her husband be dead, she is at liberty to be married to whom she will; only in the Lord.

In LAW I am sure you've heard the terms used for a legal separation. **California Family Code Div. 6, Pt. 3, Chapter 2 § 2310** defines a dissolution of marriage or legal separation as (a) irreconcilable differences or (b) permanent legal incapacity to make decisions. Which is why usually in America you hear A.

AUTHORITY OF FATHERS – *Genesis 22:1-13, 24:4* 1 And it came to pass after these things, that God did tempt Abraham, and said unto him, Abraham: and he said, Behold, *here* I *am*. 2 And he said, Take now thy son, thine only *son* Isaac, whom thou lovest, and get thee into the land of Mori´ah; and offer him there for a burnt offering upon one of the mountains which I will tell thee of. 3 And Abraham rose up early in the morning, and saddled his ass, and took two of his young men with him, and Isaac his son, and clave the wood for the burnt offering, and rose up, and went unto the place of which God had told him. 4 Then on the third day Abraham lifted up his eyes, and saw the place afar off. 5 And Abraham said unto his young men, Abide ye here with the ass; and I and the lad will go yonder and worship, and come again to you. 6 And Abraham took the wood of the burnt offering, and laid *it* upon Isaac his son; and he took the fire in his hand, and a knife; and they went both of them together. 7 And Isaac spake unto Abraham his father, and said, My father: and he said, Here *am* I, my son. And he said, Behold the fire and the wood: but where *is* the lamb for a burnt offering? **8** And Abraham said, My son, God will provide himself a lamb for a burnt offering: so they went both of them together.

9 And they came to the place which God had told him of; and Abraham built an altar there, and laid the wood in order, and bound Isaac his son, and laid him on the altar upon the wood. **10** And Abraham stretched forth his hand, and took the knife to slay his son. **11** And the angel of the Lord called unto him out of heaven, and said, Abraham, Abraham: and he said, Here *am* I. **12** And he said, Lay not thine hand upon the lad, neither do thou any thing unto him: for now I know that thou fearest God, seeing thou hast not withheld thy son, thine only *son*, from me. **13** And Abraham lifted up his eyes, and looked, and behold behind *him* a ram caught in a thicket by his horns: and Abraham went and took the ram, and offered him up for a burnt offering in the stead of his son. **24:4** but thou shalt go unto my country, and to my kindred, and take a wife unto my son Isaac.

<u>**Numbers 30:3-5**</u> **3** If a woman also vow a vow unto the Lord, and bind *herself* by a bond, *being* in her father's house in her youth; **4** and her father hear her vow, and her bond wherewith she hath bound her soul, and her father shall hold his peace at her; then all her vows shall stand, and every bond wherewith she hath bound her soul shall stand. **5** But if her father disallow her in the day that he heareth, not any of her vows, or of her bonds wherewith she hath bound her soul, shall stand; and the Lord shall forgive her, because her father disallowed her.

Judges 11:30-39 **30** And Jephthah vowed a vow unto the Lord, and said, If thou shalt without fail deliver the children of Ammon into mine hands, **31** then it shall be, that whatsoever cometh forth of the doors of my house to meet me, when I return in peace from the children of Ammon, shall surely be the Lord's, and I will offer it up for a burnt offering. **32** So Jephthah passed over unto the children of Ammon to fight against them; and the Lord delivered them into his hands. **33** And he smote them from Aro´er, even till thou come to Minnith, *even* twenty cities, and unto the plain of the vineyards, with a very great slaughter. Thus the children of Ammon were subdued before the children of Israel.

34 And Jephthah came to Mizpeh unto his house, and, behold, his daughter came out to meet him with timbrels and with dances: and she *was his* only child; beside her he had neither son nor daughter. **35** And it came to pass, when he saw her, that he rent his clothes, and said, Alas, my daughter! thou hast brought me very low, and thou art one of them that trouble me: for I have opened my mouth unto the Lord, and I cannot go back. **36** And she said unto him, My father, *if* thou hast opened thy mouth unto the Lord, do to me according to that which hath proceeded out of thy mouth; forasmuch as the Lord hath taken vengeance for thee of thine enemies, *even* of the children of Ammon. **37** And she said unto her father, Let this thing be done for me: let me alone two months, that I may go up and down upon the mountains, and bewail my virginity, I and my fellows. **38** And he said, Go. And he sent her away *for* two months: and she went with her companions, and bewailed her virginity upon the mountains. **39** And it came to pass at the end of two months, that she returned unto her father, who did with her *according* to his vow which he had vowed: and she knew no man. And it was a custom in Israel,

Job 1:5, 9 **5** And it was so, when the days of *their* feasting were gone about, that Job sent and sanctified them, and rose up early in the morning, and offered burnt offerings *according* to the number of them all: for Job said, It may be that my sons have sinned, and cursed God in their hearts. Thus did Job continually. **9** Then Satan answered the Lord, and said, Doth Job fear God for nought?

DUTIES OF FATHERS – ***Ephesians 6:4*** And, ye fathers, provoke not your children to wrath: but bring them up in the nurture and admonition of the Lord.

Learn the LAW, follow God.

DUTIES OF HUSBANDS – ***Ephesians 5:22-30*** **22** Wives, submit yourselves unto your own husbands, as unto the Lord. **23** For the husband is the head of the wife, even as Christ is the head of the church: and he is the saviour of the body. **24** Therefore as the church is subject unto Christ, so *let* the wives *be* to their own husbands in every thing. **25** Husbands, love your wives, even as Christ also loved the church, and gave himself for it; **26** that he might sanctify and cleanse it with the washing of water by the word, **27** that he might present it to himself a glorious church, not having spot, or wrinkle, or any such thing; but that it should be holy and without blemish. **28** So ought men to love their wives as their own bodies. He that loveth his wife loveth himself. **29** For no man ever yet hated his own flesh; but nourisheth and cherisheth it, even as the Lord the church: **30** for we are members of his body, of his flesh, and of his bones.

LEVIRATE MARRIAGE – *Genesis 38:6-11* **6** And Judah took a wife for Er his firstborn, whose name *was* Tamar. **7** And Er, Judah's firstborn, was wicked in the sight of the Lord; and the Lord slew him. **8** And Judah said unto Onan, Go in unto thy brother's wife, and marry her, and raise up seed to thy brother. **9** And Onan knew that the seed should not be his; and it came to pass, when he went in unto his brother's wife, that he spilled *it* on the ground, lest that he should give seed to his brother. **10** And the thing which he did displeased the Lord: wherefore he slew him also. **11** Then said Judah to Tamar his daughter-in-law, Remain a widow at thy father's house, till Shelah my son be grown: for he said, Lest peradventure he die also, as his brethren *did.* And Tamar went and dwelt in her father's house.

Deuteronomy 25:5-10 **5** If brethren dwell together, and one of them die, and have no child, the wife of the dead shall not marry without unto a stranger: her husband's brother shall go in unto her, and take her to him to wife, and perform the duty of a husband's brother unto her. **6** And it shall be, *that* the firstborn which she beareth shall succeed in the name of his brother *which is* dead, that his name be not put out of Israel. **7** And if the man like not to take his brother's wife, then let his brother's wife go up to the gate unto the elders, and say, My husband's brother refuseth to raise up unto his brother a name in Israel, he will not perform the duty of my husband's brother. **8** Then the elders of his city shall call him, and speak unto him: and *if* he stand *to it,* and say, I like not to take her; **9** then shall his brother's wife come unto him in the presence of the elders, and loose his shoe from off his foot, and spit in his face, and shall answer and say, So shall it be done unto that man that will not build up his brother's house. **10** And his name shall be called in Israel, The house of him that hath his shoe loosed.

MARITAL FAITHFULNESS - *Deuteronomy 22:30* A man shall not take his father's wife, nor discover his father's skirt.

Matthew 19:3-9 3 The Pharisees also came unto him, tempting him, and saying unto him, Is it lawful for a man to put away his wife for every cause? 4 And he answered and said unto them, Have ye not read, that he which made *them* at the beginning made them male and female, 5 and said,

For this cause shall a man leave father and mother,

and shall cleave to his wife:

and they twain shall be one flesh?

6 Wherefore they are no more twain, but one flesh. What therefore God hath joined together, let not man put asunder. 7 They say unto him, Why did Moses then command to give a writing of divorcement, and to put her away? 8 He saith unto them, Moses because of the hardness of your hearts suffered you to put away your wives: but from the beginning it was not so. 9 And I say unto you, Whosoever shall put away his wife, except *it be* for fornication, and shall marry another, committeth adultery: and whoso marrieth her which is put away doth commit adultery.

1 Corinthians 7:2 Nevertheless, *to avoid* fornication, let every man have his own wife, and let every woman have her own husband.

MARRIAGE – *Genesis 2:18-24, 24:4, 34:14* **18** And the Lord God said, *It is* not good that the man should be alone; I will make him a help meet for him. **19** And out of the ground the Lord God formed every beast of the field, and every fowl of the air; and brought *them* unto Adam to see what he would call them: and whatsoever Adam called every living creature, that *was* the name thereof. **20** And Adam gave names to all cattle, and to the fowl of the air, and to every beast of the field; but for Adam there was not found a help meet for him. **21** And the Lord God caused a deep sleep to fall upon Adam, and he slept; and he took one of his ribs, and closed up the flesh instead thereof. **22** And the rib, which the Lord God had taken from man, made he a woman, and brought her unto the man. **23** And Adam said, This *is* now bone of my bones, and flesh of my flesh: she shall be called Woman, because she was taken out of Man. **24** Therefore shall a man leave his father and his mother, and shall cleave unto his wife: and they shall be one flesh. **24:4** but thou shalt go unto my country, and to my kindred, and take a wife unto my son Isaac. **34:14** and they said unto them, We cannot do this thing, to give our sister to one that is uncircumcised; for that *were* a reproach unto us:

Numbers 36:6 This *is* the thing which the Lord doth command concerning the daughters of Zelo´phehad, saying, Let them marry to whom they think best; only to the family of the tribe of their father shall they marry.

Judges 14:1-4, 15:1, 2 **1** And Samson went down to Timnath, and saw a woman in Timnath of the daughters of the Philistines. **2** And he came up, and told his father and his mother, and said, I have seen a woman in Timnath of the daughters of the Philistines: now therefore get her for me to wife. **3** Then his father and his mother said unto him, *Is there* never a woman among the daughters of thy brethren, or among all my people, that thou goest to take a wife of the uncircumcised Philistines? And Samson said unto his father, Get her for me; for she pleaseth me well.

4 But his father and his mother knew not that it *was* of the Lord, that he sought an occasion against the Philistines: for at that time the Philistines had dominion over Israel.

15:1, 2 1 But it came to pass within a while after, in the time of wheat harvest, that Samson visited his wife with a kid; and he said, I will go in to my wife into the chamber. But her father would not suffer him to go in. 2 And her father said, I verily thought that thou hadst utterly hated her; therefore I gave her to thy companion: *is* not her younger sister fairer than she? take her, I pray thee, instead of her.

Ephesians 5:31 For this cause shall a man leave his father and mother, and shall be joined unto his wife, and they two shall be one flesh.

CIVIL CODE: Missouri Revised Statutes Title XXX DOMESTIC RELATIONS Chapter 451 § 451.010 defines MARRIAGE as a CIVIL CONTRACT with § 451.020 banning marriages that are indeed unlawful. California Family Code Division 3 MARRIAGE Part 1 § 300 defines it as a civil contract along with what is considered consent or no consent to be married. In the New York Consolidated Laws Chapter 14 Article 3 § 11-C, officials who are SOLEMNIZED to officiate marriages are called MARRIAGE OFFICERS while other states define solemnization by the authorization of someone of the ecclesiastical government or church.

RESTRICTIONS ON MARRIAGE – *Exodus 34:15, 16*
15 Lest thou make a covenant with the inhabitants of the land, and they go a whoring after their gods, and do sacrifice

unto their gods, and *one* call thee, and thou eat of his sacrifice; **16** and thou take of their daughters unto thy sons, and their daughters go a whoring after their gods, and make thy sons go a whoring after their gods.

Leviticus 18:10, 15, 20:14, 17, 19 **10** The nakedness of thy son's daughter, or of thy daughter's daughter, *even* their nakedness thou shalt not uncover: for theirs *is* thine own nakedness. **15** Thou shalt not uncover the nakedness of thy daughter-in-law: she *is* thy son's wife; thou shalt not uncover her nakedness. ***20:14, 17, 19*** **14** And if a man take a wife and her mother, it *is* wickedness: they shall be burnt with fire, both he and they; that there be no wickedness among you. **17** And if a man shall take his sister, his father's daughter, or his mother's daughter, and see her nakedness, and she see his nakedness; it *is* a wicked thing; and they shall be cut off in the sight of their people: he hath uncovered his sister's nakedness; he shall bear his iniquity. **19** And thou shalt not uncover the nakedness of thy mother's sister, nor of thy father's sister; for he uncovereth his near kin: they shall bear their iniquity.

Numbers 36:6 This *is* the thing which the Lord doth command concerning the daughters of Zelo´phehad, saying, Let them marry to whom they think best; only to the family of the tribe of their father shall they marry.

Deuteronomy 7:1-3, 22:30 **1** When the Lord thy God shall bring thee into the land whither thou goest to possess it, and hath cast out many nations before thee, the Hittites, and the Gir´gashites, and the Amorites, and the Canaanites, and the Per´izzites, and the Hivites, and the Jeb´usites, seven nations greater and mightier than thou; **2** and when the Lord thy God shall deliver them before thee; thou shalt smite them, *and* utterly destroy them; thou shalt make no covenant with them, nor show mercy unto them: **3** neither shalt thou make marriages with them; thy daughter thou shalt not give unto his son, nor his daughter shalt thou take unto thy son. **22:30** A man shall not take his father's wife, nor discover his father's skirt.

1 Timothy 3:2 A bishop then must be blameless, the husband of one wife, vigilant, sober, of good behavior, given to hospitality, apt to teach;

Illegally solemnized marriages are punishable by law. In Missouri Revised Statutes § 451.040 Subsection (3) 5. Common-law marriages shall be null and void. In § 451.020, marriages such as incestual marriages or marriages with persons who lack capacity to get married are unlawful. In § 451.022, same sex marriages are prohibited and a license may not be issued as God would have intended. While general restrictions are not set forth in the California Family Code on marriage, Division 3, Part 1. VALIDITY OF MARRIAGE assesses whether the union is permissible to receive a marriage license, while Part 3. SOLEMNIZATION OF MARRIAGE focuses on who is capable to make the union between both parties.

RESPECT FOR PARENTS – *Exodus 20:12, 21:15, 17* **12** Honor thy father and thy mother: that thy days may be long upon the land which the Lord thy God giveth thee. **21:15** And he that smiteth his father, or his mother, shall be surely put to death. **17** And he that curseth his father, or his mother, shall surely be put to death.

CIVIL CODE: Parental respect should go without saying, but in today's America, there are many children born under premature and immature circumstances. The result is a lack of respect for the parents who have all of their time invested into the world rather than their family's well-being and foundation. **California Family Code Division 12. PARENT AND CHILD RELATIONSHIP Part 1. RIGHTS OF PARENTS**, gives the authority by law to the parents unless there are circumstances which would prevent that from happening, like a negligent or abusive parent. Missouri Revised Statutes Title XXX DOMESTIC RELATIONS overlays adoption, foster care, and child abuse in their laws but doesn't specify parental powers unless proving paternity to administer family support.

POLYGAMY - *Genesis 16:1-3, 29:21-30* 1 Now Sarai, Abram's wife, bare him no children: and she had a handmaid, an Egyptian, whose name *was* Hagar. 2 And Sarai said unto Abram, Behold now, the Lord hath restrained me from bearing: I pray thee, go in unto my maid; it may be that I may obtain children by her. And Abram hearkened to the voice of Sarai. 3 And Sarai, Abram's wife, took Hagar her maid the Egyptian, after Abram had dwelt ten years in the land of Canaan, and gave her to her husband Abram to be his wife. **29:21-30** And Jacob said unto Laban, Give *me* my wife, for my days are fulfilled, that I may go in unto her. 22 And Laban gathered together all the men of the place, and made a feast. 23 And it came to pass in the evening, that he took Le´ah his daughter, and brought her to him; and he went in unto her. 24 And Laban gave unto his daughter Le´ah Zilpah his maid *for* a handmaid. 25 And it came to pass, that in the morning, behold, it *was* Le´ah: and he said to Laban, What *is* this thou hast done unto me? did not I serve with thee for Rachel? wherefore then hast thou beguiled me? 26 And Laban said, It must not be so done in our country, to give the younger before the firstborn. 27 Fulfil her week, and we will give thee this also for the service which thou shalt serve with me yet seven other years. 28 And Jacob did so, and fulfilled her week: and he gave him Rachel his daughter to wife also. **29** And Laban gave to Rachel his daughter Bilhah his handmaid to be her maid. 30And he went in also unto Rachel, and he loved also Rachel more than Le´ah, and served with him yet seven other years.

1 Samuel 1:1, 2 **1** Now there was a certain man of Ramatha´im-zo´phim, of mount E´phra-im, and his name *was* Elka´nah, the son of Jero´ham, the son of Eli´hu, the son of Tohu, the son of Zuph, an Eph´rathite: **2** and he had two wives; the name of the one *was* Hannah, and the name of the other Penin´nah: and Penin´nah had children, but Hannah had no children.

1 Kings 11:1-8 **1** But king Solomon loved many strange women, together with the daughter of Pharaoh, women of the Moabites, Ammonites, Edomites, Zido´ni-ans, *and* Hittites; **2** of the nations *concerning* which the Lord said unto the children of Israel, Ye shall not go in to them, neither shall they come in unto you: *for* surely they will turn away your heart after their gods: Solomon clave unto these in love. **3** And he had seven hundred wives, princesses, and three hundred concubines: and his wives turned away his heart. **4** For it came to pass, when Solomon was old, *that* his wives turned away his heart after other gods: and his heart was not perfect with the Lord his God, as *was* the heart of David his father. **5** For Solomon went after Ash´toreth the goddess of the Zido´ni-ans, and after Milcom the abomination of the Ammonites. **6** And Solomon did evil in the sight of the Lord, and went not fully after the Lord, as *did* David his father. **7** Then did Solomon build a high place for Chemosh, the abomination of Moab, in the hill that *is* before Jerusalem, and for Molech, the abomination of the children of Ammon. **8** And likewise did he for all his strange wives, which burnt incense and sacrificed unto their gods.

1 Timothy 3:2 A bishop then must be blameless, the husband of one wife, vigilant, sober, of good ?behavior, given to hospitality, apt to teach;

The **Texas Penal Code Title 6 Chapter 25 OFFENSES AGAINST THE FAMILY §25.01 BIGAMY** makes it unlawful to live with or assume that you and another are married if one of you already has a spouse. Does this apply to men and women who don't consider themselves married? In civil code, men and women are free to have multiple partners, as sexual intercourse isn't considered marriage in the eyes of the law. Sexual offenses in the law are gross in comparison to unfaithful, promiscuous men and women.

TREATMENT OF SERVANTS – *Exodus 20:10, 21:2, 4, 7, 8, 20* **10** but the seventh day *is* the sabbath of the Lord thy God: *in it* thou shalt not do any work, thou, nor thy son, nor thy daughter, thy manservant, nor thy maidservant, nor thy cattle, nor thy stranger that *is* within thy gates:

21:2, 4, 7, 8, 20 If thou buy a Hebrew servant, six years he shall serve: and in the seventh he shall go out free for nothing. **4** If his master have given him a wife, and she have borne him sons or daughters; the wife and her children shall be her master's, and he shall go out by himself. **7** And if a man sell his daughter to be a maidservant, she shall not go out as the menservants do. **8** If she please not her master, who hath betrothed her to himself, then shall he let her be redeemed: to sell her unto a strange nation he shall have no power, seeing he hath dealt deceitfully with her. **20** And if a man smite his servant, or his maid, with a rod, and he die under his hand; he shall be surely punished.

Deuteronomy 24:14, 15 **14** Thou shalt not oppress a hired servant *that is* poor and needy, *whether he be* of thy brethren, or of thy strangers that *are* in thy land within thy gates: **15** at his day thou shalt give *him* his hire, neither shall the sun go down upon it; for he *is* poor, and setteth his heart upon it: lest he cry against thee unto the Lord, and it be sin unto thee.

CIVIL CODE: The protection of "human rights" are found mostly in the U.S. Code and used as a model for states and their Workforce programs, labor unions, and policies. An individual is protected under what a state deems necessary and lawful in the workplace. Under EMPLOYMENT REGULATION & SUPERVISION Division 2 of the California Labor Code, the usual protections such as unfair labor practices, labor dispute protections, and ordinary rules that we all see in our breakrooms. In the **Missouri Revised Statutes, Title XVIII**, there are sections for Health and Safety of Employees (Chapter 292), Worker's Compensation Law (Chapter 287), along with other humane protections for people and not protections for a business and its model. So in this regard, California's protection for the people is obscure at first sight. In the **Consolidated Laws of New York, Chapter 31** LABOR, Article 7 GENERAL PROVISIONS, § 212, by law, every grower or processor who employs farm workers must provide bottled water for them to drink at their own expense. So, it'll be safe to assume that New York has the people and amusement parks (Chapter 31, Article 27) in mind. Why it has to be distinguished in the Texas Statutes Labor Code **§ 21.1065 SEXUAL HARRASSMENT PROTECTIONS FOR UNPAID INTERNS,** I know not, but there you have it. The law doesn't "dis-criminate" on what issues it decides to tackle and who to protect.

DUTIES OF WIVES – *Ephesians 5:22-30* **22** Wives, submit yourselves unto your own husbands, as unto the

Lord. **23** For the husband is the head of the wife, even as Christ is the head of the church: and he is the saviour of the body. **24** Therefore as the church is subject unto Christ, so *let* the wives *be* to their own husbands in every thing. **25** Husbands, love your wives, even as Christ also loved the church, and gave himself for it; **26** that he might sanctify and cleanse it with the washing of water by the word, **27** that he might present it to himself a glorious church, not having spot, or wrinkle, or any such thing; but that it should be holy and without blemish. **28** So ought men to love their wives as their own bodies. He that loveth his wife loveth himself. **29** For no man ever yet hated his own flesh; but nourisheth and cherisheth it, even as the Lord the church: 30for we are members of his body, of his flesh, and of his bones.

CIVIL CODE: In marriage, women are protected by Consolidated Laws of New York, Chapter 14 Domestic Relations Article 4, Certain Rights and Liabilities of Husband and Wife, such as **§ 50. Property of married woman,** property she has acquired before and during marriage remains hers as if she was unmarried, but does not specify that for the man. In Missouri Revised Statutes Title XXX Chapter 451 **§ 451.290** Wife deemed **FEMME SOLE**, same rule as mentioned above in New York Law.

KINDS AND POWERS OF GOVERNMENTS

RIGHTS OF ALIENS – *Exodus 12:49* One law shall be to him that is homeborn, and unto the stranger that sojourneth among you.

Leviticus 24:22 Ye shall have one manner of law, as well for the stranger, as for one of your own country: for I am the LORD your God.

CONSTITUTIONAL LAW: United States Constitution Amendment 14 (1868) §1. All persons born or naturalized in the United States, and subject to the jurisdiction thereof, are citizens of the United States and of the State wherein they reside. No State shall make or enforce any law which shall abridge the privileges or immunities of citizens of the United Stes; nor shall any State deprive any person of life, liberty, or property, without due process of law; nor deny to any person within its jurisdiction the equal protection of the laws.

ELDERS – *Numbers 11:16, 24* 16 And over the host of the tribe of the children of Zebulun *was* Eliab the son of Helon. 24 And over the host of the tribe of the children of Benjamin *was* Abidan the son of Gideoni.

Deuteronomy 22:15, 27:1 22:15 then shall the father of the damsel, and her mother, take and bring forth the tokens of the damsel's virginity unto the elders of the city in the gate: 27:1 And Moses with the elders of Israel commanded the people, saying, Keep all the commandments which I command you this day.

Judges 8:16, 11:5-11 8:16 And he took the elders of the city, and thorns of the wilderness, and briers, and with them he taught the men of Succoth. 11:5-11 And it was so, that when the children of Ammon made war against Israel, the elders of Gil´e-ad went to fetch Jephthah out of the land of Tob: 6

and they said unto Jephthah, Come, and be our captain, that we may fight with the children of Ammon. 7 And Jephthah said unto the elders of Gil´e-ad, Did not ye hate me, and expel me out of my father's house? and why are ye come unto me now when ye are in distress? 8 And the elders of Gil´e-ad said unto Jephthah, Therefore we turn again to thee now, that thou mayest go with us, and fight against the children of Ammon, and be our head over all the inhabitants of Gil´e-ad. 9 And Jephthah said unto the elders of Gil´e-ad, If ye bring me home again to fight against the children of Ammon, and the Lord deliver them before me, shall I be your head? 10 And the elders of Gil´e-ad said unto Jephthah, The Lord be witness between us, if we do not so according to thy words. 11 Then Jephthah went with the elders of Gil´e-ad, and the people made him head and captain over them: and Jephthah uttered all his words before the Lord in Mizpeh.

Ezra 10:8 and that whosoever would not come within three days, according to the counsel of the princes and the elders, all his substance should be forfeited, and himself separated from the congregation of those that had been carried away.

U.S. Constitution Article 1, Section 3 Clause 3 "No person shall be a Senator who shall not have attained to the Age of thirty Years, and been nine Years a Citizen of the United States" **Article II §1 (5)** No person except a natural born Citizen, or a Citizen of the United States, at the time of the Adoption of this Constitution, shall be eligible to the Office of President; neither shall any Person be eligible to that Office who shall not have attained to the Age of thirty five Years, and been fourteen Years a Resident within the United States.

AARON'S ROD: According to *Gillespie,* **Aaron's Rod Blossoming,** *p. 18,* "There is no mention of elderships constituted of pastors and ruling elders (without any bishop having pre-eminence over the rest), neither in the canon law, nor decretals of popes, nor in the book of the canons of the Roman church;"

GOVERNORS - *Ezra 5:3, 6, 6:6, 8:36* **5:3** At the same time came to them Tat´nai, governor on this side the river, and She´thar-boz´nai, and their companions, and said thus unto them, Who hath commanded you to build this house, and to make up this wall? **6** The copy of the letter that Tat´nai, governor on this side the river, and She´thar-boz´nai, and his companions the Aphar´sachites, which *were* on this side the river, sent unto Dari´us the king: **6:6** Now *therefore,* Tat´nai, governor beyond the river, She´thar-boz´nai, and your companions the Aphar´sachites, which *are* beyond the river, be ye far from thence: **8:36** And they delivered the king's commissions unto the king's lieutenants, and to the governors on this side the river: and they furthered the people, and the house of God.

Esther 3:12 Then were the king's scribes called on the thirteenth day of the first month, and there was written according to all that Haman had commanded unto the king's lieutenants, and to the governors that *were* over every province, and to the rulers of every people of every province according to the writing thereof, and *to* every people after their language; in the name of king Ahasue´rus was it written, and sealed with the king's ring.

Matthew 27:2 and when they had bound him, they led *him* away, and delivered him to Pontius Pilate the governor.

Luke 20:20 And they watched *him*, and sent forth spies, which should feign themselves just men, that they might take hold of his words, that so they might deliver him unto the power and authority of the governor.

Acts 23:26 Claudius Lys´i-as unto the most excellent governor Felix *sendeth* greeting.

CIVIL CODE: According to the National Governors Association and State constitutions, **GOVERNORS** have many roles and responsibilities in common, but the scope of gubernatorial (governmental) power varies from state to state in accordance with state constitutions, legislation, and **TRADITION**, which is the act of delivering into the hands of another. Governors are the **HEADS OF STATE**.

JUDGES – ***Judges 2:13-18*** **13** And they forsook the Lord, and served Ba´al and Ash´toreth. **14** And the anger of the Lord was hot against Israel, and he delivered them into the hands of spoilers that spoiled them, and he sold them into the hands of their enemies round about, so that they could not any longer stand before their enemies. **15** Whithersoever they went out, the hand of the Lord was against them for evil, as the Lord had said, and as the Lord had sworn unto them: and they were greatly distressed.

16 Nevertheless the Lord raised up judges, which delivered them out of the hand of those that spoiled them. **17** And yet they would not hearken unto their judges, but they went a whoring after other gods, and bowed themselves unto them: they turned quickly out of the way which their fathers walked in, obeying the commandments of the Lord; *but* they did not so. **18** And when the Lord raised them up judges, then the Lord was with the judge, and delivered them out of the hand of their enemies all the days of the judge: for it repented the Lord because of their groanings by reason of them that oppressed them and vexed them.

CONSTITUTIONAL LAW: Article III, § 1. of the U.S. Constitution says, "The judicial Power of the United States, shall be vested in one supreme Court, and in such inferior Courts as the Congress may from time to time ordain and establish. The Judges, both of the supreme and inferior Courts, shall hold their Offices during good Behaviour, and shall, at stated Times, receive for their Services a Compensation, which shall not be diminished during their Continuance in Office."

LIEUTENANTS - *Ezra 8:36* And they delivered the king's commissions unto the king's lieutenants, and to the governors on this side the river: and they furthered the people, and the house of God.

Esther 3:12 Then were the king's scribes called on the thirteenth day of the first month, and there was written according to all that Haman had commanded unto the king's lieutenants, and to the governors that *were* over every province, and to the rulers of every people of every province according to the writing thereof, and *to* every people after their language; in the name of king Ahasue´rus was it written, and sealed with the king's ring.

MILITARY LAW: A LIEUTENANT in LAW is a ranking commissioned officer who has leadership responsibilities in military, fire, emergency and police departments. The description of duties varies in rank and department in which a LIEUTENANT is assigned, specifically codified command structures.

MONARCHY - *1 Samuel 10:24, 25* 24 And Samuel said to all the people, See ye him whom the Lord hath chosen, that *there is* none like him among all the people? And all the people shouted, and said, God save the king.

25 Then Samuel told the people the manner of the kingdom, and wrote *it* in a book, and laid *it* up before the Lord. And Samuel sent all the people away, every man to his house. 2

1 Kings 7:7 Then he made a porch for the throne where he might judge, *even* the porch of judgment: and *it was* covered with cedar from one side of the floor to the other.

2 Kings 15:1, 19 1 In the twenty and seventh year of Jerobo´am king of Israel began Azari´ah son of Amazi´ah king of Judah to reign. 19 *And* Pul the king of Assyria came against the land: and Men´ahem gave Pul a thousand talents of silver, that his hand might be with him to confirm the kingdom in his hand.

The MONARCHY is a CONSTITUTIONAL form of government by which a hereditary sovereign reigns as the head of state of the "United Kingdom", the Crown Dependencies, British Overseas Territories. The MONARCH and their immediate family undertake various official, ceremonial, diplomatic and representational duties. The monarchy is 'CONSTITUTIONAL' meaning, although formally the monarch still has authority over the government which is known as His/Her Majesty's Government – this power may only be used according to laws enacted in Parliament and within constraints of convention and precedent. Thus in practice the monarch's role, including that of Head of the British Armed Forces, is limited to functions such as bestowing honours and appointing the prime minister, which are performed in a non-partisan manner.

PATRIARCHAL - *Genesis 22:1-14* 1 And it came to pass after these things, that God did tempt Abraham, and said unto him, Abraham: and he said, Behold, *here* I *am*. 2 And he said, Take now thy son, thine only *son* Isaac, whom thou lovest, and get thee into the land of Mori´ah; and offer him there for a burnt offering upon one of the mountains which I will tell thee of. 3 And Abraham rose up early in the morning, and saddled his ass, and took two of his young men with him, and Isaac his son, and clave the wood for the burnt offering, and rose up, and went unto the place of which God had told him. 4 Then on the third day Abraham lifted up his eyes, and saw the place afar off. 5 And Abraham said unto his young men, Abide ye here with the ass; and I and the lad will go yonder and worship, and come again to you. 6 And Abraham took the wood of the burnt offering, and laid *it* upon Isaac his son; and he took the fire in his hand, and a knife; and they went both of them together. 7 And Isaac spake unto Abraham his father, and said, My father: and he said, Here *am* I, my son. And he said, Behold the fire and the wood: but where *is* the lamb for a burnt offering? 8 And Abraham said, My son, God will provide himself a lamb for a burnt offering: so they went both of them together.

9 And they came to the place which God had told him of; and Abraham built an altar there, and laid the wood in order, and bound Isaac his son, and laid him on the altar upon the wood. 10 And Abraham stretched forth his hand, and took the knife to slay his son. 11 And the angel of the Lord called unto him out of heaven, and said, Abraham, Abraham: and he said, Here *am* I. 12 And he said, Lay not thine hand upon the lad, neither do thou any thing unto him: for now I know that thou fearest God, seeing thou hast not withheld thy son, thine only *son*, from me. 13 And

Abraham lifted up his eyes, and looked, and behold behind *him* a ram caught in a thicket by his horns: and Abraham went and took the ram, and offered him up for a burnt offering in the stead of his son. **14** And Abraham called the name of that place Jehovah-ji´reh: as it is said *to* this day, In the mount of the Lord it shall be seen.

Judges 11:30-39 **30** And Jephthah vowed a vow unto the Lord, and said, If thou shalt without fail deliver the children of Ammon into mine hands, **31** then it shall be, that whatsoever cometh forth of the doors of my house to meet me, when I return in peace from the children of Ammon, shall surely be the Lord's, and I will offer it up for a burnt offering. **32** So Jephthah passed over unto the children of Ammon to fight against them; and the Lord delivered them into his hands. **33** And he smote them from Aro´er, even till thou come to Minnith, *even* twenty cities, and unto the plain of the vineyards, with a very great slaughter. Thus the children of Ammon were subdued before the children of Israel.

34 And Jephthah came to Mizpeh unto his house, and, behold, his daughter came out to meet him with timbrels and with dances: and she *was his* only child; beside her he had neither son nor daughter. **35** And it came to pass, when he saw her, that he rent his clothes, and said, Alas, my daughter! thou hast brought me very low, and thou art one of them that trouble me: for I have opened my mouth unto the Lord, and I cannot go back. **36** And she said unto him, My father, *if* thou hast opened thy mouth unto the Lord, do to me according to that which hath proceeded out of thy mouth; forasmuch as the Lord hath taken vengeance for thee of thine enemies, *even* of the children of Ammon. **37**And she said unto her father, Let this thing be done for me: let me alone two months, that I may go up and down upon the mountains, and bewail my virginity, I and my fellows. **38** And he said, Go. And he sent her away *for* two months: and she went with her companions, and bewailed her virginity upon the mountains. **39** And it came to pass at the end of two months, that she returned unto her father, who did with her *according* to his vow which he had vowed: and she knew no man. And it was a custom in Israel,

Job 1:5 And it was so, when the days of *their* feasting were gone about, that Job sent and sanctified them, and rose up early in the morning, and offered burnt offerings *according* to the number of them all: for Job said, It may be that my sons have sinned, and cursed God in their hearts. Thus did Job continually.

Placing what God placed in my heart and mind to type here, "Where to start, in regard to the PATRIARCH." A Father, Head of Household under Christ. A Kingship.

PRINCES – *1 Kings 14:7* Go, tell Jerobo´am, Thus saith the Lord God of Israel, Forasmuch as I exalted thee from among the people, and made thee prince over my people Israel,

A prince in law is a male ruler under the king, grand prince, and grand duke. A title of nobility or to mean a ruler of a territory that is sovereign or quasi-sovereign.

SATRAPS – *Ezra 8:36* And they delivered the king's commissions unto the king's lieutenants, and to the governors on this side the river: and they furthered the people, and the house of God.

Esther 3:12 Then were the king's scribes called on the thirteenth day of the first month, and there was written according to all that Haman had commanded unto the king's lieutenants, and to the governors that *were* over every province, and to the rulers of every people of every province according to the writing thereof, and *to* every people after their language; in the name of king Ahasue´rus was it written, and sealed with the king's ring.

A SATRAP defined by Noah Webster 1828 is a Persian Admiral; or generally, the governor of a province. A commander in chief over MARITIME JURISDICTION. Subject to EMBARASSMENT from other countries, the United States created the rank of ADMIRAL in 1862, around the time of the HOMESTEAD ACT. A FLEET ADMIRAL ranks higher than an ADMIRAL in the UNITED STATES NAVY and receive active duty pay for LIFE.

THEOCRATIC – *Exodus 18:13-26, 19:3-8* 13 And it came to pass on the morrow, that Moses sat to judge the people: and the people stood by Moses from the morning unto the evening. 14 And when Moses' father-in-law saw all that he did to the people, he said, What *is* this thing that thou doest to the people? Why sittest thou thyself alone, and all the people stand by thee from morning unto even? 15 And Moses said unto his father-in-law, Because the people come unto me to inquire of God: 16 when they have a matter, they come unto me; and I judge between one and another, and I do make *them* know the statutes of God, and his laws. 17 And Moses' father-in-law said unto him, The thing that thou doest *is* not good. 18 Thou wilt surely wear away, both thou, and this people that *is* with thee: for this thing *is* too heavy for thee; thou art not able to perform it thyself alone. 19 Hearken now unto my voice, I will give thee counsel, and God shall be with thee: Be thou for the people to Godward, that thou mayest bring the causes unto God: 20 and thou shalt teach them ordinances and laws, and shalt show them the way wherein they must walk, and the work that they must do. **21** Moreover thou shalt provide out of all the people able men, such as fear God, men of truth, hating covetousness; and place *such* over them, *to be* rulers of thousands, *and* rulers of hundreds, rulers of fifties, and rulers of tens: **22** and let them judge the people at all seasons: and it shall be, *that* every great matter they shall bring unto thee, but every small matter they shall judge: so shall it be easier for thyself, and they shall bear *the burden* with thee. **23** If thou shalt do this thing, and God command thee *so*, then thou shalt be able to endure, and all this people shall also go to their place in peace.

24 So Moses hearkened to the voice of his father-in-law, and did all that he had said. **25** And Moses chose able men out of all Israel, and made them heads over the people, rulers of thousands, rulers of hundreds, rulers of fifties, and rulers of tens. **26** And they judged the people at all seasons: the hard causes they brought unto Moses, but every small matter they judged themselves. **19:3-8** And Moses went up unto God, and the Lord called unto him out of the mountain, saying, Thus shalt thou say to the house of Jacob, and tell the children of Israel; **4** Ye have seen what I did unto the Egyptians, and *how* I bare you on eagles' wings, and brought you unto myself. **5** Now therefore, if ye will obey my voice indeed, and keep my covenant, then ye shall be a peculiar treasure unto me above all people: for all the earth *is* mine: **6** and ye shall be unto me a kingdom of priests, and a holy nation. These *are* the words which thou shalt speak unto the children of Israel.

7 And Moses came and called for the elders of the people, and laid before their faces all these words which the Lord commanded him. **8** And all the people answered together, and said, All that the Lord hath spoken we will do. And Moses returned the words of the people unto the Lord.

Deuteronomy 17:14-20, 18:15-19 Instructions concerning a King

14 When thou art come unto the land which the Lord thy God giveth thee, and shalt possess it, and shalt dwell therein, and shalt say, I will set a king over me, like as all the nations that *are* about me; **15** thou shalt in any wise set *him* king over thee, whom the Lord thy God shall choose: *one* from among thy brethren shalt thou set king over thee: thou mayest not set a stranger over thee, which *is* not thy brother. **16** But he shall not multiply horses to himself, nor cause the people to return to Egypt, to the end that he should multiply horses: forasmuch as the Lord hath said unto you, Ye shall henceforth return no more that way. **17** Neither shall he multiply wives to himself, that his heart turn not away: neither shall he greatly multiply to himself silver and gold.

18 And it shall be, when he sitteth upon the throne of his kingdom, that he shall write him a copy of this law in a book out of *that which is* before the priests the Levites: **19** and it shall be with him, and he shall read therein all the days of his life; that he may learn to fear the Lord his God, to keep all the words of this law and these statutes, to do them: **20** that his heart be not lifted up above his brethren, and that he turn not aside from the commandment, *to* the right hand, or *to* the left: to the end that he may prolong *his* days in his kingdom, he, and his children, in the midst of Israel.

*(18:15-19)***15** The Lord thy God will raise up unto thee a Prophet from the midst of thee, of thy brethren, like unto me; unto him ye shall hearken; **16** according to all that thou desiredst of the Lord thy God in Horeb in the day of the

assembly, saying, Let me not hear again the voice of the Lord my God, neither let me see this great fire any more, that I die not. **17** And the Lord said unto me, They have well-*spoken that* which they have spoken. **18** I will raise them up a Prophet from among their brethren, like unto thee, and will put my words in his mouth; and he shall speak unto them all that I shall command him. **19** And it shall come to pass, *that* whosoever will not hearken unto my words which he shall speak in my name, I will require *it* of him.

THEOCRACY IN LAW - The Holy Roman Empire, a Popish THEOCRACY which practices CANON LAW of the CATHOLIC CHURCH. This order of LAW was known to be the first MODERN WESTERN LEGAL SYSTEM and oldest continuing functioning legal system right now in the West. They derive their power from Satan Peter (Saint Peter), the only one Jesus the Christ called Satan in **Matthew 16:23,** who is channeled through the Pope. Peter hung himself upside down on a Cross and deified himself after death as the rebirth of Christ allegorically. This is the false power behind the **Cestui Que Vie Trusts of 1666.**

TAX LAWS

BY CAESAR – *Matthew 22:16-21* **16** And they sent out unto him their disciples with the Hero´di-ans, saying, Master, we know that thou art true, and teachest the way of God in truth, neither carest thou for any *man*: for thou regardest not the person of men. **17** Tell us therefore, What thinkest thou? Is it lawful to give tribute unto Caesar, or not? **18** But Jesus perceived their wickedness, and said, Why tempt ye me, ye hypocrites? **19** Show me the tribute money. And they brought unto him a penny. **20** And he saith unto them, Whose *is* this image and superscription? **21** They say unto him, Caesar's. Then saith he unto them, Render therefore unto Caesar the things which are Caesar's; and unto God the things that are God's.

Augustus "OCTAVIAN" Caesar, adopted son of Julius Caesar, rose to power in founding the ROMAN EMPIRE. Having unrivaled financial power in Rome, Octavian commanded VAST financial resources. After donating mass amounts of money to the **AERARIUM SATURNI**, Octavian had failed to encourage Senators to finance building and maintenance of networks of roads (highways) in Italy. A **PUBLIC REVENUE REFORM** was created as a direct taxation to **ROME** pursuant to collecting **TRIBUTES** from each local province. The public revenue reform increased Rome's revenue from its **TERRITORIAL ACQUISTIONS**, with taxing determined by population **CENSUS**, with a fixed quota for each province. **PRIVATE TAX FARMING** was replaced by **CIVIL SERVICE TAX COLLECTORS**. Augustus also took over **EGYPT** (who God has saved and delivered us from) and shifted it to a **ROMAN** form of government.

CENSUS FOR – *Numbers 1:1-47, 4:1-3, 26:2* And the Lord spake unto Moses in the wilderness of Si´nai, in the tabernacle of the congregation, on the first *day* of the second month, in the second year after they were come out of the land of Egypt, saying, **2** Take ye the sum of all the congregation of the children of Israel, after their families, by the house of their fathers, with the number of *their* names, every male by their polls; **3** from twenty years old and upward, all that are able to go forth to war in Israel: thou and Aaron shall number them by their armies. **4** And with you there shall be a man of every tribe; every one head of the house of his fathers. **5** And these *are* the names of the men that shall stand with you: of *the tribe of* Reuben; Eli´zur the son of Shede´ur. **6** Of Simeon; Shelu´mi-el the son of Zurishad´dai. **7** Of Judah; Nahshon the son of Ammin´adab. **8** Of Is´sachar; Nethan´e-el the son of Zu´ar. **9** Of Zeb´ulun; Eli´ab the son of Helon. **10** Of the children of Joseph: of E´phra-im; Elish´ama the son of Ammi´hud: of Manas´seh; Gama´li-el the son of

Pedah´zur. **11** Of Benjamin; Ab´idan the son of Gideo´ni. **12** Of Dan; Ahi-e´zer the son of Ammishad´dai. **13** Of Asher; Pag´i-el the son of Ocran. **14** Of Gad; Eli´asaph the son of Deu´el. **15** Of Naph´tali; Ahi´ra the son of Enan. **16** These *were* the renowned of the congregation, princes of the tribes of their fathers, heads of thousands in Israel.

17 And Moses and Aaron took these men which are expressed by *their* names: **18** and they assembled all the congregation together on the first *day* of the second month, and they declared their pedigrees after their families, by the house of their fathers, according to the number of the names, from twenty years old and upward, by their polls. **19** As the Lord commanded Moses, so he numbered them in the wilderness of Si´nai.

20 And the children of Reuben, Israel's eldest son, by their generations, after their families, by the house of their fathers, according to the number of the names, by their polls, every male from twenty years old and upward, all that were able to go forth to war; **21** those that were numbered of them, *even* of the tribe of Reuben, *were* forty and six thousand and five hundred.

22 Of the children of Simeon, by their generations, after their families, by the house of their fathers, those that were numbered of them, according to the number of the names, by their polls, every male from twenty years old and upward, all that were able to go forth to war; **23** those that were numbered of them, *even* of the tribe of Simeon, *were* fifty and nine thousand and three hundred.

24 Of the children of Gad, by their generations, after their families, by the house of their fathers, according to the number of the names, from twenty years old and upward, all that were able to go forth to war; **25** those that were numbered of them, *even* of the tribe of Gad, *were* forty and five thousand six hundred and fifty.

26 Of the children of Judah, by their generations, after their families, by the house of their fathers, according to the number of the names, from twenty years old and upward, all that were able to go forth to war; **27** those that were numbered of them, *even* of the tribe of Judah, *were* threescore and fourteen thousand and six hundred.

28 Of the children of Is´sachar, by their generations, after their families, by the house of their fathers, according to the number of the names, from twenty years old and upward, all that were able to go forth to war; **29** those that were numbered of them, *even* of the tribe of Is´sachar, *were* fifty and four thousand and four hundred.

30 Of the children of Zeb´ulun, by their generations, after their families, by the house of their fathers, according to the number of the names, from twenty years old and upward, all that were able to go forth to war; **31** those that were numbered of them, *even* of the tribe of Zeb´ulun, *were* fifty and seven thousand and four hundred.

32 Of the children of Joseph, *namely*, of the children of E´phra-im, by their generations, after their families, by the house of their fathers, according to the number of the names, from twenty years old and upward, all that were able to go forth to war; **33** those that were numbered of them, *even* of the tribe of E´phra-im, *were* forty thousand and five hundred.

34 Of the children of Manas´seh, by their generations, after their families, by the house of their fathers, according to the number of the names, from twenty years old and upward, all that were able to go forth to war; **35** those that were numbered of them, *even* of the tribe of Manas´seh, *were* thirty and two thousand and two hundred.

36 Of the children of Benjamin, by their generations, after their families, by the house of their fathers, according to the number of the names, from twenty years old and upward, all that were able to go forth to war; **37** those that were numbered of them, *even* of the tribe of Benjamin, *were* thirty and five thousand and four hundred.

38 Of the children of Dan, by their generations, after their families, by the house of their fathers, according to the number of the names, from twenty years old and upward, all that were able to go forth to war; **39**those that were numbered of them, *even* of the tribe of Dan, *were* threescore and two thousand and seven hundred.

40 Of the children of Asher, by their generations, after their families, by the house of their fathers, according to the number of the names, from twenty years old and upward, all that were able to go forth to war; **41** those that were numbered of them, *even* of the tribe of Asher, *were* forty and one thousand and five hundred.

42 Of the children of Naph´tali, throughout their generations, after their families, by the house of their fathers, according to the number of the names, from twenty years old and upward, all that were able to go forth to war; **43** those that were numbered of them, *even* of the tribe of Naph´tali, *were* fifty and three thousand and four hundred.

44 These *are* those that were numbered, which Moses and Aaron numbered, and the princes of Israel, *being* twelve men: each one was for the house of his fathers. **45** So were all those that were numbered of the children of Israel, by the house of their fathers, from twenty years old and upward, all that were able to go forth to war in Israel; **46** even all they that were numbered were six hundred thousand and three thousand and five hundred and fifty. **47** But the Levites after the tribe of their fathers were not numbered among them. ***4:1-3*** **1** And the Lord spake unto Moses and unto Aaron, saying, **2** Take the sum of the sons of Kohath from among the sons of Levi, after their families, by the house of their fathers, **3** from thirty years old and upward even until fifty years old, all that enter into the host, to do the work in the tabernacle of the congregation. ***26:2*** Take the sum of all the congregation of the children of Israel, from twenty years old and upward, throughout their fathers' house, all that are able to go to war in Israel.

2 Samuel 24:1-9 **1** And again the anger of the Lord was kindled against Israel, and he moved David against them to say, Go, number Israel and Judah. **2** For the king said to Jo´ab the captain of the host, which *was* with him, Go now through all the tribes of Israel, from Dan even to Beer-sheba, and number ye the people, that I may know the number of the people. **3** And Jo´ab said unto the king, Now the Lord thy God add unto the people, how many soever they be, a hundredfold, and that the eyes of my lord the king may see *it*: but why doth my lord the king delight in this thing? **4** Notwithstanding the king's word prevailed against Jo´ab, and against the captains of the host. And Jo´ab and the captains of the host went out from the presence of the king, to number the people of Israel. **5** And they passed over Jordan, and pitched in Aro´er, on the right side of the city that *lieth* in the midst of the river of Gad, and toward Jazer: **6** then they came to Gil´e-ad, and to the land of Tahtim-hod´shi; and they came to Dan-ja´an, and about to

Zidon, **7** and came to the stronghold of Tyre, and to all the cities of the Hivites, and of the Canaanites: and they went out to the south of Judah, *even* to Beer-sheba. **8** So when they had gone through all the land, they came to Jerusalem at the end of nine months and twenty days. **9** And Jo´ab gave up the sum of the number of the people unto the king: and there were in Israel eight hundred thousand valiant men that drew the sword; and the men of Judah *were* five hundred thousand men.

Luke 2:1-3 **1** And it came to pass in those days, that there went out a decree from Caesar Augustus, that all the world should be taxed. **2** (*And* this taxing was first made when Cyre´ni-us was governor of Syria.) **3** And all went to be taxed, every one into his own city.

ROMAN LAW: Again, the measures of taxation in the reign of Augustus (CAESAR) were determined by population census, with fixed quotas for each province. CITIZENS of Rome and Italy paid INDIRECT taxes, while DIRECT taxes were taken from the provinces. INDIRECT TAXES included a 4% tax on SLAVES, a 1% tax on goods sold at auction, and 5% tax on the inheritance of estates valued at over 100,000 sesterces by persons other than the next of kin according to the **Encyclopedia of the Roman Empire,** *p. 404, Bunson, 1994.*

FOR CHARITY – *Deuteronomy 14:28, 29, 26:12-15* **28** At the end of three years thou shalt bring forth all the tithe of thine increase the same year, and shalt lay *it* up within thy gates: **29** and the Levite, (because he hath no part nor inheritance with thee,) and the stranger, and the fatherless, and the widow, which *are* within thy gates, shall come, and shall eat and be satisfied; that the Lord thy God may bless thee in all the work of thine hand which thou doest. *26:12-*

15 **12** When thou hast made an end of tithing all the tithes of thine increase the third year, *which is* the year of tithing, and hast given *it* unto the Levite, the stranger, the fatherless, and the widow, that they may eat within thy gates, and be filled; **13** then thou shalt say before the Lord thy God, I have brought away the hallowed things out of *mine* house, and also have given them unto the Levite, and unto the stranger, to the fatherless, and to the widow, according to all thy commandments which thou hast commanded me: I have not transgressed thy commandments, neither have I forgotten *them*: **14** I have not eaten thereof in my mourning, neither have I taken away *aught* thereof for *any* unclean *use*, nor given *aught* thereof for the dead: *but* I have hearkened to the voice of the Lord my God, *and* have done according to all that thou hast commanded me. **15** Look down from thy holy habitation, from heaven, and bless thy people Israel, and the land which thou hast given us, as thou swarest unto our fathers, a land that floweth with milk and honey.

CIVIL CODE: The IRS states under Substantiation of Contributions "a donor can deduct a charitable contribution of $250 or more only if the donor has a written acknowledgement from the charitable organization." Charitable organizations are organized and operated exclusively for religious, charitable, scientific, testing for public safety, literary, educational, or other specified purposes and that meet certain other requirements are tax exempt under Internal Revenue Code § 501(c)(3). Speaking from experience, most charitable contributions are for tax write offs coming from businesses or sole proprietors.

COLLECTIONS - *Matthew 9:9-13* **9** And as Jesus passed forth from thence, he saw a man, named Matthew, sitting at the receipt of custom: and he saith unto him, Follow me. And he arose, and followed him.

10 And it came to pass, as Jesus sat at meat in the house, behold, many publicans and sinners came and sat down with him and his disciples. **11** And when the Pharisees saw *it*, they said unto his disciples, Why eateth your master with publicans and sinners? **12** But when Jesus heard *that*, he said unto them, They that be whole need not a physician, but they that are sick. **13** But go ye and learn what *that* meaneth, I will have mercy, and not sacrifice: for I am not come to call the righteous, but sinners to repentance.

<u>**Luke 19:1-10**</u> **1** And *Jesus* entered and passed through Jericho. **2** And, behold, *there was* a man named Zacche´us, which was the chief among the publicans, and he was rich. **3** And he sought to see Jesus who he was; and could not for the press, because he was little of stature. **4** And he ran before, and climbed up into a sycamore tree to see him; for he was to pass that *way*. **5** And when Jesus came to the place, he looked up, and saw him, and said unto him, Zacche´us, make haste, and come down; for today I must abide at thy house. **6** And he made haste, and came down, and received him joyfully. **7** And when they saw *it*, they all murmured, saying, That he was gone to be guest with a man that is a sinner. **8** And Zacche´us stood, and said unto the Lord; Behold, Lord, the half of my goods I give to the poor; and if I have taken any thing from any man by false accusation, I restore *him* fourfold. **9** And Jesus said unto him, This day is salvation come to this house, forasmuch as he also is a son of Abraham. **10** For the Son of man is come to seek and to save that which was lost.

CIVIL CODE: To repent in the world, one must atone and take responsibility for every mistake that they made or was an accomplice to another person's mistake. With that being said the U.S. Government Revenue **COLLECTIONS** sheet from Fiscal Data at treasury.gov, recently updated

07/21/2023, provides a daily overview of federal revenue collections such as individual and corporate income tax deposits, customs duties, fees for government service, fines, and loan repayments. These collections can be made through either electronic or non-electronic transactions by mail, internet, bank, or over the counter channels. They're public and again, for assuring the payment of taxes meant to fund the community and give back unto God but instead, used for war in other countries.

EMERGENCY - *2 Kings 23:35* And Jehoi´akim gave the silver and the gold to Pharaoh; but he taxed the land to give the money according to the commandment of Pharaoh: he exacted the silver and the gold of the people of the land, of every one according to his taxation, to give *it* unto Pha´raoh-ne´choh.

CIVIL LAW: Well, in times of war, purchase WAR BONDS. Originating from the Commissioner of Internal Revenue, a federal office created in 1862 (CIVIL WAR), THE INTERNAL REVENUE SERVICE was created to fund the AMERICAN CIVIL WAR. The "temporary" measure funded over a 1/5 of the Union's war expenses. Sound like an emergency to tax the public?

EXEMPTIONS - *Ezra 7:24* Also we certify you, that, touching any of the priests and Levites, singers, porters, Neth´inim, or ministers of this house of God, it shall not be lawful to impose toll, tribute, or custom, upon them.

At the IRS, there are two types of EXEMPTIONS, nothing in which has anything to do with status or nomenclature, they are the following: personal exemptions for taxpayer and spouse and dependency exemptions for dependents. Tax Foundation notes how an organization can be granted a TAX-EXEMPT status if they meet requirements in **§ 501**

(c) of the tax code but none of the revenue may be used to benefit private shareholders or individuals.

METHOD OF - *__Luke 2:1-5__* **1** And it came to pass in those days, that there went out a decree from Caesar Augustus, that all the world should be taxed. **2** (*And* this taxing was first made when Cyre´ni-us was governor of Syria.) **3** And all went to be taxed, every one into his own city. **4** And Joseph also went up from Galilee, out of the city of Nazareth, into Judea, unto the city of David, which is called Bethlehem, (because he was of the house and lineage of David,) **5** to be taxed with Mary his espoused wife, being great with child.

CIVIL CODE: Introducing **The Revenue Act of 1913, Underwood Tariff, and/or the Underwood-Simmons Act,** which RE-established a federal income tax after the taxing of the people for "American Civil War" in 1862, ending a decade later. The act was sponsored by Oscar Underwood, passed by the **63rd U.S. Congress**, signed into law by Woodrow (Pope Pius) Wilson. Just in time for the Federal Reserve.

FOR REDEMPTION - *__Leviticus 27:1-13__* **1** And the Lord spake unto Moses, saying, **2** Speak unto the children of Israel, and say unto them, When a man shall make a singular vow, the persons *shall be* for the Lord by thy estimation. **3** And thy estimation shall be of the male from twenty years old even unto sixty years old, even thy estimation shall be fifty shekels of silver, after the shekel of the sanctuary. **4** And if it *be* a female, then thy estimation shall be thirty shekels. **5** And if *it be* from five years old even unto twenty years old, then thy estimation shall be of the male twenty shekels, and for the female ten shekels. **6** And if *it be* from a month old even unto five years old, then thy estimation shall be of the male five shekels of silver, and for the female thy estimation *shall be* three shekels of silver. **7** And if *it be* from sixty years old and above; if *it be* a male, then thy estimation shall be fifteen shekels, and for the female ten shekels. **8** But if he be poorer than thy estimation, then he shall present himself before the priest, and the priest shall value him; according to his ability that vowed shall the priest value him.

9 And if *it be* a beast, whereof men bring an offering unto the Lord, all that *any man* giveth of such unto the Lord shall be holy. **10** He shall not alter it, nor change it, a good for a bad, or a bad for a good: and if he shall at all change beast for beast, then it and the exchange thereof shall be holy. **11** And if *it be* any unclean beast, of which they do not offer a sacrifice unto the Lord, then he shall present the beast before the priest: **12** and the priest shall value it, whether it be good or bad: as thou valuest it, *who art* the priest, so shall it be. **13** But if he will at all redeem it, then he shall add a fifth *part* thereof unto thy estimation.

COMMERCIAL LAW: REDEMPTION is defined as "the return of mutual fund shares or of money invested in a fixed-income security on or before its maturity date." Now mutual funds can get into depth about where the money has been invested and going over the past few centuries. When it comes to an American's Social Security Number and CUSIP ID, these are tradable financial assets in the form of SECURITIES. A MUTUAL FUND is an investment fund with funds pooled in from multiple investors to purchase SECURITIES.

SIZE OF - *1 Samuel 8:10-18* **10** And Samuel told all the words of the Lord unto the people that asked of him a king. **11** And he said, This will be the manner of the king that shall reign over you: He will take your sons, and appoint *them* for himself, for his chariots, and *to be* his horsemen; and *some* shall run before his chariots. **12** And he will appoint him captains over thousands, and captains over fifties; and *will set them* to ear his ground, and to reap his harvest, and to make his instruments of war, and instruments of his chariots. **13** And he will take your daughters *to be* confectionaries, and *to be* cooks, and *to be* bakers. **14** And he will take your fields, and your vineyards, and your oliveyards, *even* the best *of them*, and give *them* to his servants. **15** And he will take the tenth of your seed, and of your vineyards, and give to his officers, and to his servants. **16** And he will take your menservants, and your maidservants, and your goodliest young men, and your asses, and put *them* to his work. **17** He will take the tenth of your sheep: and ye shall be his servants. **18** And ye shall cry out in that day because of your king which ye shall have chosen you; and the Lord will not hear you in that day.

JURISDICTION: Since the State has TERRITORIAL JURISDICTION over CITIZENS, the power has to be distributed to avoid the power being centralized. That is what a MUNICIPALITY is, self-government and jurisdiction adhering to local and national laws. *If this particular MUNICIPALITY wishes to impose a tax or fee that satisfies an area of governance, it can do so.*

FOR SUPPORT OF KING – *1 Kings 4:7, 27, 28* 7 And Solomon had twelve officers over all Israel, which provided victuals for the king and his household: each man his month in a year made provision. **27** And those officers provided victuals for king Solomon, and for all that came unto king Solomon's table, every man in his month: they lacked nothing. **28** Barley also and straw for the horses and dromedaries brought they unto the place where *the officers* were, every man according to his charge.

Nehemiah 5:1-5 **1** And there was a great cry of the people and of their wives against their brethren the Jews. **2** For there were that said, We, our sons, and our daughters, *are* many: therefore we take up corn *for them*, that we may eat, and live. **3** *Some* also there were that said, We have mortgaged our lands, vineyards, and houses, that we might buy corn, because of the dearth. **4** There were also that said, We have borrowed money for the king's tribute, *and that upon* our lands and vineyards. **5** Yet now our flesh *is* as the flesh of our brethren, our children as their children: and, lo, we bring into bondage our sons and our daughters to be servants, and *some* of our daughters are brought into bondage *already*: neither *is it* in our power *to redeem them*; for other men have our lands and vineyards.

THE POINT: The point is to be of good moral support. Love one another and help your fellow man.

FOR TABERNACLE OR TEMPLE – *Exodus 30:11-16*
11 And the Lord spake unto Moses, saying, **12** When thou takest the sum of the children of Israel after their number, then shall they give every man a ransom for his soul unto the Lord, when thou numberest them; that there be no plague among them, when *thou* numberest them. **13** This they shall give, every one that passeth among them that are numbered, half a shekel after the shekel of the sanctuary: (a shekel *is* twenty gerahs:) a half shekel *shall be* the offering of the Lord. **14** Every one that passeth among them that are numbered, from twenty years old and above, shall give an offering unto the Lord. **15** The rich shall not give more, and the poor shall not give less, than half a shekel, when *they* give an offering unto the Lord, to make an atonement for your souls. **16** And thou shalt take the atonement money of the children of Israel, and shalt appoint it for the service of the tabernacle of the congregation; that it

may be a memorial unto the children of Israel before the Lord, to make an atonement for your souls.

Deuteronomy 14:22-27 **22** Thou shalt truly tithe all the increase of thy seed, that the field bringeth forth year by year. **23** And thou shalt eat before the Lord thy God, in the place which he shall choose to place his name there, the tithe of thy corn, of thy wine, and of thine oil, and the firstlings of thy herds and of thy flocks; that thou mayest learn to fear the Lord thy God always. **24** And if the way be too long for thee, so that thou art not able to carry it; *or* if the place be too far from thee, which the Lord thy God shall choose to set his name there, when the Lord thy God hath blessed thee: **25** then shalt thou turn *it* into money, and bind up the money in thine hand, and shalt go unto the place which the Lord thy God shall choose: **26** and thou shalt bestow that money for whatsoever thy soul lusteth after, for oxen, or for sheep, or for wine, or for strong drink, or for whatsoever thy soul desireth: and thou shalt eat there before the Lord thy God, and thou shalt rejoice, thou, and thine household, **27** and the Levite that *is* within thy gates; thou shalt not forsake him: for he hath no part nor inheritance with thee.

2 Chronicles 24:6, 9, 31:4-12 **6** And the king called for Jehoi´ada the chief, and said unto him, Why hast thou not required of the Levites to bring in out of Judah and out of Jerusalem the collection, *according to the commandment* of Moses the servant of the Lord, and of the congregation of Israel, for the tabernacle of witness? **9** And they made a proclamation through Judah and Jerusalem, to bring in to the Lord the collection *that* Moses the servant of God *laid* upon Israel in the wilderness. ***31:4-12*** **4** Moreover he commanded the people that dwelt in Jerusalem to give the portion of the priests and the Levites, that they might be encouraged in the law of the Lord. **5** And as soon as the commandment came abroad, the children of Israel brought in abundance the firstfruits of corn, wine, and oil, and honey, and of all the increase of the field; and the tithe of all *things* brought they in abundantly. **6** And *concerning* the children of Israel and Judah, that dwelt in the cities of Judah, they also brought in the tithe of oxen and sheep, and the tithe of holy things which were consecrated unto the Lord their God, and laid *them* by heaps. **7** In the third month they began to lay the foundation of the heaps, and finished *them* in the seventh month. **8** And when Hezeki´ah and the princes came and saw the heaps, they blessed the Lord, and his people Israel. **9** Then Hezeki´ah questioned with the priests and the Levites concerning the heaps. **10** And Azari´ah the chief priest of the house of Zadok answered him, and said, Since *the people* began to bring the offerings into the house of the Lord, we have had enough to eat, and have left plenty: for the Lord hath blessed his people; and that which is left *is* this great store.

11 Then Hezeki´ah commanded to prepare chambers in the house of the Lord; and they prepared *them*, **12** and brought in the offerings and the tithes and the dedicated *things* faithfully: over which Conani´ah the Levite *was* ruler, and Shim´e-i his brother *was* the next.

TAXATION: WAREHOUSES, when identified in modern times, are places where men and women make 10-17 dollars an hour forklifting vacuums and car radios out of an organized, aisled, large storehouse of items ready for purchase. Did you know that **warehouses** used to be for more communal purposes? Identically to the Scriptures, **warehouses** were used to store excess amounts of food and goods according to the commandment of Moses, for the tabernacle of witnesses. There were family or community storage pits, which is what a ***warehouse*** was. Due to the **LEVY OF DUTIES**, space had to be made in these ***warehouses*** for the surplus of goods that were involved in trade and commerce.

MILITARY LAWS

AGE OF SERVICE – *<u>Numbers 1:2, 3</u>* **2** Take ye the sum of all the congregation of the children of Israel, after their families, by the house of their fathers, with the number of *their* names, every male by their polls; **3** from twenty years old and upward, all that are able to go forth to war in Israel: thou and Aaron shall number them by their armies.

CIVIL CODE: THE SELECTIVE SERVICE SYSTEM (SSS), as mentioned, requires by law ALL MALE CITIZENS and immigrant non-citizens who are between the ages of 18-25 to register within 30 days of their 18th birthday to the SSS. Your registration can guarantee a draft into military combat if ever needed with the looming threat of prison time for refusal of duties to Serapis.

BOOTY - *<u>Numbers 31:9, 26-52</u>* **31:9** And the children of Israel took *all* the women of Mid´i-an captives, and their little ones, and took the spoil of all their cattle, and all their flocks, and all their goods. *26-52* **26** Take the sum of the prey that was taken, *both* of man and of beast, thou, and Ele-a´zar the priest, and the chief fathers of the congregation: **27** and divide the prey into two parts; between them that took the war upon them, who went out to battle, and between all the congregation. **28** And levy a tribute unto the Lord of the men of war which went out to battle: one soul of five hundred, *both* of the persons, and of the beeves, and of the asses, and of the sheep: **29** take *it* of their half, and give *it* unto Ele-a´zar the priest, *for* a heave offering of the Lord. **30** And of the children of Israel's half, thou shalt take one portion of fifty, of the persons, of the beeves, of the asses, and of the flocks, of all manner of beasts, and give them unto the Levites, which keep the charge of the tabernacle of the Lord. **31** And Moses and Ele-a´zar the priest did as the Lord commanded Moses.

32 And the booty, *being* the rest of the prey which the men of war had caught, was six hundred thousand and seventy thousand and five thousand sheep, **33** and threescore and twelve thousand beeves, **34** and threescore and one thousand asses, **35** and thirty and two thousand persons in all, of women that had not known man by lying with him. **36** And the half, *which was* the portion of them that went out to war, was in number three hundred thousand and seven and thirty thousand and five hundred sheep: **37** and the Lord's tribute of the sheep was six hundred and threescore and fifteen. **38** And the beeves *were* thirty and six thousand; of which the Lord's tribute *was* threescore and twelve. **39** And the asses *were* thirty thousand and five hundred; of which the Lord's tribute *was* threescore and one. **40** And the persons *were* sixteen thousand; of which the Lord's tribute *was* thirty and two persons. **41** And Moses gave the tribute, *which was* the Lord's heave offering, unto Ele-a´zar the priest, as the Lord commanded Moses.

42 And of the children of Israel's half, which Moses divided from the men that warred, **43** (now the half *that pertained unto* the congregation was three hundred thousand and thirty thousand *and* seven thousand and five hundred sheep, **44** and thirty and six thousand beeves, **45** and thirty thousand asses and five hundred, **46** and sixteen thousand persons,) **47** even of the children of Israel's half, Moses took one portion of fifty, *both* of man and of beast, and gave them unto the Levites, which kept the charge of the tabernacle of the Lord; as the Lord commanded Moses.

48 And the officers which *were* over thousands of the host, the captains of thousands, and captains of hundreds, came near unto Moses: **49** and they said unto Moses, Thy servants have taken the sum of the men of war which *are* under our charge, and there lacketh not one man of us. **50** We have therefore brought an oblation for the Lord, what every man hath gotten, of jewels of gold, chains, and bracelets, rings, earrings, and tablets, to make an atonement for our souls before the Lord. **51** And Moses and Ele-a´zar the priest took the gold of them, *even* all wrought jewels. **52** And all the gold of the offering that they offered up to the Lord, of the captains of thousands, and of the captains of hundreds, was sixteen thousand seven hundred and fifty shekels.

Deuteronomy 20:14 but the women, and the little ones, and the cattle, and all that is in the city, *even* all the spoil thereof, shalt thou take unto thyself; and thou shalt eat the spoil of thine enemies, which the Lord thy God hath given thee.

Joshua 6:19 But all the silver, and gold, and vessels of brass and iron, *are* consecrated unto the Lord: they shall come into the treasury of the Lord.

1 Samuel 30:22-25 **22** Then answered all the wicked men, and *men* of Be´li-al, of those that went with David, and said, Because they went not with us, we will not give them *aught* of the spoil that we have recovered, save to every man his wife and his children, that they may lead *them* away, and depart. **23** Then said David, Ye shall not do so, my brethren, with that which the Lord hath given us, who hath preserved us, and delivered the company that came against us into our hand. **24** For who will hearken unto you in this matter? but as his part *is* that goeth down to the battle, so *shall* his part *be* that tarrieth by the stuff: they shall part alike. **25** And it was *so* from that day forward, that he made it a statute and an ordinance for Israel unto this day.

CIVIL CODE: Once again in 10 U.S. Code **§ 2579 – War booty,** The Secretary of Defense prescribes the regulations for the handling of battlefield objects when the United States is operating in a theater of operations.

BURIAL OF DEAD – *1 Kings 11:15* For it came to pass, when David was in Edom, and Jo´ab the captain of the host was gone up to bury the slain, after he had smitten every male in Edom;

CIVIL GOVERNMENT: According to va.gov, eligibility for a military burial constitutes of one of the following qualifying factors to be true: The person qualifying is a Veteran who didn't receive **DISHONORABLE DISCHARGE**, is a service member who died while on active duty, active duty for training, or inactive duty for training, is a surviving spouse or spouse of Veteran (even if they remarried), or is the minor child of a Veteran, even the unmarried adult dependent child of a Veteran.

CAPTURED CHILDREN – *Numbers 31:9* And the children of Israel took *all* the women of Mid´i-an captives, and their little ones, and took the spoil of all their cattle, and all their flocks, and all their goods.

Deuteronomy 20:14 but the women, and the little ones, and the cattle, and all that is in the city, *even* all the spoil thereof, shalt thou take unto thyself; and thou shalt eat the spoil of thine enemies, which the Lord thy God hath given thee.

MODERN WARFARE: Interestingly enough and analogous to the topic, I found a high number of articles that are written about **CHILD SOLDIERS** involved in World War II. I am referring to Hitler's Youth, SS Youth Division, and all forms of **SCOUTING**. To get back to the point, a **CAPTURED CHILD** looks like the heavily and easily influenced, propagandized, world-loving free spirit who likes to live in the moment and know no law or history. How have they captured our children in this time of war? Cartoons, video game violence, the playground (picking up bad habits from foreign children or encountering prejudice behavior), colorful products, beauty, and chemically induced foods.

CAPTURED WOMEN - *Numbers 31:9* And the children of Israel took *all* the women of Mid´i-an captives, and their little ones, and took the spoil of all their cattle, and all their flocks, and all their goods.

Deuteronomy 20:14 but the women, and the little ones, and the cattle, and all that is in the city, *even* all the spoil thereof, shalt thou take unto thyself; and thou shalt eat the spoil of thine enemies, which the Lord thy God hath given thee.

MODERN WARFARE: As the children were captured, so were our women by the serpent. Induced into vanity, the sister is inundated by the thought of beauty with no or misunderstood knowledge from the father. Caught up in a metaphorical spell of beauty and pursuit by advertising firms all over, the modern woman is far from home in her thoughts, feelings, and emotions, essentially, captured. Speaking in terms of **WARFARE**, again, the U.S. military provides support for the opposing forces women and children, whose men were killed in battle.

EXEMPTION FROM SERVICE – *Numbers 1:47-53* **47** But the Levites after the tribe of their fathers were not numbered among them. **48** For the Lord had spoken unto Moses, saying, **49** Only thou shalt not number the tribe of Levi, neither take the sum of them among the children of Israel: **50** but thou shalt appoint the Levites over the tabernacle of testimony, and over all the vessels thereof, and over all things that *belong* to it: they shall bear the tabernacle, and all the vessels thereof; and they shall minister unto it, and shall encamp round about the tabernacle. **51** And when the tabernacle setteth forward, the Levites shall take it down; and when the tabernacle is to be pitched, the Levites shall set it up: and the stranger that cometh nigh shall be put to death. **52** And the children of Israel shall pitch their tents, every man by his own camp, and every man by his own standard, throughout their hosts. **53** But the Levites shall pitch round about the tabernacle of testimony, that there be no wrath upon the congregation of the children of Israel: and the Levites shall keep the charge of the tabernacle of testimony.

Deuteronomy 20:5-8 **5** And the officers shall speak unto the people, saying, What man *is there* that hath built a new house, and hath not dedicated it? let him go and return to his house, lest he die in the battle, and another man dedicate it. **6** And what man *is he* that hath planted a vineyard, and hath not *yet* eaten of it? let him *also* go and return unto his house, lest he die in the battle, and another man eat of it. **7** And what man *is there* that hath betrothed a wife, and hath not taken her? let him go and return unto his house, lest he die in the battle, and another man take her. **8** And the officers shall speak further unto the people, and they shall say, What man *is there that is* fearful and faint-hearted? let him go and return unto his house, lest his brethren's heart faint as well as his heart.

RULES OF THE GAME: Similarly in CIVIL SERVICE, ordained ministers, men with physical disabilities must register with the Selective Service System. This is where the word "selective" can come into play because ordained ministers and men with physical disabilities are exempted from service. A "CONSCIENTIOUS OBJECTOR" may be exempt from military training and service, placed into noncombat or civilian service but not exempt from registration and draft.

HOSTAGES – *2 Kings 14:14* And he took all the gold and silver, and all the vessels that were found in the house of the Lord, and in the treasures of the king's house, and hostages, and returned to Samaria.

CIVIL CODE: In "American" history beginning in 1775, there have been only a few HOSTAGE situations that have come to light other than The Iranian Hostage Crisis in 1979, where more than 50 American soldiers were held by Iranian forces. From the Department of Justice CRM, 11. HOSTAGE TAKING (18 U.S.C. 1203) in 1984, Congress enacted the hostage taking statute to implement the International Convention Against the Taking of Hostages, becoming effective January 6, 1985. This is why you do not hear if anything of the United States holding hostages or would consider the black towns in the 1800-1900's destroyed and taken over by mobs acts of taking hostages.

INDEMNITY – *2 Kings 3:4* And Mesha king of Moab was a sheepmaster, and rendered unto the king of Israel a hundred thousand lambs, and a hundred thousand rams, with the wool.

CODE: The U.S. Army Claims Service Commander, according to Chapter 16 Foreign and Deployment Claims in the Operational Law Handbook, is responsible for TORT

CLAIMS, and according to the IRAQI CLAIMS POCKET CARD, will indemnify Iraqi civilians for property damage, injury and death caused by US Forces.

PREPARATION FOR BATTLE – *1 Samuel 7:9-11, 13:9, 28:5, 6* **9** And Samuel took a sucking lamb, and offered *it for* a burnt offering wholly unto the Lord: and Samuel cried unto the Lord for Israel; and the Lord heard him. **10** And as Samuel was offering up the burnt offering, the Philistines drew near to battle against Israel: but the Lord thundered with a great thunder on that day upon the Philistines, and discomfited them; and they were smitten before Israel. **11** And the men of Israel went out of Mizpeh, and pursued the Philistines, and smote them, until *they came* under Beth-car. **13:9** And Saul said, Bring hither a burnt offering to me, and peace offerings. And he offered the burnt offering. **28:5** And when Saul saw the host of the Philistines, he was afraid, and his heart greatly trembled. **6** And when Saul inquired of the Lord, the Lord answered him not, neither by dreams, nor by Urim, nor by prophets.

1 Kings 22:6 Then the king of Israel gathered the prophets together, about four hundred men, and said unto them, Shall I go against Ra´moth-gil´e-ad to battle, or shall I forbear? And they said, Go up; for the Lord shall deliver *it* into the hand of the king.

MILITARY LAW: The 2022 Operational Law Handbook, Chapter 2 SOURCES OF THE LAW OF ARMED CONFLICT 1. INTRODUCTION 2(E)(a)(b) FM 6-27, *The Commander's Handbook on the Law of Land Warfare* has guidance to the lawful conduct of warfare on land and to" relationships between opposing belligerents", to prepare for combat.

The GENEVA TRADITIONS under the HAGUE LAW have created an international framework for analysis, which addresses the reasons and way to prepare for armed conflict. An international armed conflict triggers rules of the Geneva Convention and a non-international armed conflict may trigger local law enforcement.

PRISONERS OF WAR – *Deuteronomy 20:10-14* **10** When thou comest nigh unto a city to fight against it, then proclaim peace unto it. **11** And it shall be, if it make thee answer of peace, and open unto thee, then it shall be, *that* all the people *that is* found therein shall be tributaries unto thee, and they shall serve thee. **12** And if it will make no peace with thee, but will make war against thee, then thou shalt besiege it: **13** and when the Lord thy God hath delivered it into thine hands, thou shalt smite every male thereof with the edge of the sword: **14** but the women, and the little ones, and the cattle, and all that is in the city, *even* all the spoil thereof, shalt thou take unto thyself; and thou shalt eat the spoil of thine enemies, which the Lord thy God hath given thee.

INTERNATIONAL LAW: The THIRD Geneva Convention set forth protections for PRISONERS OF WAR (POW), only arising during international armed conflict. **The DoD Directive 2311.01, the DoD Law of War Program,** states that U.S. forces will comply with the LOAC regardless of how the conflict is characterized.

Noted also in the Operational Law Handbook of the U.S. Military, General Washington took steps to prevent abuse to POW's and sensitive to their welfare.

The Lieber Code under President Lincoln, protected Confederate prisoners, while sending Black POW's into slavery, with 49,062 POW's perishing in POW Camps during the American Civil War alone.

Afro-Americans are currently POW's, who are royals under King George III, having their resources and blessings stolen right before their eyes.

SANITATION IN CAMP - *Deuteronomy 23:9-14* Laws of Sanitation

9 When the host goeth forth against thine enemies, then keep thee from every wicked thing.

10 If there be among you any man, that is not clean by reason of uncleanness that chanceth him by night, then shall he go abroad out of the camp, he shall not come within the camp: **11** but it shall be, when evening cometh on, he shall wash *himself* with water: and when the sun is down, he shall come into the camp *again*.

12 Thou shalt have a place also without the camp, whither thou shalt go forth abroad: **13** and thou shalt have a paddle upon thy weapon; and it shall be, when thou wilt ease thyself abroad, thou shalt dig therewith, and shalt turn back and cover that which cometh from thee: **14** for the Lord thy God walketh in the midst of thy camp, to deliver thee, and to give up thine enemies before thee; therefore shall thy camp be holy: that he see no unclean thing in thee, and turn away from thee.

CIVIL CODE: A DoD FHA Authority 10 U.S.C. §401 - Humanitarian and Civic Assistance (HCA) in conjunction with ongoing military operations such as a Crisis Action Team (CAT) consisting of a Humanitarian Assistance Coordination Center, a Humanitarian Assistance Survey Team (HAST) and a Joint Logistics Operations Center, provides basic sanitation facilities and/or rudimentary construction and repair of public facilities.

SELECTIVE SERVICE – *Numbers 31:3-6* **3** And Moses spake unto the people, saying, Arm some of yourselves unto the war, and let them go against the Mid´i-anites, and avenge the Lord of Mid´i-an. **4** Of every tribe a thousand, throughout all the tribes of Israel, shall ye send to the war. **5** So there were delivered out of the thousands of Israel, a thousand of *every* tribe, twelve thousand armed for war. **6** And Moses sent them to the war, a thousand of *every* tribe, them and Phin´ehas the son of Ele-a´zar the priest, to the war, with the holy instruments, and the trumpets to blow in his hand.

AMERICAN HISTORY: CONSCRIPTION, dating back to "times" of antiquity, comes for us in the form of the SELECTIVE SERVICE SYSTEM, requiring all able bodied, non-conscientious objecting men aged 18-25 to register with the Selective System Service within 30 days of their 18th birthday.

SIEGE OF CITIES – *Deuteronomy 20:19, 20* **19** When thou shalt besiege a city a long time, in making war against it to take it, thou shalt not destroy the trees thereof by forcing an axe against them: for thou mayest eat of them, and thou shalt not cut them down (for the tree of the field *is* man's *life*) to employ *them* in the siege: **20** only the trees which thou knowest that they *be* not trees for meat, thou shalt destroy and cut them down; and thou shalt build bulwarks against the city that maketh war with thee, until it be subdued.

THE **WILMINGTON MASSACRE OF 1898** is an example of a siege of a city, not a flooding of a town or the west coast bombs. The Lord says the meat of the trees we should eat of, and in the Wilmington Massacre, the children of God, Afro-Americans, however you want to put it, were killed, sent on trains (never to return), taken to Cape Fear out of intimidation, and had their positions usurped and history of prosperity burned. The men taking over the positions of the usurped ate the fruits of their trees and their business models.

SURRENDER OF CITIES – *Deuteronomy 20:10, 11, 16, 17* When thou comest nigh unto a city to fight against it, then proclaim peace unto it. **11** And it shall be, if it make thee answer of peace, and open unto thee, then it shall be, *that* all the people *that is* found therein shall be tributaries unto thee, and they shall serve thee. **16** But of the cities of these people, which the Lord thy God doth give thee *for* an inheritance, thou shalt save alive nothing that breatheth: **17** but thou shalt utterly destroy them; *namely*, the Hittites, and the Amorites, the Canaanites, and the Per´izzites, and the Hivites, and the Jeb´usites; as the Lord thy God hath commanded thee:

MANIFEST DESTINY: Delving into the history of the "military operation" by way of the International Committee of the Red Cross, theater of war, and mobs, which were organized forms of military, going to small towns and running the Afro-Americans out into the NIGHTMARE of MANIFEST DESTINY. Manifest Destiny excused the violence against the Indigenous Americans and gave surplus to those assimilating themselves into the United States during this time. Keep in mind there was one group of men going to war to fight in the theater of war and groups of men coming in from foreign nations to destroy, loot, and pillage cities and towns, forcing residents to surrender without the men there (off to war), being rebranded into a assimilated society.

TRIBUTE – *1 Kings 9:21* their children that were left after them in the land, whom the children of Israel also were not able utterly to destroy, upon those did Solomon levy a tribute of bondservice unto this day.

2 Kings 14:14, 18:14, 23:33 **14** And he took all the gold and silver, and all the vessels that were found in the house of the Lord, and in the treasures of the king's house, and hostages, and returned to Samaria. **18:14** And Hezeki´ah king of Judah sent to the king of Assyria to Lachish, saying, I have offended; return from me: that which thou puttest on me will I bear. And the king of Assyria appointed unto Hezeki´ah king of Judah three hundred talents of silver and thirty talents of gold. **23:33** And Pha´raoh-ne´choh put him in bands at Riblah in the land of Hamath, that he might not reign in Jerusalem; and put the land to a tribute of a hundred talents of silver, and a talent of gold.

2 Chronicles 8:8 but of their children, who were left after them in the land, whom the children of Israel consumed not, then did Solomon make to pay tribute until this day.

CIVIL CODE: The way that we pay TRIBUTE in the United States today, other than by crop, is by PERSONAL PROPERTY or PERSONAL PROPERTY TAX, which if you don't owe taxes, the only annual tax that we pay. The local government usually levies the taxes by 3%. The act of taxing goes back to the founding of the United States in 1776, when taxes were raised in most regions, mostly through PROPERTY, whereas Alexander Hamilton argued for a centralized taxed system and Thomas Jefferson argued for a LOCALLY based taxed system, citing it to be a concept of "democracy". Tax rates widely vary depending among jurisdictions.

COURT PROCEDURE

APPOINTMENT OF JUDGES - *Exodus 18:13-26*
The Appointment of Judges

(Deuteronomy 1.9-18)

13 And it came to pass on the morrow, that Moses sat to judge the people: and the people stood by Moses from the morning unto the evening. **14** And when Moses' father-in-law saw all that he did to the people, he said, What *is* this thing that thou doest to the people? Why sittest thou thyself alone, and all the people stand by thee from morning unto even? **15** And Moses said unto his father-in-law, Because the people come unto me to inquire of God: **16** when they have a matter, they come unto me; and I judge between one and another, and I do make *them* know the statutes of God, and his laws. **17** And Moses' father-in-law said unto him, The thing that thou doest *is* not good. **18** Thou wilt surely wear away, both thou, and this people that *is* with thee: for this thing *is* too heavy for thee; thou art not able to perform it thyself alone. **19** Hearken now unto my voice, I will give thee counsel, and God shall be with thee: Be thou for the people to Godward, that thou mayest bring the causes unto God: **20** and thou shalt teach them ordinances and laws, and shalt show them the way wherein they must walk, and the work that they must do. **21** Moreover thou shalt provide out of all the people able men, such as fear God, men of truth, hating covetousness; and place *such* over them, *to be* rulers of thousands, *and* rulers of hundreds, rulers of fifties, and rulers of tens: **22** and let them judge the people at all seasons: and it shall be, *that* every great matter they shall bring unto thee, but every small matter they shall judge: so shall it be easier for thyself, and they shall bear *the burden* with thee. **23** If thou shalt do this thing, and God command thee *so*, then thou shalt be able to endure, and all this people shall also go to their place in peace.

24 So Moses hearkened to the voice of his father-in-law, and did all that he had said. **25** And Moses chose able men out of all Israel, and made them heads over the people, rulers of thousands, rulers of hundreds, rulers of fifties, and rulers of tens. **26** And they judged the people at all seasons: the hard causes they brought unto Moses, but every small matter they judged themselves.

(Deuteronomy 16:18)

Judges and officers shalt thou make thee in all thy gates, which the Lord thy God giveth thee, throughout thy tribes: and they shall judge the people with just judgment.

(2 Chronicles 19:5-11)

5 And he set judges in the land throughout all the fenced cities of Judah, city by city, **6** and said to the judges, Take heed what ye do: for ye judge not for man, but for the Lord, who *is* with you in the judgment. **7** Wherefore now let the fear of the Lord be upon you; take heed and do *it*: for *there is* no iniquity with the Lord our God, nor respect of persons, nor taking of gifts.

8 Moreover in Jerusalem did Jehosh´aphat set of the Levites, and *of* the priests, and of the chief of the fathers of Israel, for the judgment of the Lord, and for controversies, when they returned to Jerusalem. **9** And he charged them, saying, Thus shall ye do in the fear of the Lord, faithfully, and with a perfect heart. **10** And what cause soever shall come to you of your brethren that dwell in their cities, between blood and blood, between law and commandment, statutes and judgments, ye shall even warn them that they trespass not against the Lord, and *so* wrath come upon you, and upon your brethren: this do, and ye shall not trespass. **11** And, behold, Amari´ah the chief priest *is* over you in all matters of the Lord; and Zebadi´ah the son of Ish´ma-el, the ruler of the house of Judah, for all the king's matters: also the Levites *shall be* officers before you. Deal courageously, and the Lord shall be with the good.

STATE AND LOCAL GOVERNMENT – In most cases, the MUNICIPAL COURT Judge is appointed by CITY COUNCIL and/or with the approval of the CITY MANAGER.

CHAPTER 1 – SUPREME COURT – United States Constitution Article III § 1 "The Judges, both of the supreme and inferior Courts, shall hold their Offices during good Behaviour,", which is for life in most cases. Supreme Court Justices are chosen by the President, with the consent of the Senate.

CHAPTER 3- COURTS OF APPEALS 28 U.S.C. § 44 states that the President shall appoint, with consent of the Senate, circuit judges for each of the 13 districts, including Federal and District of Columbia. § 45 Chief judges; precedence of judges, chief judges of the federal circuit shall be 64 years of age or under, have served for one year or more as a circuit judge, and must not have served previously as a chief judge.

CHAPTER 5 – DISTRICT COURTS §133. Appointment and number of district judges The President shall appoint, with the consent of the Senate of course, DISTRICT JUDGES for the several judicial districts, several judges being in each State and territory.

CHAPTER 7-UNITED STATES COURT OF FEDERAL CLAIMS §171 – The President shall appoint, by and with the advice and consent of the Senate, sixteen judges who shall constitute a court of record known as the United States Court of Federal Claims.

CHAPTER 11- COURT OF INTERNATIONAL TRADE The President shall appoint, by and with the advice and consent of the Senate, nine judges who shall constitute a court of record to be known as the United States Court of International Trade.

CHAPTER 43 – UNITED STATES MAGISTRATES (PREVIOUSLY UNITED STATES MAGISTRATE

JUDGES) – The Judges of each United States district court and the district court and the district courts of the Virgin Islands, Guam, and the Northern Mariana Islands shall appoint United States magistrate judges in such numbers and to serve at such locations within the judicial districts as the Judicial Conference may determine under this chapter.

THE 45ᵀᴴ CLAUSE OF THE MAGNA CARTA: We will appoint as justices, constables, sheriffs, or bailiffs only such as KNOW THE LAW OF THE REALM and mean to observe it well.

BEHAVIOR OF JUDGES *(Exodus 23:6-8)*

6 Thou shalt not wrest the judgment of thy poor in his cause. 7 Keep thee far from a false matter; and the innocent and righteous slay thou not: for I will not justify the wicked. 8 And thou shalt take no gift: for the gift blindeth the wise, and perverteth the words of the righteous.

(Deuteronomy 16:18-20)

18 Judges and officers shalt thou make thee in all thy gates, which the Lord thy God giveth thee, throughout thy tribes: and they shall judge the people with just judgment. 19 Thou shalt not wrest judgment; thou shalt not respect persons, neither take a gift: for a gift doth blind the eyes of the wise, and pervert the words of the righteous. 20 That which is altogether just shalt thou follow, that thou mayest live, and inherit the land which the Lord thy God giveth thee.

CIVIL CODE: 28 U.S.C. §144 Bias or prejudice of judge "the judge before whom the matter is pending has a personal bias or prejudice either against him or in favor of any adverse party, such judge shall proceed no further therein,", with another judge presiding over the case. You may only file this type of AFFIDAVIT once. **§ 354. Action by judicial council** (B) FOR ARTICLE III JUDGES says that if a judge is the subject of the complaint during good behavior, can certify disability of the judge pursuant to the procedures or request that the judge voluntarily retire. (C) FOR MAGISTRATE JUDGES., states that if the judge is the subject of the complaint, the chief judge under direction of the judicial council will take the appropriate action.

LOCATION OF COURTS *(Deuteronomy 21:19, 25:7)*

21:19 then shall his father and his mother lay hold on him, and bring him out unto the elders of his city, and unto the gate of his place;

25:7 And if the man like not to take his brother's wife, then let his brother's wife go up to the gate unto the elders, and say, My husband's brother refuseth to raise up unto his brother a name in Israel, he will not perform the duty of my husband's brother.

(1 Kings 7:7)

Then he made a porch for the throne where he might judge, *even* the porch of judgment: and *it was* covered with cedar from one side of the floor to the other.

AARON'S ROD BLOSSOMING: According to *Sanhedrin* and other sources located in *Aaron's Rod Blossoming,* "There were there (in Jerusalem) three assemblies of judges,- one sitting at the entry to the mountain of the sanctuary, another sitting at the door of the court, the third sitting in the conclave made of cut stone."

CIVIL PROCEDURE: In cities, precincts, and/or municipalities, there are distinct court buildings (usually noticeable) made of granite, keeping reminiscent the ideals of the original Court.

COURT OF APPEALS *(Exodus 18:26)*

And they judged the people at all seasons: the hard causes they brought unto Moses, but every small matter they judged themselves.

(Deuteronomy 17:8-11)

8 If there arise a matter too hard for thee in judgment, between blood and blood, between plea and plea, and between stroke and stroke, *being* matters of controversy within thy gates: then shalt thou arise, and get thee up into the place which the Lord thy God shall choose; **9** and thou shalt come unto the priests the Levites, and unto the judge that shall be in those days, and inquire; and they shall show thee the sentence of judgment: **10** and thou shalt do according to the sentence, which they of that place which the Lord shall choose shall show thee; and thou shalt observe to do according to all that they inform thee: **11** according to the sentence of the law which they shall teach thee, and according to the judgment which they shall tell thee, thou shalt do: thou shalt not decline from the sentence which they shall show thee, *to* the right hand, nor *to* the left.

CIVIL CODE: 28 U.S.C. Chapter 3 COURTS OF APPEALS **§ 42** allots Supreme Court Justices to Circuit Courts. **§ 43 (b)** Each court of appeals shall consist of the circuit judges of the circuit in REGULAR ACTIVE

SERVICE. §48 Terms of court (b) Each court of appeals may hold "SPECIAL SESSIONS" ay any place within its circuit as the nature of the business may require, and upon such notice as the court orders.

COURT OF ORIGINAL JURISDICTION *(Deuteronomy 25:1, 2)*

1 If there be a controversy between men, and they come unto judgment, that *the judges* may judge them; then they shall justify the righteous, and condemn the wicked. 2 And it shall be, if the wicked man *be* worthy to be beaten, that the judge shall cause him to lie down, and to be beaten before his face, according to his fault, by a certain number.

CIVIL CODE: PART IV- JURISDICTION AND VENUE Chapter 81 SUPREME COURT 28 U.S.C. § 1251(a) The Supreme Court shall have ORIGINAL and EXCLUSIVE JURISDICTION of all controversies between two or more States.

EXECUTION OF SENTENCE *(Deuteronomy 17:5-7)*

5 then shalt thou bring forth that man or that woman, which have committed that wicked thing, unto thy gates, *even* that man or that woman, and shalt stone them with stones, till they die. 6 At the mouth of two witnesses, or three witnesses, shall he that is worthy of death be put to death; *but* at the mouth of one witness he shall not be put to death. 7 The hands of the witnesses shall be first upon him to put him to death, and afterward the hands of all the people. So thou shalt put the evil away from among you.

CIVIL CODE: Each State has their own SUPREME COURT, COURT OF APPEALS, CIRCUIT COURTS, MUNICIPAL COURTS, TRAFFIC COURTS, FAMILY

COURTS, AND SMALL CLAIMS COURTS. The best way to identify their practices is to look at the "root" from where their power is vested.

Amendment VI (1791) of the U.S. Constitution states, "In all criminal prosecutions, the accused shall enjoy the right to a speedy and public trail, by an impartial jury of the State and district wherein the crime shall have been committed, which district shall have been previously ascertained by law, and to be informed of the nature and cause of the accusation; to be confronted with the witnesses against him; to have compulsory process for obtaining witnesses in his favor, and to have the Assistance of Counsel for his defence.

39th CLAUSE OF THE MAGNA CARTA: No freemen shall be taken or imprisoned or disseized or exiled or in any way destroyed, nor will we go upon him, except by the lawful judgment of his peers or by the law of the land.

PERJURY *(Deuteronomy 19:16-19)*

16 If a false witness rise up against any man to testify against him *that which is* wrong; **17** then both the men, between whom the controversy *is*, shall stand before the Lord, before the priests and the judges, which shall be in those days; **18** and the judges shall make diligent inquisition: and, behold, *if* the witness *be* a false witness, *and* hath testified falsely against his brother; **19** then shall ye do unto him, as he had thought to have done unto his brother: so shalt thou put the evil away from among you.

CIVIL CODE: 18 U.S.C. §1621. Perjury generally – "Whoever (1) having taken an oath before a competent tribunal, officer, or person, in any case in which a law of the United States authorises an oath to be administered, that he will testify, declare, depose, or certify truly, or that any written testimony, declaration, deposition, or certificate by him subscribed , is true, willfully and contrary to such oath states or subscribe any material matter which he does not believe to be true" or any form of statement under penalty of perjury, (2) is guilty of **PERJURY** and shall, except as otherwise expressly provided by law, be fined under this title or imprisoned not more than five years, or both.

SOLOMON AS JUDGE *(1 Kings 7:7)*

Then he made a porch for the throne where he might judge, *even* the porch of judgment: and *it was* covered with cedar from one side of the floor to the other.

SOURCE OF JUDGMENT *(Deuteronomy 1:17)*

Ye shall not respect persons in judgment; *but* ye shall hear the small as well as the great; ye shall not be afraid of the face of man; for the judgment *is* God's: and the cause that is too hard for you, bring *it* unto me, and I will hear it.

JURISDICTION: The power of a court to adjudicate cases and issue orders and territory within which a court or government agency may properly exercise its power.

SUPERIOR COURT *(Deuteronomy 17:8-12)*

8 If there arise a matter too hard for thee in judgment, between blood and blood, between plea and plea, and between stroke and stroke, *being* matters of controversy within thy gates: then shalt thou arise, and get thee up into the place which the Lord thy God shall choose; **9** and thou shalt come unto the priests the Levites, and unto the judge that shall be in those days, and inquire; and they shall show thee the sentence of judgment: **10** and thou shalt do according to the sentence, which they of that place which the Lord shall choose shall show thee; and thou shalt observe to do according to all that they inform thee: **11** according to the sentence of the law which they shall teach thee, and according to the judgment which they shall tell thee, thou shalt do: thou shalt not decline from the sentence which they shall show thee, *to* the right hand, nor *to* the left. **12** And the man that will do presumptuously, and will not hearken unto the priest that standeth to minister there before the Lord thy God, or unto the judge, even that man shall die: and thou shalt put away the evil from Israel.

The Superior Court in our Land most commonly refers to the trial-level courts of many states, being local level in common cases, so in this case, we'd be discussing a trial court of GENERAL JURISDICTION.

SUPREME COURT *(Numbers 5:12-31)*

12 Speak unto the children of Israel, and say unto them, If any man's wife go aside, and commit a trespass against him, **13** and a man lie with her carnally, and it be hid from the eyes of her husband, and be kept close, and she be defiled, and *there be* no witness against her, neither she be taken *with the manner*, **14** and the spirit of jealousy come upon him, and he be jealous of his wife, and she be defiled; or if the spirit of jealousy come upon him, and he be jealous of his wife, and she be not defiled: **15** then shall the man bring his wife unto the priest, and he shall bring her offering for her, the tenth *part* of an ephah of barley meal; he shall pour no oil upon it, nor put frankincense thereon; for it *is* an offering of jealousy, an offering of memorial, bringing iniquity to remembrance.

16 And the priest shall bring her near, and set her before the Lord: **17** and the priest shall take holy water in an earthen vessel; and of the dust that is in the floor of the tabernacle the priest shall take, and put *it* into the water: **18** and the priest shall set the woman before the Lord, and uncover the woman's head, and put the offering of memorial in her hands, which *is* the jealousy offering: and the priest shall have in his hand the bitter water that causeth the curse: **19** and the priest shall charge her by an oath, and say unto the woman, If no man have lain with thee, and if thou hast not gone aside to uncleanness *with another* instead of thy husband, be thou free from this bitter water that causeth the curse: **20** but if thou hast gone aside *to another* instead of thy husband, and if thou be defiled, and some man have lain with thee besides thine husband: **21** then the priest shall charge the woman with an oath of cursing, and the priest shall say unto the woman, The Lord make thee a curse and an oath among thy people, when the Lord doth make thy thigh to rot, and thy belly to swell; **22** and this water that causeth the curse shall go into thy bowels, to make *thy* belly to swell, and *thy* thigh to rot. And the woman shall say, Amen, amen.

23 And the priest shall write these curses in a book, and he shall blot *them* out with the bitter water: **24** and he shall cause the woman to drink the bitter water that causeth the curse: and the water that causeth the curse shall enter into her, *and become* bitter. **25** Then the priest shall take the jealousy offering out of the woman's hand, and shall wave the offering before the Lord, and offer it upon the altar: **26** and the priest shall take a handful of the offering, *even* the memorial thereof, and burn *it* upon the altar, and afterward shall cause the woman to drink the water. **27** And when he hath made her to drink the water, then it shall come to pass, *that* if she be defiled, and have done trespass against her husband, that the water that causeth the curse shall enter into her, *and become* bitter, and her belly shall swell, and her thigh shall rot: and the woman shall be a curse among her people. 28 And if the woman be not defiled, but be clean; then she shall be free, and shall conceive seed.

29 This *is* the law of jealousies, when a wife goeth aside *to another* instead of her husband, and is defiled; 30 or when the spirit of jealousy cometh upon him, and he be jealous over his wife, and shall set the woman before the Lord, and the priest shall execute upon her all this law. 31 Then shall the man be guiltless from iniquity, and this woman shall bear her iniquity.

(Deuteronomy 19:17-19, 21:1-9)

17 then both the men, between whom the controversy *is*, shall stand before the Lord, before the priests and the judges, which shall be in those days; 18 and the judges shall make diligent inquisition: and, behold, *if* the witness *be* a false witness, *and* hath testified falsely against his brother; 19 then shall ye do unto him, as he had thought to have done unto his brother: so shalt thou put the evil away from among you.

(21:1-9)

1 If *one* be found slain in the land which the Lord thy God giveth thee to possess it, lying in the field, *and* it be not known who hath slain him: 2 then thy elders and thy judges shall come forth, and they shall measure unto the cities which *are* round about him that is slain: 3 and it shall be, *that* the city *which is* next unto the slain man, even the elders of that city shall take a heifer, which hath not been wrought with, *and* which hath not drawn in the yoke; 4 and

the elders of that city shall bring down the heifer unto a rough valley, which is neither eared nor sown, and shall strike off the heifer's neck there in the valley. **5** And the priests the sons of Levi shall come near; for them the Lord thy God hath chosen to minister unto him, and to bless in the name of the Lord; and by their word shall every controversy and every stroke be *tried*: **6** and all the elders of that city, *that are* next unto the slain *man*, shall wash their hands over the heifer that is beheaded in the valley: **7** and they shall answer and say, Our hands have not shed this blood, neither have our eyes seen *it*. **8** Be merciful, O Lord, unto thy people Israel, whom thou hast redeemed, and lay not innocent blood unto thy people of Israel's charge. And the blood shall be forgiven them. **9** So shalt thou put away the *guilt of* innocent blood from among you, when thou shalt do *that which is* right in the sight of the Lord.

CIVIL CODE: The SUPREME COURT is the highest court inside of a JURISDICTION such as the Supreme Court of the United States or Supreme Court of California, ALL PARTS OF FEDERAL JUDICIARY. There are instances where the name Supreme Court is inserted inside the name of a court like Kings County Supreme Court in New York that isn't a SUPREME COURT, the name is in the history of the court.

TRIAL BEFORE ELDERS *(Deuteronomy 22:15)*

then shall the father of the damsel, and her mother, take and bring forth *the tokens of* the damsel's virginity unto the elders of the city in the gate:

CIVIL PROCEDURE: While on the Land called America, there is no group of assembled, noble, established in following the law, and scholarly group of ELDERS known to the general public on behalf of all people of the Land for their true betterment, but we have a Chief Justice quoad hoc The Judiciary Act of 1789.

TYPICAL TRIAL *(1Kings 3:16-28)*

16 Then came there two women, *that were* harlots, unto the king, and stood before him. **17** And the one woman said, O my lord, I and this woman dwell in one house; and I was delivered of a child with her in the house. **18** And it came to pass the third day after that I was delivered, that this woman was delivered also: and we *were* together; *there was* no stranger with us in the house, save we two in the house. **19** And this woman's child died in the night; because she overlaid it. **20** And she arose at midnight, and took my son from beside me, while thine handmaid slept, and laid it in her bosom, and laid her dead child in my bosom. **21** And when I rose in the morning to give my child suck, behold, it was dead: but when I had considered it in the morning, behold, it was not my son, which I did bear. **22** And the other woman said, Nay; but the living *is* my son, and the dead *is* thy son. And this said, No; but the dead *is* thy son, and the living *is* my son. Thus they spake before the king.

23 Then said the king, The one saith, This *is* my son that liveth, and thy son *is* the dead: and the other saith, Nay; but thy son *is* the dead, and my son *is* the living. **24** And the king said, Bring me a sword. And they brought a sword before the king. **25** And the king said, Divide the living child in two, and give half to the one, and half to the other. **26** Then spake the woman whose the living child *was* unto the king, for her bowels yearned upon her son, and she said, O my lord, give her the living child, and in no wise slay it. But the other said, Let it be neither mine nor thine, *but* divide *it.* **27** Then the king answered and said, Give her the living child, and in no wise slay it: she *is* the mother thereof. **28** And all

Israel heard of the judgment which the king had judged; and they feared the king: for they saw that the wisdom of God *was* in him to do judgment.

18 U.S.C. § 3161 (a) In any case involving a defendant charged with an offense, the appropriate judicial officer, at the earliest practicable time, shall, after consultation with the counsel for the defendant and the attorney for the Government, set the case for trial on a day certain, or list it for trial on a weekly or other short term trial calendar at a place within the judicial district, so as to assure A SPEEDY TRIAL.

28 U.S.C. §1861 "It is the policy of the United States that all litigants in Federal courts entitled to TRIAL BY JURY shall have the right to grand and petit juries selected at random from a fair cross section of the community in the district or division wherein the court convenes." Ironically, the people DO make the final judgment in an United States Court.

NUMBER OF WITNESSES *(Deuteronomy 17:6, 7, 19:15-19)*

6 At the mouth of two witnesses, or three witnesses, shall he that is worthy of death be put to death; *but* at the mouth of one witness he shall not be put to death. **7** The hands of the witnesses shall be first upon him to put him to death, and afterward the hands of all the people. So thou shalt put the evil away from among you.

(19:15-19)

15 One witness shall not rise up against a man for any iniquity, or for any sin, in any sin that he sinneth: at the mouth of two witnesses, or at the mouth of three witnesses, shall the matter be established. **16** If a false witness rise up against any man to testify against him *that which is* wrong; **17** then both the men, between whom the controversy *is*, shall stand before the Lord, before the priests and the judges, which shall be in those days; **18** and the judges shall make diligent inquisition: and, behold, *if* the witness *be* a false witness, *and* hath testified falsely against his brother; **19** then shall ye do unto him, as he had thought to have done unto his brother: so shalt thou put the evil away from among you.

(Matthew 18:16)

But if he will not hear *thee, then* take with thee one or two more, that in the mouth of two or three witnesses every word may be established.

COURT PROCEDURE: In the stage of Discovery in our court system in America, there are three types of witnesses qua **A LAY WITNESS, AN EXPERT WITNESS,** and **CHARACTER WITNESS,** each bearing distinct qualities in the nature of court.

28 U.S.C. CHAPTER 117 – EVIDENCE; DEPOSITIONS, STATUTORY NOTES AND RELATED SUBSIDIARIES, DEPOSITIONS IN ADMIRALITY CASES "SEC. 863. The testimony of any witness may be taken in any civil cause depending in a district court by deposition de bene esse, when the witness lives at a greater distance from the place of trial than one hundred miles, etc."

LAWS OF CITIZENSHIP

OBLIGATIONS OF ALIENS – *Exodus 12:48, 49* 48 And when a stranger shall sojourn with thee, and will keep the passover to the Lord, let all his males be circumcised, and then let him come near and keep it; and he shall be as one that is born in the land: for no uncircumcised person shall eat thereof. 49 One law shall be to him that is homeborn, and unto the stranger that sojourneth among you.

Leviticus 17:8, 9, 24:22 8 And thou shalt say unto them, Whatsoever man *there be* of the house of Israel, or of the strangers which sojourn among you, that offereth a burnt offering or sacrifice, 9 and bringeth it not unto the door of the tabernacle of the congregation, to offer it unto the Lord; even that man shall be cut off from among his people.

24:22 Ye shall have one manner of law, as well for the stranger, as for one of your own country: for I *am* the Lord your God.

LIBERTY IN AMERICA: With the **First Amendment of the U.S. Constitution** prevalent in the minds of practicing religious peoples in the United States, it makes it hard to tell your neighbor to put away her giant rainbow dragon in the backyard without facing extreme communal judgment and/or a potential fine. The point isn't for me to ridicule one for their own beliefs, the point is if this is a nation under God, there's a large number of dissenters in that regard as far as following His Law. There are many traditions and practices that are quickly spread throughout communities until it becomes national over time. Kind of reminds you of COMMON LAW in the United States right? For instance, observe the laws changing incrementally over time until a decade passes, and the laws have been altered to a point unrelatable to the foundation of the *Law of the Land*.

RIGHTS OF ALIENS *(Exodus 12:48, 49, 20:10)* **48** And when a stranger shall sojourn with thee, and will keep the passover to the Lord, let all his males be circumcised, and then let him come near and keep it; and he shall be as one that is born in the land: for no uncircumcised person shall eat thereof. **49** One law shall be to him that is homeborn, and unto the stranger that sojourneth among you.

20:10 but the seventh day *is* the sabbath of the Lord thy God: *in it* thou shalt not do any work, thou, nor thy son, nor thy daughter, thy manservant, nor thy maidservant, nor thy cattle, nor thy stranger that *is* within thy gates:

Leviticus 16:29 And *this* shall be a statute forever unto you: *that* in the seventh month, on the tenth *day* of the month, ye shall afflict your souls, and do no work at all, *whether it be* one of your own country, or a stranger that sojourneth among you:

Well, the RIGHTS OF ALIENS don't extend far past the U.S. Constitution, with fluid law running rampant over the Congress of today. Why do you think so many people have come through ELLIS ISLAND, there are numerous persons coming in through the SOUTHWEST of America, and everything here in America is modeled after immigrants? There are RIGHTS for DISNEY, LGBTQFG, ILLEGAL ALIENS, and CORPORATIONS in general, leaving behind the correctness of the LORD OUR GOD, ultimately, criminalizing the LEGISLATIVE BRANCH of the modern era. With such a diverse way of life being offered to Americans through the flick of a channel or brief change of scenery, God becomes distant from such a place.

ELIGIBILITY – *Deuteronomy 23:7, 8* **7** Thou shalt not abhor an Edomite; for he *is* thy brother: thou shalt not abhor an Egyptian; because thou wast a stranger in his land. **8** The children that are begotten of them shall enter into the congregation of the Lord in their third generation.

To come into America, it seems that you need just the WILL to do it. How many stories have you heard of a family coming here with nothing, arriving with just $500 dollars and a dream or better yet, $5 and a purpose? The movie WHITEWASHED, will show you how families with no job or money, can still receive LOANS to start their businesses or mortgage a home.

EXCLUSIONS – *Deuteronomy 23:3* An Ammonite or Moabite shall not enter into the congregation of the Lord; even to their tenth generation shall they not enter into the congregation of the Lord for ever:

CIVILITER MORTUUS: If you are BLACK, you are excluded from the freedom of CIVILITY, you'll receive a large number of tickets, be placed into debt bondage, and a SLAVE under the 13TH AND 14th AMENDMENT.

FREEDOM FROM PAYING INTEREST - *Exodus 22:25* If thou lend money to *any of* my people *that is* poor by thee, thou shalt not be to him as a usurer, neither shalt thou lay upon him usury.

Deuteronomy 23:19, 20 **19** Thou shalt not lend upon usury to thy brother; usury of money, usury of victuals, usury of any thing that is lent upon usury: **20** unto a stranger thou mayest lend upon usury; but unto thy brother thou shalt not lend upon usury: that the Lord thy God may bless thee in all that thou settest thine hand to in the land whither thou goest to possess it.

JUS CIVILE: One is rewarded in CIVIL SOCIETY for timely payments, which instills trust from lenders of various sorts. What is considered a DEFERRED INTEREST, is a loan or credit card issued where your interest payments are deferred, not absolved. You'd still essentially have to pay the interest at a later date if you're late on your last payment. If you're hoping for a NO INTEREST LOAN or whichever lingo your lender is using to define the loan, you will need good to excellent credit to receive it.

MARITAL RIGHTS - *Genesis 34:14* and they said unto them, We cannot do this thing, to give our sister to one that is uncircumcised; for that *were* a reproach unto us:

Exodus 34:15, 16 **15** Lest thou make a covenant with the inhabitants of the land, and they go a whoring after their gods, and do sacrifice unto their gods, and *one* call thee, and thou eat of his sacrifice; **16** and thou take of their daughters unto thy sons, and their daughters go a whoring after their gods, and make thy sons go a whoring after their gods.

Deuteronomy 7:1-3 **1** When the Lord thy God shall bring thee into the land whither thou goest to possess it, and hath cast out many nations before thee, the Hittites, and the Gir´gashites, and the Amorites, and the Canaanites, and the Per´izzites, and the Hivites, and the Jeb´usites, seven nations greater and mightier than thou; **2** and when the Lord thy God shall deliver them before thee; thou shalt smite them, *and* utterly destroy them; thou shalt make no covenant with them, nor show mercy unto them: **3** neither shalt thou make marriages with them; thy daughter thou shalt not give unto his son, nor his daughter shalt thou take unto thy son.

The rights that belong to the FREEDMEN of Briton, spread throughout the four corners of the earth, are our marital rights when we are MARRIED TO GOD. As the bride of Christ, our obligations are to UPHOLD THE LAW and in return, you receive the blessings of the Father in our FATHERLAND. The act of marriage in the United States has nothing to do with the Father and every matter to do with CONTRACTS and PECUNIARY OBLIGATIONS which need to be made in a BASTARDISED SYSTEM.

QUALIFICATIONS FOR - *Exodus 19:5, 6* **5** Now therefore, if ye will obey my voice indeed, and keep my covenant, then ye shall be a peculiar treasure unto me above all people: for all the earth *is* mine: **6** and ye shall be unto me a kingdom of priests, and a holy nation. These *are* the words which thou shalt speak unto the children of Israel.

Priests, lawyers, judges, and high priests, all being truthful and lawful, are the men who uphold the law and speak unto the children of Israel the Word of God, being qualified and as such, a peculiar treasure amongst the people. I speak not of those who uphold jurisprudence over the truth.

RIGHT OF APPEAL – *Acts 25:11*. For if I be an offender, or have committed any thing worthy of death, I refuse not to die: but if there be none of these things whereof these accuse me, no man may deliver me unto them. I appeal unto Caesar.

JUS CIVILE: According to the JUSTICE MANUAL, Sect. 2-1.000 APPEALS IN GENERAL, "Procedures to be followed in civil and criminal appeals to United States courts of appeals from the United States district courts, (WHICH IS APPELLATE JURISDICTION, *not in Justice Manual*), are set forth in the FEDERAL RULES OF APPELLATE PROCEDURE." Each state having its own district courts are subject to the rules as well.

RIGHT TO TRIAL – *Acts 16:37-39* **37** But Paul said unto them, They have beaten us openly uncondemned, being Romans, and have cast *us* into prison; and now do they thrust us out privily? nay verily; but let them come themselves and fetch us out. **38** And the sergeants told these words unto the magistrates: and they feared, when they heard that they were Romans. **39** And they came and besought them, and brought *them* out, and desired *them* to depart out of the city.

JUS CIVILE: The 6th Amendment of the U.S. Constitution guarantees all CRIMINAL prosecutions have and enjoy the right to a SPEEDY AND PUBLIC TRIAL. In 18 U.S.C. **§3161, any case** involving a defendant charged with an offense, the appropriate judicial officer will set the case for trial on a certain day or list it for trial on a weekly or other short-term trial calendar at a place within the judicial district so as to assure a speedy trial brought forth from THE SPEEDY TRIAL ACT OF 1974.

ROMAN – *Acts 16:37, 38, 22:25-29, 23:27* **37** But Paul said unto them, They have beaten us openly uncondemned, being Romans, and have cast *us* into prison; and now do they thrust us out privily? nay verily; but let them come themselves and fetch us out. **38** And the sergeants told these words unto the magistrates: and they feared, when they heard that they were Romans. **22:25-29** And as they bound him with thongs, Paul said unto the centurion that stood by, Is it lawful for you to scourge a man that is a Roman, and uncondemned? **26** When the centurion heard *that*, he went and told the chief captain, saying, Take heed what thou doest; for this man is a Roman. **27** Then the chief captain came, and said unto him, Tell me, art thou a Roman? He said, Yea. **28** And the chief captain answered, With a great sum obtained I this freedom. And Paul said, But I was *free*-born. **29** Then straightway they departed from him which should have examined him: and the chief captain also was afraid, after he knew that he was a Roman, and because he had bound him. **23:27** This man was taken of the Jews, and should have been killed of them: then came I with an army, and rescued him, having understood that he was a Roman.

When In Rome: ROMAN LAW has taken its place in TIME IMMEMORIAL, running 1,000 years of LEGAL JURISPRUDENCE from the Twelve Tables, and the body of civil law, CORPUS JURIS (IURIS) CIVILIS, the body of the FRENCH NAPOLEONIC CODE. Rome has founded the basis of CIVIL LAW we see in America today. The Laws of the Twelve Tables is the legislation that stands at the foot of Roman law.

The CORPUS JURIS CIVILIS is a collection of works in jurisprudence, issued by Justinian I of the Byzantine Empire, also known as the Code of Justinian. The work has FOUR parts the CODE, the DIGEST, the INSTITUTES, and the NOVELLAE. The Belly of the Beast.

EASTERN CATHOLIC CANON LAW is the law of the 23 Catholic SUI JURIS particular churches of the Eastern Catholic tradition. Oriental CANON LAW includes both the common tradition among all Eastern Catholic Churches, now chiefly containing in the Code of Canons of the Eastern Churches, as well as the particular law proper to each individual sui juris particular Eastern Catholic Church. Originating with the canons of particular councils and the writings of the Eastern Church Fathers, oriental canon law developed IN CONCERT with the BYZANTINE ROMAN LAWS, leading to the compilation of nomocanons, a collection of ECCLESIASTICAL LAWS of CIVIL AND CANON LAWS.

THE HOLY ROMAN EMPIRE, A.K.A, THE HOLY ROMAN EMPIRE OF THE **GERMAN NATION** is nothing more than the NAZI PARTY disguised under the VATICAN reigning over the Americas currently, which is coming to an end.

OF SLAVES – *Exodus 21:1-11* 1 Now these are the judgments which thou shalt set before them. 2 If thou buy a Hebrew servant, six years he shall serve: and in the seventh he shall go out free for nothing. 3 If he came in by himself, he shall go out by himself: if he were married, then his wife shall go out with him. 4 If his master have given him a wife, and she have borne him sons or daughters; the wife and her children shall be her master's, and he shall go out by himself. 5 And if the servant shall plainly say, I love my master, my wife, and my children; I will not go out free: 6 then his master shall bring him unto the judges; he shall also bring him to the door, or unto the doorpost; and his master shall bore his ear through with an awl; and he shall serve him for ever.

7 And if a man sell his daughter to be a maidservant, she shall not go out as the menservants do. **8** If she please not her master, who hath betrothed her to himself, then shall he let her be redeemed: to sell her unto a strange nation he shall have no power, seeing he hath dealt deceitfully with her. **9** And if he have betrothed her unto his son, he shall deal with her after the manner of daughters. **10** If he take him another *wife*, her food, her raiment, and her duty of marriage, shall he not diminish. **11** And if he do not these three unto her, then shall she go out free without money.

Leviticus 25:39-55 **39** And if thy brother *that dwelleth* by thee be waxen poor, and be sold unto thee; thou shalt not compel him to serve as a bondservant: **40** *but* as a hired servant, *and* as a sojourner, he shall be with thee, *and* shall serve thee unto the year of jubilee: **41** and *then* shall he depart from thee, *both* he and his children with him, and shall return unto his own family, and unto the possession of his fathers shall he return. **42** For they *are* my servants, which I brought forth out of the land of Egypt: they shall not be sold as bondmen. **43** Thou shalt not rule over him with rigor; but shalt fear thy God. **44** Both thy bondmen, and thy bondmaids, which thou shalt have, *shall be* of the heathen that are round about you; of them shall ye buy bondmen and bondmaids. **45** Moreover, of the children of the strangers that do sojourn among you, of them shall ye buy, and of their families that *are* with you, which they begat in your land: and they shall be your possession. **46** And ye shall take them as an inheritance for your children after you, to inherit *them for* a possession; they shall be your bondmen for ever: but over your brethren the children of Israel, ye shall not rule one over another with rigor.

47 And if a sojourner or stranger wax rich by thee, and thy brother *that dwelleth* by him wax poor, and sell himself unto the stranger *or* sojourner by thee, or to the stock of the stranger's family: **48** after that he is sold he may be redeemed again; one of his brethren may redeem him: **49** either his uncle, or his uncle's son, may redeem him, or *any* that is nigh of kin unto him of his family may redeem him; or if he be able, he may redeem himself. **50** And he shall reckon with him that bought him from the year that he was sold to him unto the year of jubilee: and the price of his sale shall be according unto the number of years, according to the time of a hired servant shall it be with him. **51** If *there be* yet many years *behind,* according unto them he shall give again the price of his redemption out of the money that he was bought for. **52** And if there remain but few years unto the year of jubilee, then he shall count with him, *and* according unto his years shall he give him again the price of his redemption. **53** *And* as a yearly hired servant shall he be with him: *and the other* shall not rule with rigor over him in thy sight. **54** And if he be not redeemed in these *years,* then he shall go out in the year of jubilee, *both* he, and his children with him. **55** For unto me the children of Israel *are* servants; they *are* my servants whom I brought forth out of the land of Egypt: I *am* the Lord your God.

<u>Deuteronomy 15:12-18</u> **12** *And* if thy brother, a Hebrew man, or a Hebrew woman, be sold unto thee, and serve thee six years; then in the seventh year thou shalt let him go free from thee. **13** And when thou sendest him out free from thee, thou shalt not let him go away empty: **14** thou shalt furnish him liberally out of thy flock, and out of thy floor, and out of thy winepress: *of that* wherewith the Lord thy God hath blessed thee thou shalt give unto him. **15** And thou shalt remember that thou wast a bondman in the land of Egypt, and the Lord thy God redeemed thee: therefore I command thee this thing today. **16** And it shall be, if he say unto thee, I will not go away from thee; because he loveth thee and thine house, because he is well with thee; **17** then thou shalt take an awl, and thrust *it* through his ear unto the door, and he shall be thy servant for ever. And also unto thy maidservant thou shalt do likewise. **18** It shall not seem hard unto thee, when thou sendest him away free from thee; for he hath been worth a double hired servant *to thee*, in serving thee six years: and the Lord thy God shall bless thee in all that thou doest.

<u>*1 Corinthians 12:13*</u> For by one Spirit are we all baptized into one body, whether *we be* Jews or Gentiles, whether *we be* bond or free; and have been all made to drink into one Spirit.

<u>*Galatians 3:28*</u> There is neither Jew nor Greek, there is neither bond nor free, there is neither male nor female: for ye are all one in Christ Jesus.

<u>*Colossians 3:11*</u> where there is neither Greek nor Jew, circumcision nor uncircumcision, Barbarian, Scyth´i-an, bond *nor* free: but Christ *is* all, and in all.

U.S. CONSTITUTION AMENDMENT 13 (1865)
Section 1. Neither SLAVERY nor INVOLUNTARY SERVITUDE, except as a punishment for crime whereof the party shall have been duly convicted, shall exist within the United States, or any place subject to their jurisdiction. Section 2. Congress shall have power to enforce this article by appropriate legislation.

1828 WEBSTER'S DICTIONARY: **VASSAL** 1. A feudatory; a tenant; one who holds land of a superior, and who vows FIDELITY AND HOMAGE to him. A REAR VASSAL is one who holds of a lord who is himself a VASSAL. 2. A subject; a dependent 3. A servant. 4. In common language, a bondman; a political slave. To subject to control; to enslave.

SAME DICTIONARY, DIFFERENT TERM: **VESSEL.** 2. In anatomy, any tube or canal, in which the blood and other humors are contained, secreted or circulated, as the arteries, veins, lymphatics, spermatics, etc. 5. Something containing. Chosen vessel, ministers of the gospel, as appointed to bear the glad news of salvation to others; called also EARTHEN VESSELS (ADAM), on account of their weakness and frailty. 46 U.S.C. § 2106 **Liability in rem** When a VESSEL IS MADE LIABLE *IN REM* UNDER THIS SUBTITLE, THE VESSEL MAY BE LIBELED AND PROCEEDED AGAINST THE DISTRICT COURT OF THE UNITED STATES FOR ANY DISTRICT IN WHICH THE VESSEL IS FOUND. 46 U.S.C. § 2101 defines "PUBLIC VESSEL" as (33) (A) is owned, or DEMISE CHARTERED, and operated by the United States Government or a government of a foreign country and is (B) not engaged in COMMERCIAL SERVICE.

RELIGIOUS LAWS

BAPTISM *(Matthew 3:13-17, 28:19)*

13 Then cometh Jesus from Galilee to Jordan unto John, to be baptized of him. **14** But John forbade him, saying, I have need to be baptized of thee, and comest thou to me? **15** And Jesus answering said unto him, Suffer *it to be so now: for thus it becometh us to fulfil all righteousness.* Then he suffered him. **16** And Jesus, when he was baptized, went up straightway out of the water: and, lo, the heavens were opened unto him, and he saw the Spirit of God descending like a dove, and lighting upon him: **17** and lo a voice from heaven, saying, This is my beloved Son, in whom I am well pleased.

(28:19)

Go ye therefore, and teach all nations, baptizing them in the name of the Father, and of the Son, and of the Holy Ghost:

John 4:1, 2 **1** When therefore the Lord knew how the Pharisees had heard that Jesus made and baptized more disciples than John, **2** (though Jesus himself baptized not, but his disciples,)

Acts 2:38, 19:3-6 **2:38** Then Peter said unto them, Repent, and be baptized every one of you in the name of Jesus Christ for the remission of sins, and ye shall receive the gift of the Holy Ghost. *19:3-6* **3** And he said unto them, Unto what then were ye baptized? And they said, Unto John's baptism. **4** Then said Paul, John verily baptized with the baptism of repentance, saying unto the people, that they should believe on him which should come after him, that is, on Christ Jesus. **5** When they heard *this*, they were baptized in the name of the Lord Jesus. **6** And when Paul had laid *his* hands upon them, the Holy Ghost came on them; and they spake with tongues, and prophesied.

<u>*Romans 6:3, 4*</u> **3** Know ye not, that so many of us as were baptized into Jesus Christ were baptized into his death? **4** Therefore we are buried with him by baptism into death: that like as Christ was raised up from the dead by the glory of the Father, even so we also should walk in newness of life.

<u>*1 Corinthians 12:13*</u> buried with him in baptism, wherein also ye are risen with *him* through the faith of the operation of God, who hath raised him from the dead.

<u>*1 Peter 3:20, 21*</u> **20** which sometime were disobedient, when once the long-suffering of God waited in the days of Noah, while the ark was a preparing, wherein few, that is, eight souls were saved by water. **21** The like figure whereunto *even* baptism doth also now save us, (not the putting away of the filth of the flesh, but the answer of a good conscience toward God,) by the resurrection of Jesus Christ:

BLASPHEMY – <u>*Leviticus 24:10-16*</u> **10** And the son of an Israelitish woman, whose father *was* an Egyptian, went out among the children of Israel: and this son of the Israelitish *woman* and a man of Israel strove together in the camp; **11** and the Israelitish woman's son blasphemed the name *of the Lord*, and cursed. And they brought him unto

Moses: (and his mother's name *was* Shelo´mith, the daughter of Dibri, of the tribe of Dan:) **12** and they put him in ward, that the mind of the Lord might be showed them.

13 And the Lord spake unto Moses, saying, **14** Bring forth him that hath cursed without the camp; and let all that heard *him* lay their hands upon his head, and let all the congregation stone him. **15** And thou shalt speak unto the children of Israel, saying, Whosoever curseth his God shall bear his sin. **16** And he that blasphemeth the name of the Lord, he shall surely be put to death, *and* all the congregation shall certainly stone him: as well the stranger, as he that is born in the land, when he blasphemeth the name *of the Lord*, shall be put to death.

Deuteronomy 5:11 Thou shalt not take the name of the Lord thy God in vain: for the Lord will not hold *him* guiltless that taketh his name in vain.

Matthew 5:19, 20 **19** Whosoever therefore shall break one of these least commandments, and shall teach men so, he shall be called the least in the kingdom of heaven: but whosoever shall do and teach *them*, the same shall be called great in the kingdom of heaven. **20** For I say unto you, That except your righteousness shall exceed *the righteousness* of the scribes and Pharisees, ye shall in no case enter into the kingdom of heaven.

BURNT OFFERINGS – *Leviticus 1:1-17*

1 And the Lord called unto Moses, and spake unto him out of the tabernacle of the congregation, saying, **2** Speak unto the children of Israel, and say unto them, If any man of you bring an offering unto the Lord, ye shall bring your offering of the cattle, *even* of the herd, and of the flock.

3 If his offering *be* a burnt sacrifice of the herd, let him offer a male without blemish: he shall offer it of his own voluntary will at the door of the tabernacle of the congregation before the Lord. **4** And he shall put his hand upon the head of the burnt offering; and it shall be accepted for him to make atonement for him. **5** And he shall kill the bullock before the Lord: and the priests, Aaron's sons, shall bring the blood, and sprinkle the blood round about upon the altar that *is by* the door of the tabernacle of the congregation. **6** And he shall flay the burnt offering, and cut it into his pieces.

7 And the sons of Aaron the priest shall put fire upon the altar, and lay the wood in order upon the fire: **8** and the priests, Aaron's sons, shall lay the parts, the head, and the fat, in order upon the wood that *is* on the fire which *is* upon the altar: **9** but his inwards and his legs shall he wash in water: and the priest shall burn all on the altar, *to be* a burnt sacrifice, an offering made by fire, of a sweet savor unto the Lord.

10 And if his offering *be* of the flocks, *namely*, of the sheep, or of the goats, for a burnt sacrifice; he shall bring it a male without blemish. **11** And he shall kill it on the side of the altar northward before the Lord: and the priests, Aaron's sons, shall sprinkle his blood round about upon the altar. **12** And he shall cut it into his pieces, with his head and his fat: and the priest shall lay them in order on the wood that *is* on the fire which *is* upon the altar: **13** but he shall wash the inwards and the legs with water: and the priest shall bring *it* all, and burn *it* upon the altar: it *is* a burnt sacrifice, an offering made by fire, of a sweet savor unto the Lord.

14 And if the burnt sacrifice for his offering to the Lord *be* of fowls, then he shall bring his offering of turtledoves, or of young pigeons. **15** And the priest shall bring it unto the altar, and wring off his head, and burn *it* on the altar; and the blood thereof shall be wrung out at the side of the altar: **16** and he shall pluck away his crop with his feathers, and cast it beside the altar on the east part, by the place of the ashes. **17** And he shall cleave it with the wings thereof, *but* shall not divide *it* asunder: and the priest shall burn it upon the altar, upon the wood that *is* upon the fire: it *is* a burnt sacrifice, an offering made by fire, of a sweet savor unto the Lord.

Numbers 6:11, 15:3 **6:11** and the priest shall offer the one for a sin offering, and the other for a burnt offering, and make an atonement for him, for that he sinned by the dead, and shall hallow his head that same day. **15:3** and will make an offering by fire unto the Lord, a burnt offering, or a sacrifice in performing a vow, or in a freewill offering, or in your solemn feasts, to make a sweet savor unto the Lord, of the herd, or of the flock:

CHILDBIRTH SACRIFICES - ***Luke 2:22-24*** **22** And when the days of her purification according to the law of Moses were accomplished, they brought him to Jerusalem, to present *him* to the Lord; **23** (as it is written in the law of the Lord, Every male that openeth the womb shall be called holy to the Lord;) **24** and to offer a sacrifice according to that which is said in the law of the Lord, A pair of turtledoves, or two young pigeons.

CIRCUMCISION - ***Genesis 17:9-14, 34:14-17, 22*** **9** And God said unto Abraham, Thou shalt keep my covenant therefore, thou, and thy seed after thee in their generations. **10** This *is* my covenant, which ye shall keep, between me and you and thy seed after thee; Every man child among you shall be circumcised. **11** And ye shall circumcise the flesh of your foreskin; and it shall be a token of the covenant betwixt me and you. **12** And he that is eight days old shall be circumcised among you, every man child in your generations, he that is born in the house, or bought with money of any stranger, which *is* not of thy seed. **13** He that is born in thy house, and he that is bought with thy money, must needs be circumcised: and my covenant shall be in your flesh for an everlasting covenant. 14And the uncircumcised man child whose flesh of his foreskin is not circumcised, that soul shall be cut off from his people; he hath broken my covenant. **34:14-17, 22** and they said unto them, We cannot do this thing, to give our sister to one that is uncircumcised; for that *were* a reproach unto us: **15** but in this will we consent unto you: If ye will be as we *be*, that every male of you be circumcised; **16** then will we give our daughters unto you, and we will take your daughters to us, and we will dwell with you, and we will become one people. **17** But if ye will not hearken unto us, to be circumcised; then will we take our daughter, and we will be gone. **22** Only herein will the men consent unto us for to dwell with us, to be one people, if every male among us be circumcised, as they *are* circumcised.

Exodus 4:25, 26, 12:48 **25** Then Zippo´rah took a sharp stone, and cut off the foreskin of her son, and cast *it* at his feet, and said, Surely a bloody husband *art* thou to me. **26** So he let him go: then she said, A bloody husband *thou art*, because of the circumcision. **12:48** And when a stranger shall sojourn with thee, and will keep the passover to the Lord, let all his males be circumcised, and then let him come near and keep it; and he shall be as one that is born in the land: for no uncircumcised person shall eat thereof.

Luke 2:21 And when eight days were accomplished for the circumcising of the child, his name was called Jesus, which was so named of the angel before he was conceived in the womb.

Acts 15:13-29, 16:1-3 13 And after they had held their peace, James answered, saying, Men *and* brethren, hearken unto me: 14 Simeon hath declared how God at the first did visit the Gentiles, to take out of them a people for his name. 15 And to this agree the words of the prophets; as it is written,

16 After this I will return,

and will build again the tabernacle of David, which is fallen down;

and I will build again the ruins thereof,

and I will set it up:

17 that the residue of men might seek after the Lord,

and all the Gentiles, upon whom my name is called,

saith the Lord, who doeth all these things.

18 Known unto God are all his works from the beginning of the world.

19 Wherefore my sentence is, that we trouble not them, which from among the Gentiles are turned to God: 20 but that we write unto them, that they abstain from pollutions of idols, and *from* fornication, and *from* things strangled, and *from* blood. 21 For Moses of old time hath in every city them that preach him, being read in the synagogues every sabbath day.

22 Then pleased it the apostles and elders, with the whole church, to send chosen men of their own company to An´tioch with Paul and Barnabas; *namely*, Judas surnamed

Barsabas, and Silas, chief men among the brethren: **23** and they wrote *letters* by them after this manner; The apostles and elders and brethren *send* greeting unto the brethren which are of the Gentiles in An´ti-och and Syria and Cili´cia: **24** Forasmuch as we have heard, that certain which went out from us have troubled you with words, subverting your souls, saying, *Ye must* be circumcised, and keep the law; to whom we gave no *such* commandment: **25** it seemed good unto us, being assembled with one accord, to send chosen men unto you with our beloved Barnabas and Paul, **26** men that have hazarded their lives for the name of our Lord Jesus Christ. **27** We have sent therefore Judas and Silas, who shall also tell *you* the same things by mouth. **28** For it seemed good to the Holy Ghost, and to us, to lay upon you no greater burden than these necessary things; **29** that ye abstain from meats offered to idols, and from blood, and from things strangled, and from fornication: from which if ye keep yourselves, ye shall do well. Fare ye well. *16:1-3* **1** Then came he to Derbe and Lystra: and, behold, a certain disciple was there, named Timothy, the son of a certain woman, which was a Jewess, and believed; but his father *was* a Greek: **2** which was well reported of by the brethren that were at Lystra and Ico´ni-um. **3** Him would Paul have to go forth with him; and took and circumcised him because of the Jews which were in those quarters: for they knew all that his father was a Greek.

Romans 4:10, 12 **10** How was it then reckoned? when he was in circumcision, or in uncircumcision? Not in circumcision, but in uncircumcision. **12** and the father of circumcision to them who are not of the circumcision only, but who also walk in the steps of that faith of our father Abraham, which *he had* being *yet* uncircumcised.

Galatians 2:3 But neither Titus, who was with me, being a Greek, was compelled to be circumcised:

CLEAN AND UNCLEAN – *Leviticus 11:1-47* Clean and Unclean Animals

(Deuteronomy 14.3-21)

1 And the Lord spake unto Moses and to Aaron, saying unto them, 2 Speak unto the children of Israel, saying, These *are* the beasts which ye shall eat among all the beasts that *are* on the earth. 3 Whatsoever parteth the hoof, and is cloven-footed, *and* cheweth the cud, among the beasts, that shall ye eat. 4 Nevertheless, these shall ye not eat of them that chew the cud, or of them that divide the hoof: *as* the camel, because he cheweth the cud, but divideth not the hoof; he *is* unclean unto you. 5 And the coney, because he cheweth the cud, but divideth not the hoof; he *is* unclean unto you. 6 And the hare, because he cheweth the cud, but divideth not the hoof; he *is* unclean unto you. 7 And the swine, though he divide the hoof, and be cloven-footed, yet he cheweth not the cud; he *is* unclean to you. 8 Of their flesh shall ye not eat, and their carcass shall ye not touch; they *are* unclean to you.

9 These shall ye eat of all that *are* in the waters: whatsoever hath fins and scales in the waters, in the seas, and in the rivers, them shall ye eat. 10 And all that have not fins and scales in the seas, and in the rivers, of all that move in the waters, and of any living thing which *is* in the waters, they *shall be* an abomination unto you: 11 they shall be even an abomination unto you; ye shall not eat of their flesh, but ye shall have their carcasses in abomination. 12 Whatsoever hath no fins nor scales in the waters, that *shall be* an abomination unto you.

13 And these *are they which* ye shall have in abomination among the fowls; they shall not be eaten, they *are* an abomination: the eagle, and the ossifrage, and the osprey, **14** and the vulture, and the kite after his kind; **15** every raven after his kind; **16** and the owl, and the nighthawk, and the cuckoo, and the hawk after his kind, **17** and the little owl, and the cormorant, and the great owl, **18** and the swan, and the pelican, and the gier-eagle, **19** and the stork, the heron after her kind, and the lapwing, and the bat.

20 All fowls that creep, going upon *all* four, *shall be* an abomination unto you. **21** Yet these may ye eat of every flying creeping thing that goeth upon *all* four, which have legs above their feet, to leap withal upon the earth; **22** *even* these of them ye may eat; the locust after his kind, and the bald locust after his kind, and the beetle after his kind, and the grasshopper after his kind. **23** But all *other* flying creeping things, which have four feet, *shall be* an abomination unto you.

24 And for these ye shall be unclean: whosoever toucheth the carcass of them shall be unclean until the even. **25** And whosoever beareth *aught* of the carcass of them shall wash his clothes, and be unclean until the even. **26** *The carcasses* of every beast which divideth the hoof, and *is* not cloven-footed, nor cheweth the cud, *are* unclean unto you: every one that toucheth them shall be unclean. **27** And whatsoever goeth upon his paws, among all manner of beasts that go on *all* four, those *are* unclean unto you: whoso toucheth their carcass shall be unclean until the even. **28** And he that beareth the carcass of them shall wash his clothes, and be unclean until the even: they *are* unclean unto you.

29 These also *shall be* unclean unto you among the creeping things that creep upon the earth; the weasel, and the mouse, and the tortoise after his kind, **30** and the ferret, and the chameleon, and the lizard, and the snail, and the mole. **31** These *are* unclean to you among all that creep: whosoever doth touch them, when they be dead, shall be unclean until the even. **32** And upon whatsoever *any* of them, when they are dead, doth fall, it shall be unclean; whether *it be* any vessel of wood, or raiment, or skin, or sack, whatsoever vessel *it be*, wherein *any* work is done, it must be put into water, and it shall be unclean until the even; so it shall be cleansed. **33** And every earthen vessel, whereinto *any* of them falleth, whatsoever *is* in it shall be unclean; and ye shall break it. **34** Of all meat which may be eaten, *that* on which *such* water cometh shall be unclean: and all drink that may be drunk in every *such* vessel shall be unclean. **35** And every *thing* whereupon *any part* of their carcass falleth shall be unclean; *whether it be* oven, or ranges for pots, they shall be broken down: *for* they *are* unclean, and shall be unclean unto you. **36** Nevertheless a fountain or pit, *wherein there is* plenty of water, shall be clean: but that which toucheth their carcass shall be unclean. **37** And if *any part* of their carcass fall upon any sowing seed which is to be sown, it *shall be* clean. **38** But if *any* water be put upon the seed, and *any part* of their carcass fall thereon, it *shall be* unclean unto you.

39 And if any beast, of which ye may eat, die; he that toucheth the carcass thereof shall be unclean until the even. **40** And he that eateth of the carcass of it shall wash his clothes, and be unclean until the even: he also that beareth the carcass of it shall wash his clothes, and be unclean until the even.

41 And every creeping thing that creepeth upon the earth *shall be* an abomination; it shall not be eaten. **42** Whatsoever goeth upon the belly, and whatsoever goeth upon *all* four, or whatsoever hath more feet among all creeping things that creep upon the earth, them ye shall not eat; for they *are* an abomination. **43** Ye shall not make yourselves abominable with any creeping thing that creepeth, neither shall ye make yourselves unclean with them, that ye should be defiled thereby. **44** For I *am* the Lord your God: ye shall therefore sanctify yourselves, and ye shall be holy; for I *am* holy: neither shall ye defile yourselves with any manner of creeping thing that creepeth upon the earth. **45** For I *am* the Lord that bringeth you up out of the land of Egypt, to be your God: ye shall therefore be holy, for I *am* holy.

46 This *is* the law of the beasts, and of the fowl, and of every living creature that moveth in the waters, and of every creature that creepeth upon the earth: **47** to make a difference between the unclean and the clean, and between the beast that may be eaten and the beast that may not be eaten.

Numbers 19:11-22 **11** He that toucheth the dead body of any man shall be unclean seven days. **12** He shall purify himself with it on the third day, and on the seventh day he shall be clean: but if he purify not himself the third day, then the seventh day he shall not be clean. **13** Whosoever toucheth the dead body of any man that is dead, and purifieth not himself, defileth the tabernacle of the Lord; and that soul shall be cut off from Israel: because the water of separation was not sprinkled upon him, he shall be unclean; his uncleanness *is* yet upon him.

14 This *is* the law, when a man dieth in a tent: all that come into the tent, and all that *is* in the tent, shall be unclean seven days. **15** And every open vessel, which hath no covering bound upon it, *is* unclean. **16** And whosoever toucheth one that is slain with a sword in the open fields, or a dead body, or a bone of a man, or a grave, shall be unclean seven days. **17** And for an unclean *person* they shall take of the ashes of the burnt heifer of purification for sin, and running water shall be put thereto in a vessel: **18** and a clean person shall take hyssop, and dip *it* in the water, and sprinkle *it* upon the tent, and upon all the vessels, and upon the persons that were there, and upon him that touched a bone, or one slain, or one dead, or a grave: **19** and the clean *person* shall sprinkle upon the unclean on the third day, and on the seventh day: and on the seventh day he shall purify himself, and wash his clothes, and bathe himself in water, and shall be clean at even.

20 But the man that shall be unclean, and shall not purify himself, that soul shall be cut off from among the congregation, because he hath defiled the sanctuary of the Lord: the water of separation hath not been sprinkled upon him; he *is* unclean. **21** And it shall be a perpetual statute unto them, that he that sprinkleth the water of separation shall wash his clothes; and he that toucheth the water of separation shall be unclean until even. **22** And whatsoever the unclean *person* toucheth shall be unclean; and the soul that toucheth *it* shall be unclean until even.

<u>John 15:3</u> Now ye are clean through the word which I have spoken unto you.

<u>Acts 10:14, 28</u> **14** But Peter said, Not so, Lord; for I have never eaten any thing that is common or unclean. **28** And he said unto them, Ye know how that it is an unlawful thing for

a man that is a Jew to keep company, or come unto one of another nation; but God hath showed me that I should not call any man common or unclean.

CLEAN AND UNCLEAN FOODS - *Leviticus 11:1-47*

1 And the Lord spake unto Moses and to Aaron, saying unto them, 2 Speak unto the children of Israel, saying, These *are* the beasts which ye shall eat among all the beasts that *are* on the earth. 3 Whatsoever parteth the hoof, and is cloven-footed, *and* cheweth the cud, among the beasts, that shall ye eat. 4 Nevertheless, these shall ye not eat of them that chew the cud, or of them that divide the hoof: *as* the camel, because he cheweth the cud, but divideth not the hoof; he *is* unclean unto you. 5 And the coney, because he cheweth the cud, but divideth not the hoof; he *is* unclean unto you. 6 And the hare, because he cheweth the cud, but divideth not the hoof; he *is* unclean unto you. 7 And the swine, though he divide the hoof, and be cloven-footed, yet he cheweth not the cud; he *is* unclean to you. 8 Of their flesh shall ye not eat, and their carcass shall ye not touch; they *are* unclean to you.

9 These shall ye eat of all that *are* in the waters: whatsoever hath fins and scales in the waters, in the seas, and in the rivers, them shall ye eat. 10 And all that have not fins and scales in the seas, and in the rivers, of all that move in the waters, and of any living thing which *is* in the waters, they *shall be* an abomination unto you: 11 they shall be even an abomination unto you; ye shall not eat of their flesh, but ye shall have their carcasses in abomination. 12 Whatsoever hath no fins nor scales in the waters, that *shall be* an abomination unto you.

13 And these *are they which* ye shall have in abomination among the fowls; they shall not be eaten, they *are* an

abomination: the eagle, and the ossifrage, and the osprey, **14** and the vulture, and the kite after his kind; **15** every raven after his kind; **16** and the owl, and the nighthawk, and the cuckoo, and the hawk after his kind, **17** and the little owl, and the cormorant, and the great owl, **18** and the swan, and the pelican, and the gier-eagle, **19** and the stork, the heron after her kind, and the lapwing, and the bat.

20 All fowls that creep, going upon *all* four, *shall be* an abomination unto you. **21** Yet these may ye eat of every flying creeping thing that goeth upon *all* four, which have legs above their feet, to leap withal upon the earth; **22** *even* these of them ye may eat; the locust after his kind, and the bald locust after his kind, and the beetle after his kind, and the grasshopper after his kind. **23** But all *other* flying creeping things, which have four feet, *shall be* an abomination unto you.

24 And for these ye shall be unclean: whosoever toucheth the carcass of them shall be unclean until the even. **25** And whosoever beareth *aught* of the carcass of them shall wash his clothes, and be unclean until the even. **26** *The carcasses* of every beast which divideth the hoof, and *is* not cloven-footed, nor cheweth the cud, *are* unclean unto you: every one that toucheth them shall be unclean. **27** And whatsoever goeth upon his paws, among all manner of beasts that go on *all* four, those *are* unclean unto you: whoso toucheth their carcass shall be unclean until the even. **28** And he that beareth the carcass of them shall wash his clothes, and be unclean until the even: they *are* unclean unto you.

29 These also *shall be* unclean unto you among the creeping things that creep upon the earth; the weasel, and the mouse, and the tortoise after his kind, **30** and the ferret, and the chameleon, and the lizard, and the snail, and the mole. **31**

These *are* unclean to you among all that creep: whosoever doth touch them, when they be dead, shall be unclean until the even. **32** And upon whatsoever *any* of them, when they are dead, doth fall, it shall be unclean; whether *it be* any vessel of wood, or raiment, or skin, or sack, whatsoever vessel *it be*, wherein *any* work is done, it must be put into water, and it shall be unclean until the even; so it shall be cleansed. **33** And every earthen vessel, whereinto *any* of them falleth, whatsoever *is* in it shall be unclean; and ye shall break it. **34** Of all meat which may be eaten, *that* on which *such* water cometh shall be unclean: and all drink that may be drunk in every *such* vessel shall be unclean. **35** And every *thing* whereupon *any part* of their carcass falleth shall be unclean; *whether it be* oven, or ranges for pots, they shall be broken down: *for* they *are* unclean, and shall be unclean unto you. **36** Nevertheless a fountain or pit, *wherein there is* plenty of water, shall be clean: but that which toucheth their carcass shall be unclean. **37** And if *any part* of their carcass fall upon any sowing seed which is to be sown, it *shall be* clean. **38** But if *any* water be put upon the seed, and *any part* of their carcass fall thereon, it *shall be* unclean unto you.

39 And if any beast, of which ye may eat, die; he that toucheth the carcass thereof shall be unclean until the even. **40** And he that eateth of the carcass of it shall wash his clothes, and be unclean until the even: he also that beareth the carcass of it shall wash his clothes, and be unclean until the even.

41 And every creeping thing that creepeth upon the earth *shall be* an abomination; it shall not be eaten. **42** Whatsoever goeth upon the belly, and whatsoever goeth upon *all* four, or whatsoever hath more feet among all creeping things that creep upon the earth, them ye shall not eat; for they *are* an abomination. **43** Ye shall not make yourselves abominable with any creeping thing that creepeth, neither shall ye make yourselves unclean with them, that ye should be defiled thereby. **44** For I *am* the Lord your God: ye shall therefore sanctify yourselves, and ye shall be holy; for I *am* holy: neither shall ye defile yourselves with any manner of creeping thing that creepeth upon the earth. **45** For I *am* the Lord that bringeth you up out of the land of Egypt, to be your God: ye shall therefore be holy, for I *am* holy.

46 This *is* the law of the beasts, and of the fowl, and of every living creature that moveth in the waters, and of every creature that creepeth upon the earth: **47** to make a difference between the unclean and the clean, and between the beast that may be eaten and the beast that may not be eaten.

Deuteronomy 14:3-21 Clean and Unclean Food

(Leviticus 11.1-47)

3 Thou shalt not eat any abominable thing. **4** These *are* the beasts which ye shall eat: the ox, the sheep, and the goat, **5** the hart, and the roebuck, and the fallow deer, and the wild goat, and the pygarg, and the wild ox, and the chamois. **6** And every beast that parteth the hoof, and cleaveth the cleft into two claws, *and* cheweth the cud among the beasts, that ye shall eat. **7** Nevertheless these ye shall not eat, of them that chew the cud, or of them that divide the cloven hoof; *as* the camel, and the hare, and the coney: for they chew the cud, but divide not the hoof; *therefore* they *are* unclean unto you. **8** And the swine, because it divideth the hoof, yet cheweth not the cud, it *is* unclean unto you: ye shall not eat of their flesh, nor touch their dead carcass.

9 These ye shall eat, of all that *are* in the waters: all that have fins and scales shall ye eat: **10** and whatsoever hath not fins and scales ye may not eat; it *is* unclean unto you.

11 *Of* all clean birds ye shall eat. **12** But these *are they* of which ye shall not eat: the eagle, and the ossifrage, and the osprey, **13** and the glede, and the kite, and the vulture after his kind, **14** and every raven after his kind, **15** and the owl, and the nighthawk, and the cuckoo, and the hawk after his kind, **16** the little owl, and the great owl, and the swan, **17** and the pelican, and the gier-eagle, and the cormorant, **18** and the stork, and the heron after her kind, and the lapwing, and the bat. **19** And every creeping thing that flieth *is* unclean unto you: they shall not be eaten. **20** *But of* all clean fowls ye may eat.

21 Ye shall not eat *of* any thing that dieth of itself: thou shalt give it unto the stranger that *is* in thy gates, that he may eat it; or thou mayest sell it unto an alien: for thou *art* a holy people unto the Lord thy God.

Thou shalt not seethe a kid in his mother's milk.

COLLECTIONS IN CHURCH - *1 Corinthians 16:1, 2* **1** Now concerning the collection for the saints, as I have given order to the churches of Galatia, even so do ye. **2** Upon the first *day* of the week let every one of you lay by him in store, as *God* hath prospered him, that there be no gatherings when I come.

COMMUNION - *Matthew 26:26-29* **26** And as they were eating, Jesus took bread, and blessed *it*, and brake *it*, and gave *it* to the disciples, and said, Take, eat; this is my body. **27** And he took the cup, and gave thanks, and gave *it* to them, saying, Drink ye all of it; **28** for this is my blood of the new testament, which is shed for many for the remission of sins. **29** But I say unto you, I will not drink henceforth of this fruit of the vine, until that day when I drink it new with you in my Father's kingdom.

Mark 14:22-25 **22** And as they did eat, Jesus took bread, and blessed, and brake *it*, and gave to them, and said, Take, eat; this is my body. **23** And he took the cup, and when he had given thanks, he gave *it* to them: and they all drank of it. **24** And he said unto them, This is my blood of the new testament, which is shed for many. **25** Verily I say unto you, I will drink no more of the fruit of the vine, until that day that I drink it new in the kingdom of God.

Luke 22:19, 20 **19** And he took bread, and gave thanks, and brake *it*, and gave unto them, saying, This is my body which is given for you: this do in remembrance of me. **20** Likewise also the cup after supper, saying, This cup *is* the new testament in my blood, which is shed for you.

DAY OF ATONEMENT – *Exodus 30:1-10* **1** And thou shalt make an altar to burn incense upon: *of* shittim wood shalt thou make it. **2** A cubit *shall be* the length thereof, and a cubit the breadth thereof; foursquare shall it be: and two cubits *shall be* the height thereof: the horns thereof *shall be* of the same. **3** And thou shalt overlay it with pure gold, the top thereof, and the sides thereof round about, and the horns thereof; and thou shalt make unto it a crown of gold round about. **4** And two golden rings shalt thou make to it under the crown of it, by the two corners thereof, upon the two sides of it shalt thou make *it*; and they shall be for places for the staves to bear it withal. **5** And thou shalt make the staves *of* shittim wood, and overlay them with gold. **6** And thou shalt put it before the veil that *is* by the ark of the testimony, before the mercy seat that *is* over the testimony, where I will meet with thee. **7** And Aaron shall burn thereon sweet incense every morning: when he dresseth the lamps, he shall burn incense upon it. **8** And when Aaron lighteth the lamps at even, he shall burn incense upon it, a perpetual incense before the Lord throughout your generations. **9** Ye shall offer no strange incense thereon, nor burnt sacrifice, nor meat offering; neither shall ye pour drink offering thereon. **10** And Aaron shall make an atonement upon the horns of it once in a year with the blood of the sin offering of atonements; once in the year shall he make atonement upon it throughout your generations: it *is* most holy unto the Lord.

Leviticus 16:1-34, 23:26-32 **The Day of Atonement**

1 And the Lord spake unto Moses after the death of the two sons of Aaron, when they offered before the Lord, and died; **2** and the Lord said unto Moses, Speak unto Aaron thy brother, that he come not at all times into the holy *place* within the veil before the mercy seat, which *is* upon the ark; that he die not: for I will appear in the cloud upon the mercy seat. **3** Thus shall Aaron come into the holy *place*; with a young bullock for a sin offering, and a ram for a burnt offering. **4** He shall put on the holy linen coat, and he shall have the linen breeches upon his flesh, and shall be girded with a linen girdle, and with the linen mitre shall he be attired: these *are* holy garments; therefore shall he wash his flesh in water, and *so* put them on. **5** And he shall take of the congregation of the children of Israel two kids of the goats for a sin offering, and one ram for a burnt offering.

6 And Aaron shall offer his bullock of the sin offering, which *is* for himself, and make an atonement for himself, and for his house. **7** And he shall take the two goats, and present them before the Lord *at* the door of the tabernacle of the congregation. **8** And Aaron shall cast lots upon the two goats; one lot for the Lord, and the other lot for the scapegoat. **9** And Aaron shall bring the goat upon which the Lord's lot fell, and offer him *for* a sin offering. **10** But the goat, on which the lot fell to be the scapegoat, shall be presented alive before the Lord, to make an atonement with him, *and* to let him go for a scapegoat into the wilderness.

11 And Aaron shall bring the bullock of the sin offering, which *is* for himself, and shall make an atonement for himself, and for his house, and shall kill the bullock of the sin offering which *is* for himself: **12** and he shall take a censer full of burning coals of fire from off the altar before the Lord, and his hands full of sweet incense beaten small, and bring *it* within the veil: **13** and he shall put the incense upon the fire before the Lord, that the cloud of the incense may cover the mercy seat that *is* upon the testimony, that he die not: **14** and he shall take of the blood of the bullock, and sprinkle *it* with his finger upon the mercy seat eastward; and before the mercy seat shall he sprinkle of the blood with his finger seven times.

15 Then shall he kill the goat of the sin offering, that *is* for the people, and bring his blood within the veil, and do with that blood as he did with the blood of the bullock, and sprinkle it upon the mercy seat, and before the mercy seat: **16** and he shall make an atonement for the holy *place*, because of the uncleanness of the children of Israel, and because of their transgressions in all their sins: and so shall he do for the tabernacle of the congregation, that remaineth among them in the midst of their uncleanness. **17** And there shall be no man in the tabernacle of the congregation when he goeth in to make an atonement in the holy *place*, until he come out, and have made an atonement for himself, and for his household, and for all the congregation of Israel. **18** And he shall go out unto the altar that *is* before the Lord, and make an atonement for it; and shall take of the blood of the bullock, and of the blood of the goat, and put *it* upon the horns of the altar round about. **19** And he shall sprinkle of the blood upon it with his finger seven times, and cleanse it, and hallow it from the uncleanness of the children of Israel.

20 And when he hath made an end of reconciling the holy *place*, and the tabernacle of the congregation, and the altar, he shall bring the live goat: **21** and Aaron shall lay both his hands upon the head of the live goat, and confess over him all the iniquities of the children of Israel, and all their transgressions in all their sins, putting them upon the head of the goat, and shall send *him* away by the hand of a fit man into the wilderness: **22** and the goat shall bear upon him all their iniquities unto a land not inhabited: and he shall let go the goat in the wilderness.

23 And Aaron shall come into the tabernacle of the congregation, and shall put off the linen garments, which he put on when he went into the holy *place*, and shall leave them there: **24** and he shall wash his flesh with water in the holy place, and put on his garments, and come forth, and offer his burnt offering, and the burnt offering of the people, and make an atonement for himself, and for the people. **25** And the fat of the sin offering shall he burn upon the altar. **26** And he that let go the goat for the scapegoat shall wash his clothes, and bathe his flesh in water, and afterward come into the camp. **27** And the bullock *for* the sin offering, and the goat *for* the sin offering, whose blood was brought in to make atonement in the holy *place*, shall *one* carry forth without the camp; and they shall burn in the fire their skins, and their flesh, and their dung. **28** And he that burneth them shall wash his clothes, and bathe his flesh in water, and afterward he shall come into the camp.

29 And *this* shall be a statute for ever unto you: *that* in the seventh month, on the tenth *day* of the month, ye shall afflict your souls, and do no work at all, *whether it be* one of your own country, or a stranger that sojourneth among you: **30** for on that day shall *the priest* make an atonement for you, to cleanse you, *that* ye may be clean from all your sins before the Lord. **31** It *shall be* a sabbath of rest unto you, and ye shall afflict your souls, by a statute for ever. **32** And the priest, whom he shall anoint, and whom he shall consecrate to minister in the priest's office in his father's stead, shall make the atonement, and shall put on the linen clothes, *even* the holy garments: **33** and he shall make an atonement for the holy sanctuary, and he shall make an atonement for the tabernacle of the congregation, and for the altar: and he shall make an atonement for the priests, and for all the people of the congregation. **34** And this shall be an everlasting statute unto you, to make an atonement for the children of Israel for all their sins once a year. And he did as the Lord commanded Moses.

23:26-32 **26** And the Lord spake unto Moses, saying, **27** Also on the tenth *day* of this seventh month *there shall be* a day of atonement: it shall be a holy convocation unto you; and ye shall afflict your souls, and offer an offering made by fire unto the Lord. **28** And ye shall do no work in that same day: for it *is* a day of atonement, to make an atonement for you before the Lord your God. **29** For whatsoever soul *it be* that shall not be afflicted in that same day, he shall be cut off from among his people. **30** And whatsoever soul *it be* that doeth any work in that same day, the same soul will I destroy from among his people. **31** Ye shall do no manner of work: *it shall be* a statute for ever throughout your generations in all your dwellings. **32** It *shall be* unto you a sabbath of rest, and ye shall afflict your souls:

in the ninth *day* of the month at even, from even unto even, shall ye celebrate your sabbath.

Numbers 29:7-11 **7** And ye shall have on the tenth *day* of this seventh month a holy convocation; and ye shall afflict your souls: ye shall not do any work *therein.* **8** but ye shall offer a burnt offering unto the Lord *for* a sweet savor; one young bullock, one ram, *and* seven lambs of the first year; they shall be unto you without blemish. **9** And their meat offering *shall be of* flour mingled with oil, three tenth deals to a bullock, *and* two tenth deals to one ram, **10** a several tenth deal for one lamb, throughout the seven lambs: **11** one kid of the goats *for* a sin offering; beside the sin offering of atonement, and the continual burnt offering, and the meat offering of it, and their drink offerings.

Hebrews 9:6-15 **6** Now when these things were thus ordained, the priests went always into the first tabernacle, accomplishing the service *of God.* **7** But into the second *went* the high priest alone once every year, not without blood, which he offered for himself, and *for* the errors of the people: **8** the Holy Ghost this signifying, that the way into the holiest of all was not yet made manifest, while as the first tabernacle was yet standing: **9** which *was* a figure for the time then present, in which were offered both gifts and sacrifices, that could not make him that did the service perfect, as pertaining to the conscience; **10** *which stood* only in meats and drinks, and divers washings, and carnal ordinances, imposed *on them* until the time of reformation.

11 But Christ being come a high priest of good things to come, by a greater and more perfect tabernacle, not made with hands, that is to say, not of this building; **12** neither by the blood of goats and calves, but by his own blood he entered in once into the holy place, having obtained eternal redemption *for us.* **13** For if the blood of bulls and of goats, and the ashes of a heifer sprinkling the unclean, sanctifieth to the purifying of the flesh; **14** how much more shall the blood of Christ, who through the eternal Spirit offered himself without spot to God, purge your conscience from dead works to serve the living God?

15 And for this cause he is the mediator of the new testament, that by means of death, for the redemption of the transgressions *that were* under the first testament, they which are called might receive the promise of eternal inheritance.

DRINK OFFERINGS – *Numbers 28:9, 10* **9** And on the sabbath day two lambs of the first year without spot, and two tenth deals of flour *for* a meat offering, mingled with oil, and the drink offering thereof: **10** *this is* the burnt offering of every sabbath, beside the continual burnt offering, and his drink offering.

Deuteronomy 32:38 which did eat the fat of their sacrifices,

and drank the wine of their drink offerings?

Let them rise up and help you,

and be your protection.

EATING – *Exodus 22:31* And ye shall be holy men unto me: neither shall ye eat *any* flesh *that is* torn of beasts in the fields; ye shall cast it to the dogs.

Leviticus 3:17, 19:23-25 **3:17** *It shall be* a perpetual statute for your generations throughout all your dwellings, that ye eat neither fat nor blood. *19:23-25* **23** And when ye shall come into the land, and shall have planted all manner of trees for food, then ye shall count the fruit thereof as uncircumcised: three years shall it be as uncircumcised unto you: it shall not be eaten of. **24** But in the fourth year all the fruit thereof shall be holy to praise the Lord *withal.* **25** And in the fifth year shall ye eat of the fruit thereof, that it may yield unto you the increase thereof: I *am* the Lord your God.

EUCHARIST - *Matthew 26:26-29* **26** And as they were eating, Jesus took bread, and blessed *it*, and brake *it*, and gave *it* to the disciples, and said, Take, eat; this is my body. **27** And he took the cup, and gave thanks, and gave *it* to them, saying, Drink ye all of it; **28** for this is my blood of the new testament, which is shed for many for the remission of sins. **29** But I say unto you, I will not drink henceforth of this fruit of the vine, until that day when I drink it new with you in my Father's kingdom.

Luke 22:17-20 **17** And he took the cup, and gave thanks, and said, Take this, and divide *it* among yourselves: **18** for I say unto you, I will not drink of the fruit of the vine, until the kingdom of God shall come. **19** And he took bread, and gave thanks, and brake *it*, and gave unto them, saying, This is my body which is given for you: this do in remembrance of me. **20** Likewise also the cup after supper, saying, This cup *is* the new testament in my blood, which is shed for you.

WORSHIP OF FALSE GODS - *Exodus 20:1-5, 22:20*

1 And God spake all these words, saying,

2 I *am* the Lord thy God, which have brought thee out of the land of Egypt, out of the house of bondage.

3 Thou shalt have no other gods before me.

4 Thou shalt not make unto thee any graven image, or any likeness *of any thing* that *is* in heaven above, or that *is* in the

earth beneath, or that *is* in the water under the earth: 5 thou shalt not bow down thyself to them, nor serve them: for I the Lord thy God *am* a jealous God, visiting the iniquity of the fathers upon the children unto the third and fourth *generation* of them that hate me;

22:20 He that sacrificeth unto *any* god, save unto the Lord only, he shall be utterly destroyed.

FASTS - *Luke 18:12* I fast twice in the week, I give tithes of all that I possess.

FEAST OF HARVEST - *Exodus 23:16* And the feast of the harvest, the firstfruits of thy labours, which thou hast sown in the field: and the feast of ingathering, *which is* in the end of the year, when thou hast gathered in thy labours out of the field.

FEAST OF INGATHERING - *Exodus 23:16* And the feast of the harvest, the firstfruits of thy labours, which thou hast sown in the field: and the feast of ingathering, *which is* in the end of the year, when thou hast gathered in thy labours out of the field.

FEAST OF TABERNACLES - *Leviticus 23:33-44* 33 And the Lord spake unto Moses, saying, 34 Speak unto the children of Israel, saying, The fifteenth day of this seventh month *shall be* the feast of tabernacles *for* seven days unto the Lord. 35 On the first day *shall be* a holy convocation: ye shall do no servile work *therein*. 36 Seven days ye shall offer an offering made by fire unto the Lord; on the eighth day shall be a holy convocation unto you, and ye shall offer an offering made by fire unto the Lord: it *is* a solemn assembly; *and* ye shall do no servile work *therein*.

37 These *are* the feasts of the Lord, which ye shall proclaim *to be* holy convocations, to offer an offering made by fire unto the Lord, a burnt offering, and a meat offering, a sacrifice, and drink offerings, every thing upon his day: **38** beside the sabbaths of the Lord, and beside your gifts, and beside all your vows, and beside all your freewill offerings, which ye give unto the Lord.

39 Also in the fifteenth day of the seventh month, when ye have gathered in the fruit of the land, ye shall keep a feast unto the Lord seven days: on the first day *shall be* a sabbath, and on the eighth day *shall be* a sabbath. **40** And ye shall take you on the first day the boughs of goodly trees, branches of palm trees, and the boughs of thick trees, and willows of the brook; and ye shall rejoice before the Lord your God seven days. **41** And ye shall keep it a feast unto the Lord seven days in the year: *it shall be* a statute for ever in your generations; ye shall celebrate it in the seventh month. **42** Ye shall dwell in booths seven days; all that are Israelites born shall dwell in booths: **43** that your generations may know that I made the children of Israel to dwell in booths, when I brought them out of the land of Egypt: I *am* the Lord your God.

44 And Moses declared unto the children of Israel the feasts of the Lord.

<u>*Numbers 29:12-40*</u> **12** And on the fifteenth day of the seventh month ye shall have a holy convocation; ye shall do no servile work, and ye shall keep a feast unto the Lord seven days: **13** and ye shall offer a burnt offering, a sacrifice made by fire, of a sweet savor unto the Lord; thirteen young bullocks, two rams, *and* fourteen lambs of the first year; they shall be without blemish: **14** and their meat offering *shall be of* flour mingled with oil, three tenth deals

unto every bullock of the thirteen bullocks, two tenth deals to each ram of the two rams, **15** and a several tenth deal to each lamb of the fourteen lambs: **16** and one kid of the goats *for* a sin offering; beside the continual burnt offering, his meat offering, and his drink offering.

17 And on the second day *ye shall offer* twelve young bullocks, two rams, fourteen lambs of the first year without spot: **18** and their meat offering and their drink offerings for the bullocks, for the rams, and for the lambs, *shall be* according to their number, after the manner: **19** and one kid of the goats *for* a sin offering; beside the continual burnt offering, and the meat offering thereof, and their drink offerings.

20 And on the third day eleven bullocks, two rams, fourteen lambs of the first year without blemish: **21** and their meat offering and their drink offerings for the bullocks, for the rams, and for the lambs, *shall be* according to their number, after the manner: **22** and one goat *for* a sin offering; beside the continual burnt offering, and his meat offering, and his drink offering.

23 And on the fourth day ten bullocks, two rams, *and* fourteen lambs of the first year without blemish: **24** their meat offering and their drink offerings for the bullocks, for the rams, and for the lambs, *shall be* according to their number, after the manner: **25** and one kid of the goats *for* a sin offering; beside the continual burnt offering, his meat offering, and his drink offering.

26 And on the fifth day nine bullocks, two rams, *and* fourteen lambs of the first year without spot: **27** and their meat offering and their drink offerings for the bullocks, for the rams, and for the lambs, *shall be* according to their number, after the manner: **28** and one goat *for* a sin offering; beside the continual burnt offering, and his meat offering, and his drink offering.

29 And on the sixth day eight bullocks, two rams, *and* fourteen lambs of the first year without blemish: **30** and their meat offering and their drink offerings for the bullocks, for the rams, and for the lambs, *shall be* according to their number, after the manner: **31** and one goat *for* a sin offering; beside the continual burnt offering, his meat offering, and his drink offering.

32 And on the seventh day seven bullocks, two rams, *and* fourteen lambs of the first year without blemish: **33** and their meat offering and their drink offerings for the bullocks, for the rams, and for the lambs, *shall be* according to their number, after the manner: **34** and one goat *for* a sin offering; beside the continual burnt offering, his meat offering, and his drink offering.

35 On the eighth day ye shall have a solemn assembly: ye shall do no servile work *therein*: **36** but ye shall offer a burnt offering, a sacrifice made by fire, of a sweet savor unto the Lord: one bullock, one ram, seven lambs of the first year without blemish: **37** their meat offering and their drink offerings for the bullock, for the ram, and for the lambs, *shall be* according to their number, after the manner: **38** and one goat *for* a sin offering; beside the continual burnt offering, and his meat offering, and his drink offering.

39 These *things* ye shall do unto the Lord in your set feasts, beside your vows, and your freewill offerings, for your burnt offerings, and for your meat offerings, and for your drink offerings, and for your peace offerings.

40 And Moses told the children of Israel according to all that the Lord commanded Moses.

Deuteronomy 16:13-17, 31:10-13 **13** Thou shalt observe the feast of tabernacles seven days, after that thou hast gathered in thy corn and thy wine: **14** and thou shalt rejoice in thy feast, thou, and thy son, and thy daughter, and thy manservant, and thy maidservant, and the Levite, the stranger, and the fatherless, and the widow, that *are* within thy gates. **15** Seven days shalt thou keep a solemn feast unto the Lord thy God in the place which the Lord shall choose: because the Lord thy God shall bless thee in all thine increase, and in all the works of thine hands, therefore thou shalt surely rejoice.

16 Three times in a year shall all thy males appear before the Lord thy God in the place which he shall choose; in the feast of unleavened bread, and in the feast of weeks, and in the feast of tabernacles: and they shall not appear before the Lord empty: **17** every man *shall give* as he is able, according to the blessing of the Lord thy God which he hath given thee. ***31:10-13*** **10** And Moses commanded them, saying, At the end of *every* seven years, in the solemnity of the year of release, in the feast of tabernacles, **11** when all Israel is come to appear before the Lord thy God in the place which he shall choose, thou shalt read this law before all Israel in their hearing. **12** Gather the people together, men, and women, and children, and thy stranger that *is* within thy gates, that they may hear, and that they may learn, and fear the Lord your God, and observe to do all the words of this law: **13** and *that* their children, which have not known *any thing*, may hear, and learn to fear the Lord your God, as long as ye live in the land whither ye go over Jordan to possess it.

FEAST OF THE NEW MOON – *Numbers 10:10, 28:11-15* **10:10** Also in the day of your gladness, and in your solemn days, and in the beginnings of your months, ye shall blow with the trumpets over your burnt offerings, and over the sacrifices of your peace offerings; that they may be to you for a memorial before your God: I *am* the Lord your God. *28:11-15* **11** And in the beginnings of your months ye shall offer a burnt offering unto the Lord; two young bullocks, and one ram, seven lambs of the first year without spot; **12** and three tenth deals of flour *for* a meat offering, mingled with oil, for one bullock; and two tenth deals of flour *for* a meat offering, mingled with oil, for one ram; **13** and a several tenth deal of flour mingled with oil *for* a meat offering unto one lamb; *for* a burnt offering of a sweet savor, a sacrifice made by fire unto the Lord. **14** And their drink offerings shall be half a hin of wine unto a bullock, and the third *part* of a hin unto a ram, and a fourth *part* of a hin unto a lamb: this *is* the burnt offering of every month throughout the months of the year. **15** And one kid of the goats for a sin offering unto the Lord shall be offered, beside the continual burnt offering, and his drink offering.

Psalm 81:3 Blow up the trumpet in the new moon, in the time appointed, on our solemn feast day.

Isaiah 66:23 And it shall come to pass, *that* from one new moon to another, and from one sabbath to another, shall all flesh come to worship before me, saith the Lord.

Ezekiel 46:3 Likewise the people of the land shall worship at the door of this gate before the Lord in the sabbaths and in the new moons.

Amos 8:5 saying, When will the new moon be gone, that we may sell corn? and the sabbath, that we may set forth wheat, making the ephah small, and the shekel great, and falsifying the balances by deceit?

FEAST OF UNLEAVENED BREAD – *Exodus 24:18*
And Moses went into the midst of the cloud, and gat him up into the mount: and Moses was in the mount forty days and forty nights.

FEAST OF WEEKS – *Deuteronomy 16:9-12*
9 Seven weeks shalt thou number unto thee: begin to number the seven weeks from *such time as* thou beginnest *to put* the sickle to the corn. **10** And thou shalt keep the feast of weeks unto the Lord thy God with a tribute of a freewill offering of thine hand, which thou shalt give *unto the Lord thy God*, according as the Lord thy God hath blessed thee: **11** and thou shalt rejoice before the Lord thy God, thou, and thy son, and thy daughter, and thy manservant, and thy maidservant, and the Levite that *is* within thy gates, and the stranger, and the fatherless, and the widow, that *are* among you, in the place which the Lord thy God hath chosen to place his name there. **12** And thou shalt remember that thou wast a bondman in Egypt: and thou shalt observe and do these statutes.

FIRSTBORN – *Exodus 13:2, 34:19, 20*
13:2 Sanctify unto me all the firstborn, whatsoever openeth the womb among the children of Israel, *both* of man and of beast: it *is* mine. *34:19, 20* **19** All that openeth the matrix *is* mine; and every firstling among thy cattle, *whether* ox or sheep, *that is male*. **20** But the firstling of an ass thou shalt redeem with a lamb: and if thou redeem *him* not, then shalt thou break his neck. All the firstborn of thy sons thou shalt redeem. And none shall appear before me empty.

FIRSTFRUITS – *Exodus 34:26* The first of the firstfruits of thy land thou shalt bring unto the house of the Lord thy God. Thou shalt not seethe a kid in his mother's milk.

Deuteronomy 18:3, 4 **3** And this shall be the priest's due from the people, from them that offer a sacrifice, whether *it be* ox or sheep; and they shall give unto the priest the shoulder, and the two cheeks, and the maw. **4** The firstfruit *also* of thy corn, of thy wine, and of thine oil, and the first of the fleece of thy sheep, shalt thou give him.

FREEWILL OFFERINGS – *Leviticus 22:17-25* **17** And the Lord spake unto Moses, saying, **18** Speak unto Aaron, and to his sons, and unto all the children of Israel, and say unto them, Whatsoever *he be* of the house of Israel, or of the strangers in Israel, that will offer his oblation for all his vows, and for all his freewill offerings, which they will offer unto the Lord for a burnt offering; **19** *ye shall offer* at your own will a male without blemish, of the beeves, of the sheep, or of the goats. **20** *But* whatsoever hath a blemish, *that* shall ye not offer: for it shall not be acceptable for you. **21** And whosoever offereth a sacrifice of peace offerings unto the Lord to accomplish *his* vow, or a freewill offering in beeves or sheep, it shall be perfect to be accepted; there shall be no blemish therein. **22** Blind, or broken, or maimed, or having a wen, or scurvy, or scabbed, ye shall not offer these unto the Lord, nor make an offering by fire of them upon the altar unto the Lord. **23** Either a bullock or a lamb that hath any thing superfluous or lacking in his parts, that mayest thou offer *for* a freewill offering; but for a vow it shall not be accepted. **24** Ye shall not offer unto the Lord that which is bruised, or crushed, or broken, or cut; neither shall ye make *any offering thereof* in your land. **25** Neither from a stranger's hand shall ye offer the bread of your God of any of these; because their corruption *is* in them, *and* blemishes *be* in them: they shall not be accepted for you.

Numbers 15:3 and will make an offering by fire unto the Lord, a burnt offering, or a sacrifice in performing a vow, or in a freewill offering, or in your solemn feasts, to make a sweet savor unto the Lord, of the herd, or of the flock:

GOD IS RULER – *Exodus 19:3-8* 3 And Moses went up unto God, and the Lord called unto him out of the mountain, saying, Thus shalt thou say to the house of Jacob, and tell the children of Israel; 4 Ye have seen what I did unto the Egyptians, and *how* I bare you on eagles' wings, and brought you unto myself. 5 Now therefore, if ye will obey my voice indeed, and keep my covenant, then ye shall be a peculiar treasure unto me above all people: for all the earth *is* mine: 6 and ye shall be unto me a kingdom of priests, and a holy nation. These *are* the words which thou shalt speak unto the children of Israel.

7 And Moses came and called for the elders of the people, and laid before their faces all these words which the Lord commanded him. 8 And all the people answered together, and said, All that the Lord hath spoken we will do. And Moses returned the words of the people unto the Lord.

GUILT OFFERINGS – *Leviticus 5:1-19* 1 And if a soul sin, and hear the voice of swearing, and *is* a witness, whether he hath seen or known *of it*; if he do not utter *it*, then he shall bear his iniquity. 2 Or if a soul touch any unclean thing, whether *it be* a carcass of an unclean beast, or a carcass of unclean cattle, or the carcass of unclean creeping things, and *if* it be hidden from him; he also shall be unclean, and guilty. 3 Or if he touch the uncleanness of man, whatsoever uncleanness *it be* that a man shall be defiled withal, and it be hid from him; when he knoweth *of it*, then he shall be guilty. **4** Or if a soul swear, pronouncing with *his* lips to do evil, or to do good, whatsoever *it be* that a man shall pronounce with an oath, and it be hid from him; when he knoweth *of it*, then he shall be guilty in one of these. **5** And it shall be, when he shall be guilty in one of these *things*, that he shall confess that he hath sinned in that *thing*: **6** and he shall bring his trespass offering unto the Lord for his sin which he hath sinned, a female from the flock, a lamb, or a kid of the goats, for a sin offering; and the priest shall make an atonement for him concerning his sin.

7 And if he be not able to bring a lamb, then he shall bring for his trespass, which he hath committed, two turtledoves, or two young pigeons, unto the Lord; one for a sin offering, and the other for a burnt offering. **8** And he shall bring them unto the priest, who shall offer *that* which *is* for the sin offering first, and wring off his head from his neck, but shall not divide *it* asunder: **9** and he shall sprinkle of the blood of the sin offering upon the side of the altar; and the rest of the blood shall be wrung out at the bottom of the altar: it *is* a sin offering. **10** And he shall offer the second *for* a burnt offering, according to the manner: and the priest shall make an atonement for him for his sin which he hath sinned, and it shall be forgiven him.

11 But if he be not able to bring two turtledoves, or two young pigeons, then he that sinned shall bring for his offering the tenth part of an ephah of fine flour for a sin offering; he shall put no oil upon it, neither shall he put *any* frankincense thereon: for it *is* a sin offering. **12** Then shall he bring it to the priest, and the priest shall take his handful of it, *even* a memorial thereof, and burn *it* on the altar, according to the offerings made by fire unto the Lord: it *is* a sin offering. **13** And the priest shall make an atonement for him as touching his sin that he hath sinned in one of these, and it shall be forgiven him: and *the remnant* shall be the priest's, as a meat offering.

Trespass Offerings

14 And the Lord spake unto Moses, saying, **15** If a soul commit a trespass, and sin through ignorance, in the holy things of the Lord; then he shall bring for his trespass unto the Lord a ram without blemish out of the flocks, with thy estimation by shekels of silver, after the shekel of the sanctuary, for a trespass offering: **16** and he shall make amends for the harm that he hath done in the holy thing, and shall add the fifth part thereto, and give it unto the priest: and the priest shall make an atonement for him with the ram of the trespass offering, and it shall be forgiven him.

17 And if a soul sin, and commit any of these things which are forbidden to be done by the commandments of the Lord; though he wist *it* not, yet is he guilty, and shall bear his iniquity. **18** And he shall bring a ram without blemish out of the flock, with thy estimation, for a trespass offering, unto the priest: and the priest shall make an atonement for him concerning his ignorance wherein he erred and wist *it* not, and it shall be forgiven him. **19** It *is* a trespass offering: he hath certainly trespassed against the Lord.

HEAVE OFFERINGS – *Exodus 29:26, 27* **26** And thou shalt take the breast of the ram of Aaron's consecration, and wave it *for* a wave offering before the Lord: and it shall be thy part. **27** And thou shalt sanctify the breast of the wave offering, and the shoulder of the heave offering, which is waved, and which is heaved up, of the ram of the consecration, *even* of *that* which *is* for Aaron, and of *that* which is for his sons:

HUMAN SACRIFICE – *Genesis 22:1-19* **1** And it came to pass after these things, that God did tempt Abraham, and said unto him, Abraham: and he said, Behold, *here* I *am*. **2** And he said, Take now thy son, thine only *son* Isaac, whom thou lovest, and get thee into the land of Mori´ah; and offer him there for a burnt offering upon one of the mountains which I will tell thee of. **3** And Abraham rose up early in the morning, and saddled his ass, and took two of his young men with him, and Isaac his son, and clave the wood for the burnt offering, and rose up, and went unto the place of which God had told him. **4** Then on the third day Abraham lifted up his eyes, and saw the place afar off. **5** And Abraham said unto his young men, Abide ye here with the ass; and I and the lad will go yonder and worship, and come again to you. **6** And Abraham took the wood of the burnt offering, and laid *it* upon Isaac his son; and he took the fire in his hand, and a knife; and they went both of them together. **7** And Isaac spake unto Abraham his father, and said, My father: and he said, Here *am* I, my son. And he said, Behold the fire and the wood: but where *is* the lamb for a burnt offering? **8** And Abraham said, My son, God will provide himself a lamb for a burnt offering: so they went both of them together.

9 And they came to the place which God had told him of; and Abraham built an altar there, and laid the wood in order, and bound Isaac his son, and laid him on the altar upon the wood. **10** And Abraham stretched forth his hand, and took the knife to slay his son. **11** And the angel of the Lord called unto him out of heaven, and said, Abraham, Abraham: and he said, Here *am* I. **12** And he said, Lay not thine hand upon the lad, neither do thou any thing unto him: for now I know that thou fearest God, seeing thou hast not withheld thy son, thine only *son*, from me. **13** And

Abraham lifted up his eyes, and looked, and behold behind *him* a ram caught in a thicket by his horns: and Abraham went and took the ram, and offered him up for a burnt offering in the stead of his son. **14** And Abraham called the name of that place Jehovah-ji´reh: as it is said *to* this day, In the mount of the Lord it shall be seen.

15 And the angel of the Lord called unto Abraham out of heaven the second time, **16** and said, By myself have I sworn, saith the Lord, for because thou hast done this thing, and hast not withheld thy son, thine only *son*, **17** that in blessing I will bless thee, and in multiplying I will multiply thy seed as the stars of the heaven, and as the sand which *is* upon the seashore; and thy seed shall possess the gate of his enemies; **18** and in thy seed shall all the nations of the earth be blessed; because thou hast obeyed my voice. **19** So Abraham returned unto his young men, and they rose up and went together to Beer-sheba; and Abraham dwelt at Beer-sheba.

JUBILEE - *Leviticus 25:8-55* **8** And thou shalt number seven sabbaths of years unto thee, seven times seven years; and the space of the seven sabbaths of years shall be unto thee forty and nine years. **9** Then shalt thou cause the trumpet of the jubilee to sound on the tenth *day* of the seventh month, in the day of atonement shall ye make the trumpet sound throughout all your land. **10** And ye shall hallow the fiftieth year, and proclaim liberty throughout *all* the land unto all the inhabitants thereof: it shall be a jubilee unto you; and ye shall return every man unto his possession, and ye shall return every man unto his family. **11** A jubilee shall that fiftieth year be unto you: ye shall not sow, neither reap that which groweth of itself in it, nor gather *the grapes* in it of thy vine undressed. **12** For it *is* the jubilee; it shall be holy unto you: ye shall eat the increase thereof out of the field.

13 In the year of this jubilee ye shall return every man unto his possession. **14** And if thou sell aught unto thy neighbor, or buyest *aught* of thy neighbor's hand, ye shall not oppress one another: **15** according to the number of years after the jubilee thou shalt buy of thy neighbor, *and* according unto the number of years of the fruits he shall sell unto thee: **16** according to the multitude of years thou shalt increase the price thereof, and according to the fewness of years thou shalt diminish the price of it: for *according* to the number *of the years* of the fruits doth he sell unto thee. **17** Ye shall not therefore oppress one another; but thou shalt fear thy God: for I *am* the Lord your God.

18 Wherefore ye shall do my statutes, and keep my judgments, and do them; and ye shall dwell in the land in safety. **19** And the land shall yield her fruit, and ye shall eat your fill, and dwell therein in safety. **20** And if ye shall say, What shall we eat the seventh year? behold, we shall not sow, nor gather in our increase: **21** then I will command my blessing upon you in the sixth year, and it shall bring forth fruit for three years. **22** And ye shall sow the eighth year, and eat *yet* of old fruit until the ninth year; until her fruits come in ye shall eat *of* the old *store*. **23** The land shall not be sold for ever: for the land *is* mine; for ye *are* strangers and sojourners with me. **24** And in all the land of your possession ye shall grant a redemption for the land.

25 If thy brother be waxen poor, and hath sold away *some* of his possession, and if any of his kin come to redeem it, then shall he redeem that which his brother sold. **26** And if the man have none to redeem it, and himself be able to redeem it; **27** then let him count the years of the sale thereof, and restore the overplus unto the man to whom he sold it; that he may return unto his possession. **28** But if he be not able to restore *it* to him, then that which is sold shall remain in the hand of him that hath bought it until the year of jubilee: and in the jubilee it shall go out, and he shall return unto his possession.

29 And if a man sell a dwelling house in a walled city, then he may redeem it within a whole year after it is sold; *within* a full year may he redeem it. **30** And if it be not redeemed within the space of a full year, then the house that *is* in the walled city shall be established for ever to him that bought it throughout his generations: it shall not go out in the jubilee. **31** But the houses of the villages which have no wall round about them shall be counted as the fields of the country: they may be redeemed, and they shall go out in the jubilee. **32** Notwithstanding the cities of the Levites, *and* the houses of the cities of their possession, may the Levites redeem at any time. **33** And if a man purchase of the Levites, then the house that was sold, and the city of his possession, shall go out in *the year of* jubilee: for the houses of the cities of the Levites *are* their possession among the children of Israel. **34** But the field of the suburbs of their cities may not be sold; for it *is* their perpetual possession.

35 And if thy brother be waxen poor, and fallen in decay with thee; then thou shalt relieve him: *yea, though he be* a stranger, or a sojourner; that he may live with thee. **36** Take thou no usury of him, or increase: but fear thy God; that thy brother may live with thee. **37** Thou shalt not give him thy money upon usury, nor lend him thy victuals for increase. **38** I *am* the Lord your God, which brought you forth out of the land of Egypt, to give you the land of Canaan, *and* to be your God.

39 And if thy brother *that dwelleth* by thee be waxen poor, and be sold unto thee; thou shalt not compel him to serve as a bondservant: **40** *but* as a hired servant, *and* as a sojourner, he shall be with thee, *and* shall serve thee unto the year of jubilee: **41** and *then* shall he depart from thee, *both* he and his children with him, and shall return unto his own family, and unto the possession of his fathers shall he return. **42** For they *are* my servants, which I brought forth out of the land of Egypt: they shall not be sold as bondmen. **43** Thou shalt not rule over him with rigor; but shalt fear thy God. **44** Both thy bondmen, and thy bondmaids, which thou shalt have, *shall be* of the heathen that are round about you; of them shall ye buy bondmen and bondmaids. **45** Moreover, of the children of the strangers that do sojourn among you, of them shall ye buy, and of their families that *are* with you, which they begat in your land: and they shall be your possession. **46** And ye shall take them as an inheritance for your children after you, to inherit *them for* a possession; they shall be your bondmen for ever: but over your brethren the children of Israel, ye shall not rule one over another with rigor.

47 And if a sojourner or stranger wax rich by thee, and thy brother *that dwelleth* by him wax poor, and sell himself unto the stranger *or* sojourner by thee, or to the stock of the stranger's family: **48** after that he is sold he may be redeemed again; one of his brethren may redeem him: **49** either his uncle, or his uncle's son, may redeem him, or *any* that is nigh of kin unto him of his family may redeem him; or if he be able, he may redeem himself. **50** And he shall reckon with him that bought him from the year that he was sold to him unto the year of jubilee: and the price of his sale shall be according unto the number of years, according to the time of a hired servant shall it be with him. **51** If *there be* yet many years *behind*, according unto them he shall give again the price of his redemption out of the money that he was bought for. **52** And if there remain but few years unto the year of jubilee, then he shall count with him, *and* according unto his years shall he give him again the price of his redemption. **53** *And* as a yearly hired servant shall he be with him: *and the other* shall not rule with rigor over him in thy sight. **54** And if he be not redeemed in these *years*, then he shall go out in the year of jubilee, *both* he, and his children with him. **55** For unto me the children of Israel *are* servants; they *are* my servants whom I brought forth out of the land of Egypt: I *am* the Lord your God.

JUDGMENTS FROM GOD – *Deuteronomy 1:17* Ye shall not respect persons in judgment; *but* ye shall hear the small as well as the great; ye shall not be afraid of the face of man; for the judgment *is* God's: and the cause that is too hard for you, bring *it* unto me, and I will hear it.

EXEMPTION OF LEVITES – *Numbers 1:49* Only thou shalt not number the tribe of Levi, neither take the sum of them among the children of Israel:

LORD AS JUDGE – *Numbers 5:12-31* **12** Speak unto the children of Israel, and say unto them, If any man's wife go aside, and commit a trespass against him, **13** and a man lie with her carnally, and it be hid from the eyes of her husband, and be kept close, and she be defiled, and *there be* no witness against her, neither she be taken *with the manner*; **14** and the spirit of jealousy come upon him, and he be jealous of his wife, and she be defiled; or if the spirit of jealousy come upon him, and he be jealous of his wife, and she be not defiled: **15** then shall the man bring his wife unto the priest, and he shall bring her offering for her, the tenth *part* of an ephah of barley meal; he shall pour no oil upon it, nor put frankincense thereon; for it *is* an offering of jealousy, an offering of memorial, bringing iniquity to remembrance.

16 And the priest shall bring her near, and set her before the Lord: **17** and the priest shall take holy water in an earthen vessel; and of the dust that is in the floor of the tabernacle the priest shall take, and put *it* into the water: **18** and the priest shall set the woman before the Lord, and uncover the woman's head, and put the offering of memorial in her hands, which *is* the jealousy offering: and the priest shall have in his hand the bitter water that causeth the curse: **19** and the priest shall charge her by an oath, and say unto the woman, If no man have lain with thee, and if thou hast not gone aside to uncleanness *with another* instead of thy husband, be thou free from this bitter water that causeth the curse: **20** but if thou hast gone aside *to another* instead of thy husband, and if thou be defiled, and some man have lain with thee besides thine husband: **21** then the priest shall charge the woman with an oath of cursing, and the priest shall say unto the woman, The Lord make thee a curse and an oath among thy people, when the Lord doth make thy thigh to rot, and thy belly to swell; **22** and this water that causeth the curse shall go into thy bowels, to make *thy* belly to swell, and *thy* thigh to rot. And the woman shall say, Amen, amen.

23 And the priest shall write these curses in a book, and he shall blot *them* out with the bitter water: **24** and he shall cause the woman to drink the bitter water that causeth the curse: and the water that causeth the curse shall enter into her, *and become* bitter. **25** Then the priest shall take the jealousy offering out of the woman's hand, and shall wave the offering before the Lord, and offer it upon the altar: **26** and the priest shall take a handful of the offering, *even* the memorial thereof, and burn *it* upon the altar, and afterward shall cause the woman to drink the water. **27** And when he hath made her to drink the water, then it shall come to pass, *that* if she be defiled, and have done trespass against her husband, that the water that causeth the curse shall enter into her, *and become* bitter, and her belly shall swell, and her thigh shall rot: and the woman shall be a curse among her people. **28** And if the woman be not defiled, but be clean; then she shall be free, and shall conceive seed.

29 This *is* the law of jealousies, when a wife goeth aside *to another* instead of her husband, and is defiled; **30** or when the spirit of jealousy cometh upon him, and he be jealous over his wife, and shall set the woman before the Lord, and the priest shall execute upon her all this law. **31** Then shall the man be guiltless from iniquity, and this woman shall bear her iniquity.

Deuteronomy 19:17-19, 21:1-9 **17** then both the men, between whom the controversy *is*, shall stand before the Lord, before the priests and the judges, which shall be in those days; **18** and the judges shall make diligent inquisition: and, behold, *if* the witness *be* a false witness, *and* hath testified falsely against his brother; **19** then shall ye do unto him, as he had thought to have done unto his brother: so shalt thou put the evil away from among you. *21:1-9*
Settlement for an Unknown Murderer's Crime

1 If *one* be found slain in the land which the Lord thy God giveth thee to possess it, lying in the field, *and* it be not known who hath slain him: **2** then thy elders and thy judges shall come forth, and they shall measure unto the cities which *are* round about him that is slain: **3** and it shall be, *that* the city *which is* next unto the slain man, even the elders of that city shall take a heifer, which hath not been wrought with, *and* which hath not drawn in the yoke; **4** and the elders of that city shall bring down the heifer unto a rough valley, which is neither eared nor sown, and shall strike off the heifer's neck there in the valley. **5** And the priests the sons of Levi shall come near; for them the Lord thy God hath chosen to minister unto him, and to bless in the name of the Lord; and by their word shall every controversy and every stroke be *tried*: **6** and all the elders of that city, *that are* next unto the slain *man*, shall wash their hands over the heifer that is beheaded in the valley: **7** and they shall answer and say, Our hands have not shed this blood, neither have our eyes seen *it*. **8** Be merciful, O Lord, unto thy people Israel, whom thou hast redeemed, and lay not innocent blood unto thy people of Israel's charge. And the blood shall be forgiven them. 9So shalt thou put away the *guilt of* innocent blood from among you, when thou shalt do *that which is* right in the sight of the Lord.

LORD'S SUPPER – *1 Corinthians 11:18-34* **18** For first of all, when ye come together in the church, I hear that there be divisions among you; and I partly believe it. **19** For there must be also heresies among you, that they which are approved may be made manifest among you. **20** When ye come together therefore into one place, *this* is not to eat the Lord's supper. **21** For in eating every one taketh before *other* his own supper: and one is hungry, and another is drunken. **22** What! have ye not houses to eat and to drink in? or despise ye the church of God, and shame them that have not? What shall I say to you? shall I praise you in this? I praise *you* not.

The Institution of the Lord's Supper

(Matthew 26.26-29;Mark 14.22-25;Luke 22.14-20)

23 For I have received of the Lord that which also I delivered unto you, That the Lord Jesus, the *same* night in which he was betrayed, took bread: **24** and when he had given thanks, he brake *it*, and said, Take, eat; this is my body, which is broken for you: this do in remembrance of me. **25** After the same manner also *he took* the cup, when he had supped, saying, This cup is the new testament in my blood: this do ye, as oft as ye drink *it*, in remembrance of me. **26** For as often as ye eat this bread, and drink this cup, ye do show the Lord's death till he come.

Partaking of the Supper Unworthily

27 Wherefore whosoever shall eat this bread, and drink *this* cup of the Lord, unworthily, shall be guilty of the body and blood of the Lord. **28** But let a man examine himself, and so let him eat of *that* bread, and drink of *that* cup. **29** For he that eateth and drinketh unworthily, eateth and drinketh damnation to himself, not discerning the Lord's body. **30** For this cause many *are* weak and sickly among you, and many sleep. **31** For if we would judge ourselves, we should not be judged. **32** But when we are judged, we are chastened of the Lord, that we should not be condemned with the world.

33 Wherefore, my brethren, when ye come together to eat, tarry one for another. **34** And if any man hunger, let him eat at home; that ye come not together unto condemnation. And the rest will I set in order when I come.

MEAT OFFERING – *Leviticus 2:1-11* **1** And when any will offer a meat offering unto the Lord, his offering shall be *of* fine flour; and he shall pour oil upon it, and put frankincense thereon. **2** And he shall bring it to Aaron's sons the priests: and he shall take thereout his handful of the flour thereof, and of the oil thereof, with all the frankincense thereof; and the priest shall burn the memorial of it upon the altar, *to be* an offering made by fire, of a sweet savor unto the Lord: **3** and the remnant of the meat offering *shall be* Aaron's and his sons': *it is* a thing most holy of the offerings of the Lord made by fire.

4 And if thou bring an oblation of a meat offering baked in the oven, *it shall be* unleavened cakes of fine flour mingled with oil, or unleavened wafers anointed with oil. **5** And if thy oblation *be* a meat offering *baked* in a pan, it shall be *of* fine flour unleavened, mingled with oil. **6** Thou shalt part it in pieces, and pour oil thereon: it *is* a meat offering. **7** And if thy oblation *be* a meat offering *baked* in the frying pan, it shall be made *of* fine flour with oil. **8** And thou shalt bring the meat offering that is made of these things unto the Lord: and when it is presented unto the priest, he shall bring it unto the altar. **9** And the priest shall take from the meat offering a memorial thereof, and shall burn *it* upon the altar: *it is* an offering made by fire, of a sweet savor unto the Lord. **10** And that which is left of the meat offering *shall be* Aaron's and his sons': *it is* a thing most holy of the offerings of the Lord made by fire.

11 No meat offering, which ye shall bring unto the Lord, shall be made with leaven: for ye shall burn no leaven, nor any honey, in any offering of the Lord made by fire.

<u>Numbers 28:9, 10</u> **9** And on the sabbath day two lambs of the first year without spot, and two tenth deals of flour *for* a meat offering, mingled with oil, and the drink offering thereof: **10** *this is* the burnt offering of every sabbath, beside the continual burnt offering, and his drink offering.

MEMORIAL OFFERING – *Leviticus 2:2, 9, 16* 2 And he shall bring it to Aaron's sons the priests: and he shall take thereout his handful of the flour thereof, and of the oil thereof, with all the frankincense thereof; and the priest shall burn the memorial of it upon the altar, *to be* an offering made by fire, of a sweet savor unto the Lord: **9** And the priest shall take from the meat offering a memorial thereof, and shall burn *it* upon the altar: *it is* an offering made by fire, of a sweet savor unto the Lord. **16** And the priest shall burn the memorial of it, *part* of the beaten corn thereof, and *part* of the oil thereof, with all the frankincense thereof: *it is* an offering made by fire unto the Lord.

MERCY PREFERRED – *Matthew 9:13, 12:7* 9:13 But go ye and learn what *that* meaneth, I will have mercy, and not sacrifice: for I am not come to call the righteous, but sinners to repentance. **12:7** But if ye had known what *this* meaneth, I will have mercy, and not sacrifice, ye would not have condemned the guiltless.

NAZARITES – *Numbers 6:1-21* The Law for the Nazarite

1 And the Lord spake unto Moses, saying, **2** Speak unto the children of Israel, and say unto them, When either man or woman shall separate *themselves* to vow a vow of a Nazarite, to separate *themselves* unto the Lord; **3** he shall separate *himself* from wine and strong drink, and shall drink no vinegar of wine, or vinegar of strong drink, neither shall he drink any liquor of grapes, nor eat moist grapes, or dried. **4** All the days of his separation shall he eat nothing that is made of the vine tree, from the kernels even to the husk.

5 All the days of the vow of his separation there shall no razor come upon his head: until the days be fulfilled, in the which he separateth *himself* unto the Lord, he shall be holy, *and* shall let the locks of the hair of his head grow.

6 All the days that he separateth *himself* unto the Lord he shall come at no dead body. **7** He shall not make himself unclean for his father, or for his mother, for his brother, or for his sister, when they die: because the consecration of his God *is* upon his head. **8** All the days of his separation he *is* holy unto the Lord.

9 And if any man die very suddenly by him, and he hath defiled the head of his consecration; then he shall shave his head in the day of his cleansing, on the seventh day shall he shave it. **10** And on the eighth day he shall bring two turtles, or two young pigeons, to the priest, to the door of the tabernacle of the congregation: **11** and the priest shall offer the one for a sin offering, and the other for a burnt offering, and make an atonement for him, for that he sinned by the dead, and shall hallow his head that same day. **12** And he shall consecrate unto the Lord the days of his separation, and shall bring a lamb of the first year for a trespass offering: but the days that were before shall be lost, because his separation was defiled.

13 And this *is* the law of the Nazarite: when the days of his separation are fulfilled, he shall be brought unto the door of the tabernacle of the congregation: **14** and he shall offer his offering unto the Lord, one he lamb of the first year without blemish for a burnt offering, and one ewe lamb of the first year without blemish for a sin offering, and one ram without blemish for peace offerings, **15** and a basket of unleavened bread, cakes of fine flour mingled with oil, and wafers of unleavened bread anointed with oil, and their meat offering, and their drink offerings. **16** And the priest shall bring *them* before the Lord, and shall offer his sin offering, and his burnt offering: **17** and he shall offer the ram *for* a sacrifice of peace offerings unto the Lord, with the basket of unleavened bread: the priest shall offer also his meat offering, and his drink offering. **18** And the Nazarite shall shave the head of his separation *at* the door of the tabernacle of the congregation, and shall take the hair of the head of his separation, and put *it* in the fire which *is* under the sacrifice of the peace offerings. **19** And the priest shall take the sodden shoulder of the ram, and one unleavened cake out of the basket, and one unleavened wafer, and shall put *them* upon the hands of the Nazarite, after *the hair of* his separation is shaven: **20** and the priest shall wave them *for* a wave offering before the Lord: this *is* holy for the priest, with the wave breast and heave shoulder: and after that the Nazarite may drink wine.

21 This *is* the law of the Nazarite who hath vowed, *and of* his offering unto the Lord for his separation, besides *that* that his hand shall get: according to the vow which he vowed, so he must do after the law of his separation.

OFFERINGS – *Genesis 4:3-5* **3** And in process of time it came to pass, that Cain brought of the fruit of the ground an offering unto the Lord. **4** And Abel, he also brought of the firstlings of his flock and of the fat thereof. And the Lord had respect unto Abel and to his offering: **5** but unto Cain and to his offering he had not respect. And Cain was very wroth, and his countenance fell.

Leviticus 1:1-3, 7:3-8 1 And the Lord called unto Moses, and spake unto him out of the tabernacle of the congregation, saying, **2** Speak unto the children of Israel, and say unto them, If any man of you bring an offering unto the Lord, ye shall bring your offering of the cattle, even of the herd, and of the flock.

3 If his offering be a burnt sacrifice of the herd, let him offer a male without blemish: he shall offer it of his own voluntary will at the door of the tabernacle of the congregation before the Lord.

7:3-8 **3** Likewise this *is* the law of the trespass offering: it *is* most holy. 2In the place where they kill the burnt offering shall they kill the trespass offering: and the blood thereof shall he sprinkle round about upon the altar. **3** And he shall offer of it all the fat thereof; the rump, and the fat that covereth the inwards, **4** and the two kidneys, and the fat that *is* on them, which *is* by the flanks, and the caul *that is* above the liver, with the kidneys, it shall he take away: **5** and the priest shall burn them upon the altar *for* an offering made by fire unto the Lord: it *is* a trespass offering. **6** Every male among the priests shall eat thereof: it shall be eaten in the holy place: it *is* most holy. **7** As the sin offering *is*, so *is* the trespass offering: *there is* one law for them: the priest that maketh atonement therewith shall have *it*. **8** And the priest that offereth any man's burnt offering, *even* the priest shall have to himself the skin of the burnt offering which he hath offered.

OFFERINGS OF FIRSTFRUITS – *Leviticus 2:12-16*

12 As for the oblation of the firstfruits, ye shall offer them unto the Lord: but they shall not be burnt on the altar for a sweet savor. **13** And every oblation of thy meat offering shalt thou season with salt; neither shalt thou suffer the salt of the covenant of thy God to be lacking from thy meat offering: with all thine offerings thou shalt offer salt.

14 And if thou offer a meat offering of thy firstfruits unto the Lord, thou shalt offer for the meat offering of thy firstfruits green ears of corn dried by the fire, *even* corn beaten out of full ears. **15** And thou shalt put oil upon it, and lay frankincense thereon: it *is* a meat offering. **16** And the priest shall burn the memorial of it, *part* of the beaten corn thereof, and *part* of the oil thereof, with all the frankincense thereof: *it is* an offering made by fire unto the Lord.

***Deuteronomy 26:2, 10* 26:2** that thou shalt take of the first of all the fruit of the earth, which thou shalt bring of thy land that the Lord thy God giveth thee, and shalt put *it* in a basket, and shalt go unto the place which the Lord thy God shall choose to place his name there. **10** And now, behold, I have brought the firstfruits of the land, which thou, O Lord, hast given me. And thou shalt set it before the Lord thy God, and worship before the Lord thy God:

OIL OFFERINGS – *Genesis 28:18* And Jacob rose up early in the morning, and took the stone that he had put *for* his pillows, and set it up *for* a pillar, and poured oil upon the top of it.

PASSOVER – *Exodus 12:1-14, 21-27* The Passover

1 And the Lord spake unto Moses and Aaron in the land of Egypt, saying, **2** This month *shall be* unto you the beginning of months: it *shall be* the first month of the year to you. **3** Speak ye unto all the congregation of Israel, saying, In the tenth *day* of this month they shall take to them every man a lamb, according to the house of *their* fathers, a lamb for a house: **4** and if the household be too little for the lamb, let him and his neighbor next unto his house take *it* according to the number of the souls; every man according to his eating shall make your count for the lamb. **5** Your lamb shall be without blemish, a male of the first year: ye shall take *it* out from the sheep, or from the goats: **6** and ye shall keep it up until the fourteenth day of the same month: and the whole assembly of the congregation of Israel shall kill it in the evening. **7** And they shall take of the blood, and strike *it* on the two side posts and on the upper doorpost of the houses, wherein they shall eat it. **8** And they shall eat the flesh in that night, roast with fire, and unleavened bread; *and* with bitter *herbs* they shall eat it. **9** Eat not of it raw, nor sodden at all with water, but roast *with* fire; his head with his legs, and with the purtenance thereof. **10** And ye shall let nothing of it remain until the morning; and that which remaineth of it until the morning ye shall burn with fire. **11** And thus shall ye eat it; *with* your loins girded, your shoes on your feet, and your staff in your hand; and ye shall eat it in haste: it *is* the Lord's passover. **12** For I will pass through the land of Egypt this night, and will smite all the firstborn in the land of Egypt, both man and beast; and against all the gods of Egypt I will execute judgment: I *am* the Lord. **13** And the blood shall be to you for a token upon the houses where ye *are*: and when I see the blood, I will pass over you, and the plague shall not be upon you to destroy *you*, when I smite the land of Egypt.

14 And this day shall be unto you for a memorial; and ye shall keep it a feast to the Lord throughout your generations: ye shall keep it a feast by an ordinance for ever.

21-27 **21** Then Moses called for all the elders of Israel, and said unto them, Draw out and take you a lamb according to your families, and kill the passover. **22** And ye shall take a bunch of hyssop, and dip *it* in the blood that *is* in the basin, and strike the lintel and the two side posts with the blood that *is* in the basin; and none of you shall go out at the door of his house until the morning. **23** For the Lord will pass through to smite the Egyptians; and when he seeth the blood upon the lintel, and on the two side posts, the Lord will pass over the door, and will not suffer the destroyer to come in unto your houses to smite *you*. **24** And ye shall observe this thing for an ordinance to thee and to thy sons for ever. **25** And it shall come to pass, when ye be come to the land which the Lord will give you, according as he hath promised, that ye shall keep this service. **26** And it shall come to pass, when your children shall say unto you, What mean ye by this service? **27** That ye shall say, It *is* the sacrifice of the Lord's passover, who passed over the houses of the children of Israel in Egypt, when he smote the Egyptians, and delivered our houses. And the people bowed the head and worshipped.

Deuteronomy 16:1-8 **1** Observe the month of Abib, and keep the passover unto the Lord thy God: for in the month of Abib the Lord thy God brought thee forth out of Egypt by night. **2** Thou shalt therefore sacrifice the passover unto the Lord thy God, of the flock and the herd, in the place which the Lord shall choose to place his name there. **3** Thou shalt eat no leavened bread with it; seven days shalt thou eat unleavened bread therewith, *even* the bread of affliction; for thou camest forth out of the land of Egypt in haste: that thou mayest remember the day when thou camest forth out of the land of Egypt all the days of thy life. **4** And there shall be no leavened bread seen with thee in all thy coast seven days; neither shall there *any thing* of the flesh, which thou sacrificedst the first day at even, remain all night until the morning. **5** Thou mayest not sacrifice the passover within any of thy gates, which the Lord thy God giveth thee: **6** but at the place which the Lord thy God shall choose to place his name in, there thou shalt sacrifice the passover at even, at the going down of the sun, at the season that thou camest forth out of Egypt. **7** And thou shalt roast and eat *it* in the place which the Lord thy God shall choose: and thou shalt turn in the morning, and go unto thy tents. **8** Six days thou shalt eat unleavened bread: and on the seventh day *shall be* a solemn assembly to the Lord thy God: thou shalt do no work *therein*.

Ezekiel 45:21-24 **21** In the first *month*, in the fourteenth day of the month, ye shall have the passover, a feast of seven days; unleavened bread shall be eaten. **22** And upon that day shall the prince prepare for himself and for all the people of the land a bullock *for* a sin offering. **23** And seven days of the feast he shall prepare a burnt offering to the Lord, seven bullocks and seven rams without blemish daily the seven days; and a kid of the goats daily *for* a sin offering. **24** And he shall prepare a meat offering of an ephah for a bullock, and an ephah for a ram, and a hin of oil for an ephah.

Luke 22:7-18 Jesus Eats the Passover with His Disciples

(Matthew 26.17-29;Mark 14.12-25;John 13.21-30;1 Corinthians 11.23-26)

7 Then came the day of unleavened bread, when the passover must be killed. **8** And he sent Peter and John, saying, Go and prepare us the passover, that we may eat. **9** And they said unto him, Where wilt thou that we prepare? **10** And he said unto them, Behold, when ye are entered into the city, there shall a man meet you, bearing a pitcher of water; follow him into the house where he entereth in. **11** And ye shall say unto the goodman of the house, The Master saith unto thee, Where is the guest chamber, where I shall eat the passover with my disciples? **12** And he shall show you a large upper room furnished: there make ready. **13** And they went, and found as he had said unto them: and they made ready the passover.

14 And when the hour was come, he sat down, and the twelve apostles with him. **15** And he said unto them, With desire I have desired to eat this passover with you before I suffer: **16** for I say unto you, I will not any more eat thereof, until it be fulfilled in the kingdom of God. **17** And he took the cup, and gave thanks, and said, Take this, and divide *it* among yourselves: **18** for I say unto you, I will not drink of the fruit of the vine, until the kingdom of God shall come.

PEACE OFFERINGS – *Leviticus 3:1-17* Peace Offerings

1 And if his oblation *be* a sacrifice of peace offering, if he offer *it* of the herd, whether *it be* a male or female, he shall offer it without blemish before the Lord. **2** And he shall lay his hand upon the head of his offering, and kill it *at* the door of the tabernacle of the congregation: and Aaron's sons the priests shall sprinkle the blood upon the altar round about. **3** And he shall offer of the sacrifice of the peace offering an offering made by fire unto the Lord; the fat that covereth the inwards, and all the fat that *is* upon the inwards, **4** and the two kidneys, and the fat that *is* on them, which *is* by the flanks, and the caul above the liver, with the kidneys, it shall he take away. **5** And Aaron's sons shall burn it on the altar upon the burnt sacrifice, which *is* upon the wood that *is* on the fire: *it is* an offering made by fire, of a sweet savor unto the Lord.

6 And if his offering for a sacrifice of peace offering unto the Lord *be* of the flock, male or female, he shall offer it without blemish. **7** If he offer a lamb for his offering, then shall he offer it before the Lord. **8** And he shall lay his hand upon the head of his offering, and kill it before the tabernacle of the congregation: and Aaron's sons shall sprinkle the blood thereof round about upon the altar. **9** And he shall offer of the sacrifice of the peace offering an offering made by fire unto the Lord; the fat thereof, *and* the whole rump, it shall he take off hard by the backbone; and the fat that covereth the inwards, and all the fat that *is* upon the inwards, **10** and the two kidneys, and the fat that *is* upon them, which *is* by the flanks, and the caul above the liver, with the kidneys, it shall he take away. **11** And the priest shall burn it upon the altar: *it is* the food of the offering made by fire unto the Lord.

12 And if his offering *be* a goat, then he shall offer it before the Lord. **13** And he shall lay his hand upon the head of it, and kill it before the tabernacle of the congregation: and the sons of Aaron shall sprinkle the blood thereof upon the altar round about. **14** And he shall offer thereof his offering, *even* an offering made by fire unto the Lord; the fat that covereth the inwards, and all the fat that *is* upon the inwards, **15** and the two kidneys, and the fat that *is* upon them, which *is* by the flanks, and the caul above the liver, with the kidneys, it shall he take away. **16** And the priest shall burn them upon the altar: *it is* the food of the offering made by fire for a sweet savor: all the fat *is* the Lord's. **17** *It shall be* a perpetual statute for your generations throughout all your dwellings, that ye eat neither fat nor blood.

PENTECOST - *Leviticus 23:15-21* **15** And ye shall count unto you from the morrow after the sabbath, from the day that ye brought the sheaf of the wave offering; seven sabbaths shall be complete: **16** even unto the morrow after the seventh sabbath shall ye number fifty days; and ye shall offer a new meat offering unto the Lord. **17** Ye shall bring out of your habitations two wave loaves of two tenth deals: they shall be of fine flour; they shall be baked with leaven; *they are* the firstfruits unto the Lord. **18** And ye shall offer with the bread seven lambs without blemish of the first year, and one young bullock, and two rams: they shall be *for* a burnt offering unto the Lord, with their meat offering, and their drink offerings, *even* an offering made by fire, of sweet savor unto the Lord. **19** Then ye shall sacrifice one kid of the goats for a sin offering, and two lambs of the first year for a sacrifice of peace offerings. **20** And the priest shall wave them with the bread of the firstfruits *for* a wave offering before the Lord, with the two lambs: they shall be holy to the Lord for the priest. **21**And ye shall proclaim on the selfsame day, *that* it may be a holy convocation unto you: ye shall do no servile work *therein: it shall be* a statute for ever in all your dwellings throughout your generations.

Acts 2:1-4 **1** And when the day of Pentecost was fully come, they were all with one accord in one place. **2** And suddenly there came a sound from heaven as of a rushing mighty wind, and it filled all the house where they were sitting. **3** And there appeared unto them cloven tongues like as of fire, and it sat upon each of them. **4** And they were all filled with the Holy Ghost, and began to speak with other tongues, as the Spirit gave them utterance.

POLL TAX – *Exodus 30:12-16* **12** When thou takest the sum of the children of Israel after their number, then shall they give every man a ransom for his soul unto the Lord, when thou numberest them; that there be no plague among them, when *thou* numberest them. **13** This they shall give, every one that passeth among them that are numbered, half a shekel after the shekel of the sanctuary: (a shekel *is* twenty gerahs:) a half shekel *shall be* the offering of the Lord. **14** Every one that passeth among them that are numbered, from twenty years old and above, shall give an offering unto the Lord. **15** The rich shall not give more, and the poor shall not give less, than half a shekel, when *they* give an offering unto the Lord, to make an atonement for your souls. **16** And thou shalt take the atonement money of the children of Israel, and shalt appoint it for the service of the tabernacle of the congregation; that it may be a memorial unto the children of Israel before the Lord, to make an atonement for your souls.

PURIFICATION – *Leviticus 12:1-8, 14:1-32, 15:1-33* The Purification of Women after Childbirth

1 And the Lord spake unto Moses, saying, **2** Speak unto the children of Israel, saying, If a woman have conceived seed, and borne a man child, then she shall be unclean seven days; according to the days of the separation for her infirmity shall she be unclean. **3** And in the eighth day the flesh of his foreskin shall be circumcised. **4** And she shall then continue in the blood of her purifying three and thirty days; she shall touch no hallowed thing, nor come into the sanctuary, until the days of her purifying be fulfilled. **5** But if she bear a maid child, then she shall be unclean two weeks, as in her separation: and she shall continue in the blood of her purifying threescore and six days.

6 And when the days of her purifying are fulfilled, for a son, or for a daughter, she shall bring a lamb of the first year for a burnt offering, and a young pigeon, or a turtledove, for a sin offering, unto the door of the tabernacle of the congregation, unto the priest: **7** who shall offer it before the Lord, and make an atonement for her; and she shall be cleansed from the issue of her blood. This *is* the law for her that hath borne a male or a female. **8** And if she be not able to bring a lamb, then she shall bring two turtles, or two young pigeons; the one for the burnt offering, and the other for a sin offering: and the priest shall make an atonement for her, and she shall be clean.

14:1-32 **1** And the Lord spake unto Moses, saying, **2** This shall be the law of the leper in the day of his cleansing: He shall be brought unto the priest: **3** and the priest shall go forth out of the camp; and the priest shall look, and, behold, *if* the plague of leprosy be healed in the leper; **4** then shall the priest command to take for him that is to be cleansed two birds alive *and* clean, and cedar wood, and scarlet, and hyssop: **5** and the priest shall command that one of the birds be killed in an earthen vessel over running water. **6** As for the living bird, he shall take it, and the cedar wood, and the scarlet, and the hyssop, and shall dip them and the living bird in the blood of the bird *that was* killed over the running water: **7** and he shall sprinkle upon him that is to be cleansed from the leprosy seven times, and shall pronounce him clean, and shall let the living bird loose into the open field. **8** And he that is to be cleansed shall wash his clothes, and shave off all his hair, and wash himself in water, that he may be clean: and after that he shall come into the camp, and shall tarry abroad out of his tent seven days. **9** But it shall be on the seventh day, that he shall shave all his hair off his head and his beard and his eyebrows, even all his hair he shall shave off: and he shall wash his clothes, also he shall wash his flesh in water, and he shall be clean.

10 And on the eighth day he shall take two he lambs without blemish, and one ewe lamb of the first year without blemish, and three tenth deals of fine flour *for* a meat offering, mingled with oil, and one log of oil: **11** and the priest that maketh *him* clean shall present the man that is to be made clean, and those things, before the Lord, *at* the door of the tabernacle of the congregation. **12** And the priest shall take one he lamb, and offer him for a trespass offering, and the log of oil, and wave them *for* a wave offering before the Lord: **13** and he shall slay the lamb in the place where he shall kill the sin offering and the burnt offering, in the holy place: for as the sin offering *is* the priest's, *so is* the trespass offering: it *is* most holy: **14** and the priest shall take *some* of the blood of the trespass offering, and the priest shall put *it* upon the tip of the right ear of him that is to be cleansed, and upon the thumb of his right hand, and upon the great toe of his right foot. **15** And the priest shall take *some* of the log of oil, and pour *it* into the palm of his own left hand: **16** and the priest shall dip his right finger in the oil that *is* in his left hand, and shall sprinkle of the oil with his finger seven times before the Lord: **17** and of the rest of the oil that *is* in his hand shall the priest put upon the tip of the right ear of him that is to be cleansed, and upon the thumb of his right hand, and upon the great toe of his right foot, upon the blood of the trespass offering: **18** and the remnant of the oil that *is* in the priest's hand he shall pour upon the head of him that is to be cleansed: and the priest shall make an atonement for him before the Lord. **19** And the priest shall offer the sin offering, and make an atonement for him that is to be cleansed from his uncleanness; and afterward he shall kill the burnt offering: **20** and the priest shall offer the burnt offering and the meat offering upon the altar: and the priest shall make an atonement for him, and he shall be clean.

21 And if he *be* poor, and cannot get so much; then he shall take one lamb *for* a trespass offering to be waved, to make an atonement for him, and one tenth deal of fine flour mingled with oil for a meat offering, and a log of oil; **22** and two turtledoves, or two young pigeons, such as he is able to get; and the one shall be a sin offering, and the other a burnt offering. **23** And he shall bring them on the eighth day for his cleansing unto the priest, unto the door of the tabernacle of the congregation, before the Lord. **24** And the priest shall take the lamb of the trespass offering, and the log of oil, and the priest shall wave them *for* a wave offering before the Lord: **25** and he shall kill the lamb of the trespass offering, and the priest shall take *some* of the blood of the trespass offering, and put *it* upon the tip of the right ear of him that is to be cleansed, and upon the thumb of his right hand, and upon the great toe of his right foot. **26** And the priest shall pour of the oil into the palm of his own left hand: **27** and the priest shall sprinkle with his right finger *some* of the oil that *is* in his left hand seven times before the Lord: **28** and the priest shall put of the oil that *is* in his hand upon the tip of the right ear of him that is to be cleansed, and upon the thumb of his right hand, and upon the great toe of his right foot, upon the place of the blood of the trespass offering: **29** and the rest of the oil that *is* in the priest's hand he shall put upon the head of him that is to be cleansed, to make an atonement for him before the Lord. **30** And he shall offer the one of the turtledoves, or of the young pigeons, such as he can get; **31** *even* such as he is able to get, the one *for* a sin offering, and the other *for* a burnt offering, with the meat offering: and the priest shall make an atonement for him that is to be cleansed before the Lord. **32** This *is* the law *of him* in whom *is* the plague of leprosy, whose hand is not able to get *that which pertaineth* to his cleansing.

15:1-33 Unclean Discharges from the Body

1 And the Lord spake unto Moses and to Aaron, saying, **2** Speak unto the children of Israel, and say unto them, When any man hath a running issue out of his flesh, *because of* his issue he *is* unclean. **3** And this shall be his uncleanness in his issue: whether his flesh run with his issue, or his flesh be stopped from his issue, it *is* his uncleanness. **4** Every bed, whereon he lieth that hath the issue, is unclean: and every thing, whereon he sitteth, shall be unclean. **5** And whosoever toucheth his bed shall wash his clothes, and bathe *himself* in water, and be unclean until the even. **6** And he that sitteth on *any* thing whereon he sat that hath the issue shall wash his clothes, and bathe *himself* in water, and be unclean until the even. **7** And he that toucheth the flesh of him that hath the issue shall wash his clothes, and bathe *himself* in water, and be unclean until the even. **8** And if he that hath the issue spit upon him that is clean; then he shall wash his clothes, and bathe *himself* in water, and be unclean until the even. **9** And what saddle soever he rideth upon that hath the issue shall be unclean. **10** And whosoever toucheth any thing that was under him shall be unclean until the even: and he that beareth *any of* those things shall wash his clothes, and bathe *himself* in water, and be unclean until the even. **11** And whomsoever he toucheth that hath the issue, and hath not rinsed his hands in water, he shall wash his clothes, and bathe *himself* in water, and be unclean until the even. **12** And the vessel of earth, that he toucheth which hath the issue, shall be broken: and every vessel of wood shall be rinsed in water.

13 And when he that hath an issue is cleansed of his issue, then he shall number to himself seven days for his cleansing, and wash his clothes, and bathe his flesh in running water, and shall be clean. **14** And on the eighth day he shall take to him two turtledoves, or two young pigeons, and come before the Lord unto the door of the tabernacle of the congregation, and give them unto the priest: **15** and the priest shall offer them, the one *for* a sin offering, and the other *for* a burnt offering; and the priest shall make an atonement for him before the Lord for his issue.

16 And if any man's seed of copulation go out from him, then he shall wash all his flesh in water, and be unclean until the even. **17** And every garment, and every skin, whereon is the seed of copulation, shall be washed with water, and be unclean until the even. **18** The woman also with whom man shall lie *with* seed of copulation, they shall *both* bathe *themselves* in water, and be unclean until the even.

19 And if a woman have an issue, *and* her issue in her flesh be blood, she shall be put apart seven days: and whosoever toucheth her shall be unclean until the even. **20** And every thing that she lieth upon in her separation shall be unclean: every thing also that she sitteth upon shall be unclean. **21** And whosoever toucheth her bed shall wash his clothes, and bathe *himself* in water, and be unclean until the even. **22** And whosoever toucheth any thing that she sat upon shall wash his clothes, and bathe *himself* in water, and be unclean until the even. **23** And if it *be* on *her* bed, or on any thing whereon she sitteth, when he toucheth it, he shall be unclean until the even. **24** And if any man lie with her at all, and her flowers be upon him, he shall be unclean seven days; and all the bed whereon he lieth shall be unclean.

25 And if a woman have an issue of her blood many days out of the time of her separation, or if it run beyond the time of her separation; all the days of the issue of her uncleanness shall be as the days of her separation: she *shall be* unclean. **26** Every bed whereon she lieth all the days of her issue shall be unto her as the bed of her separation: and whatsoever she sitteth upon shall be unclean, as the uncleanness of her separation. **27** And whosoever toucheth those things shall be unclean, and shall wash his clothes, and bathe *himself* in water, and be unclean until the even. **28** But if she be cleansed of her issue, then she shall number to herself seven days, and after that she shall be clean. **29** And on the eighth day she shall take unto her two turtles, or two young pigeons, and bring them unto the priest, to the door of the tabernacle of the congregation. **30** And the priest shall offer the one *for* a sin offering, and the other *for* a burnt offering; and the priest shall make an atonement for her before the Lord for the issue of her uncleanness.

31 Thus shall ye separate the children of Israel from their uncleanness; that they die not in their uncleanness, when they defile my tabernacle that *is* among them.

32 This *is* the law of him that hath an issue, and *of him* whose seed goeth from him, and is defiled therewith; **33** and of her that is sick of her flowers, and of him that hath an issue, of the man, and of the woman, and of him that lieth with her that is unclean.

Numbers 19:1-22 **The Purification of the Unclean**

1 And the Lord spake unto Moses and unto Aaron, saying, **2** This *is* the ordinance of the law which the Lord hath commanded, saying, Speak unto the children of Israel, that they bring thee a red heifer without spot, wherein *is* no blemish, *and* upon which never came yoke. **3** And ye shall give her unto Ele-a´zar the priest, that he may bring her forth without the camp, and *one* shall slay her before his face: **4** and Ele-a´zar the priest shall take of her blood with his finger, and sprinkle of her blood directly before the tabernacle of the congregation seven times. **5** And *one* shall burn the heifer in his sight; her skin, and her flesh, and her blood, with her dung, shall he burn: **6** and the priest shall take cedar wood, and hyssop, and scarlet, and cast *it* into the midst of the burning of the heifer. **7** Then the priest shall wash his clothes, and he shall bathe his flesh in water, and afterward he shall come into the camp, and the priest shall be unclean until the even. **8** And he that burneth her shall wash his clothes in water, and bathe his flesh in water, and shall be unclean until the even. **9** And a man *that is* clean shall gather up the ashes of the heifer, and lay *them* up without the camp in a clean place, and it shall be kept for the congregation of the children of Israel for a water of separation: it *is* a purification for sin. **10** And he that gathereth the ashes of the heifer shall wash his clothes, and be unclean until the even: and it shall be unto the children of Israel, and unto the stranger that sojourneth among them, for a statute for ever.

11 He that toucheth the dead body of any man shall be unclean seven days. **12** He shall purify himself with it on the third day, and on the seventh day he shall be clean: but if he purify not himself the third day, then the seventh day he shall not be clean. **13** Whosoever toucheth the dead body of any man that is dead, and purifieth not himself, defileth the tabernacle of the Lord; and that soul shall be cut off from Israel: because the water of separation was not sprinkled upon him, he shall be unclean; his uncleanness *is* yet upon him.

14 This *is* the law, when a man dieth in a tent: all that come into the tent, and all that *is* in the tent, shall be unclean seven days. **15** And every open vessel, which hath no covering bound upon it, *is* unclean. **16** And whosoever toucheth one that is slain with a sword in the open fields, or a dead body, or a bone of a man, or a grave, shall be unclean seven days. **17** And for an unclean *person* they shall take of the ashes of the burnt heifer of purification for sin, and running water shall be put thereto in a vessel: **18** and a clean person shall take hyssop, and dip *it* in the water, and sprinkle *it* upon the tent, and upon all the vessels, and upon the persons that were there, and upon him that touched a bone, or one slain, or one dead, or a grave: **19** and the clean *person* shall sprinkle upon the unclean on the third day, and on the seventh day: and on the seventh day he shall purify himself, and wash his clothes, and bathe himself in water, and shall be clean at even.

20 But the man that shall be unclean, and shall not purify himself, that soul shall be cut off from among the congregation, because he hath defiled the sanctuary of the Lord: the water of separation hath not been sprinkled upon him; he *is* unclean. **21** And it shall be a perpetual statute unto them, that he that sprinkleth the water of separation shall wash his clothes; and he that toucheth the water of separation shall be unclean until even. **22** And whatsoever the unclean *person* toucheth shall be unclean; and the soul that toucheth *it* shall be unclean until even.

Luke 2:21-24 **21** And when eight days were accomplished for the circumcising of the child, his name was called Jesus, which was so named of the angel before he was conceived in the womb.

22 And when the days of her purification according to the law of Moses were accomplished, they brought him to Jerusalem, to present *him* to the Lord; **23** (as it is written in the law of the Lord, Every male that openeth the womb shall be called holy to the Lord;) **24** and to offer a sacrifice according to that which is said in the law of the Lord, A pair of turtledoves, or two young pigeons.

PURIM – ***Esther 9:20-32*** **20** And Mor´decai wrote these things, and sent letters unto all the Jews that *were* in all the provinces of the king Ahasue´rus, *both* nigh and far, **21** to establish *this* among them, that they should keep the fourteenth day of the month Adar, and the fifteenth day of the same, yearly, **22** as the days wherein the Jews rested from their enemies, and the month which was turned unto them from sorrow to joy, and from mourning into a good day: that they should make them days of feasting and joy, and of sending portions one to another, and gifts to the poor.

23 And the Jews undertook to do as they had begun, and as Mor´decai had written unto them; **24** because Haman the son of Hammeda´tha, the A´gagite, the enemy of all the Jews, had devised against the Jews to destroy them, and had cast Pur, that *is*, the lot, to consume them, and to destroy them; **25** but when *Esther* came before the king, he commanded by letters that his wicked device, which he devised against the Jews, should return upon his own head, and that he and his sons should be hanged on the gallows. **26** Wherefore they called these days Purim after the name of Pur. Therefore for all the words of this letter, and *of that* which they had seen concerning this matter, and which had come unto them, **27** the Jews ordained, and took upon them, and upon their seed, and upon all such as joined themselves unto them, so as it should not fail, that they would keep these two days according to their writing, and according to their *appointed* time every year; **28** and *that* these days *should be* remembered and kept throughout every generation, every family, every province, and every city; and *that* these days of Purim should not fail from among the Jews, nor the memorial of them perish from their seed.

29 Then Esther the queen, the daughter of Ab´ihail, and Mor´decai the Jew, wrote with all authority, to confirm this second letter of Purim. **30** And he sent the letters unto all the Jews, to the hundred twenty and seven provinces of the kingdom of Ahasue´rus, *with* words of peace and truth, **31** to confirm these days of Purim in their times *appointed*, according as Mor´decai the Jew and Esther the queen had enjoined them, and as they had decreed for themselves and for their seed, the matters of the fastings and their cry. **32** And the decree of Esther confirmed these matters of Purim; and it was written in the book.

SABBATH - *Genesis 2:1-3* **1** Thus the heavens and the earth were finished, and all the host of them. **2** And on the seventh day God ended his work which he had made; and he rested on the seventh day from all his work which he had made. 3 And God blessed the seventh day, and sanctified it: because that in it he had rested from all his work which God created and made.

Exodus 16:23, 20:8-11, 31:14-17 **16:23** And he said unto them, This *is that* which the Lord hath said, Tomorrow *is* the rest of the holy sabbath unto the Lord: bake *that* which ye will bake *today*, and seethe that ye will seethe; and that which remaineth over lay up for you to be kept until the morning. ***20:8-11*** **8** Remember the sabbath day, to keep it holy. **9** Six days shalt thou labor, and do all thy work: **10** but the seventh day *is* the sabbath of the Lord thy God: *in it* thou shalt not do any work, thou, nor thy son, nor thy daughter, thy manservant, nor thy maidservant, nor thy cattle, nor thy stranger that *is* within thy gates: **11** for *in* six days the Lord made heaven and earth, the sea, and all that in them *is*, and rested the seventh day: wherefore the Lord blessed the sabbath day, and hallowed it. ***31:14-17*** **14** And Moses was wroth with the officers of the host, *with* the captains over thousands, and captains over hundreds, which came from the battle. **15** And Moses said unto them, Have ye saved all the women alive? **16** Behold, these caused the children of Israel, through the counsel of Ba´laam, to commit trespass against the Lord in the matter of Pe´or, and there was a plague among the congregation of the Lord. **17** Now therefore kill every male among the little ones, and kill every woman that hath known man by lying with him.

Leviticus 23:3, 24:5-9 **23:3** Six days shall work be done: but the seventh day *is* the sabbath of rest, a holy convocation; ye shall do no work *therein*: it *is* the sabbath of the Lord in all your dwellings. ***24:5-9*** **5** And thou shalt take fine flour, and bake twelve cakes thereof: two tenth deals shall be in one cake. **6** And thou shalt set them in two rows, six on a row, upon the pure table before the Lord. **7** And thou shalt put pure frankincense upon *each* row, that it may be on the bread for a memorial, *even* an offering made by fire unto the Lord. **8** Every sabbath he shall set it in order before the Lord continually, *being taken* from the children of Israel by an everlasting covenant. **9** And it shall be Aaron's and his sons'; and they shall eat it in the holy place: for it *is* most holy unto him of the offerings of the Lord made by fire by a perpetual statute.

<u>Numbers 15:32-36, 28:9, 10</u> **The Stoning of a Sabbath Breaker**

32 And while the children of Israel were in the wilderness, they found a man that gathered sticks upon the sabbath day. **33** And they that found him gathering sticks brought him unto Moses and Aaron, and unto all the congregation. **34** And they put him in ward, because it was not declared what should be done to him. **35** And the Lord said unto Moses, The man shall be surely put to death: all the congregation shall stone him with stones without the camp. **36** And all the congregation brought him without the camp, and stoned him with stones, and he died; as the Lord commanded Moses.

28:9, 10 **9** And on the sabbath day two lambs of the first year without spot, and two tenth deals of flour *for* a meat offering, mingled with oil, and the drink offering thereof: **10** *this is* the burnt offering of every sabbath, beside the continual burnt offering, and his drink offering.

Deuteronomy 5:12-15 **12** Keep the sabbath day to sanctify it, as the Lord thy God hath commanded thee. **13** Six days thou shalt labor, and do all thy work: **14** but the seventh day *is* the sabbath of the Lord thy God: *in it* thou shalt not do any work, thou, nor thy son, nor thy daughter, nor thy manservant, nor thy maidservant, nor thine ox, nor thine ass, nor any of thy cattle, nor thy stranger that *is* within thy gates; that thy manservant and thy maidservant may rest as well as thou. **15** And remember that thou wast a servant in the land of Egypt, and *that* the Lord thy God brought thee out thence through a mighty hand and by a stretched out arm: therefore the Lord thy God commanded thee to keep the sabbath day.

Nehemiah 10:31, 13:15-22 **10:31** and *if* the people of the land bring ware or any victuals on the sabbath day to sell, *that* we would not buy it of them on the sabbath, or on the holy day: and *that* we would leave the seventh year, and the exaction of every debt.

_13:15-22_ **15** In those days saw I in Judah *some* treading winepresses on the sabbath, and bringing in sheaves, and lading asses; as also wine, grapes, and figs, and all *manner of* burdens, which they brought into Jerusalem on the sabbath day: and I testified *against them* in the day wherein they sold victuals. **16** There dwelt men of Tyre also therein, which brought fish, and all manner of ware, and sold on the sabbath unto the children of Judah, and in Jerusalem. **17** Then I contended with the nobles of Judah, and said unto them, What evil thing *is* this that ye do, and profane the sabbath day? **18** Did not your fathers thus, and did not our God bring all this evil upon us, and upon this city? yet ye bring more wrath upon Israel by profaning the sabbath.

19 And it came to pass, that when the gates of Jerusalem began to be dark before the sabbath, I commanded that the gates should be shut, and charged that they should not be opened till after the sabbath: and *some* of my servants set I at the gates, *that* there should no burden be brought in on the sabbath day. **20** So the merchants and sellers of all kind of ware lodged without Jerusalem once or twice. **21** Then I testified against them, and said unto them, Why lodge ye about the wall? if ye do *so* again, I will lay hands on you. From that time forth came they no *more* on the sabbath. **22** And I commanded the Levites, that they should cleanse themselves, and *that* they should come *and* keep the gates, to sanctify the sabbath day. Remember me, O my God, *concerning* this also, and spare me according to the greatness of thy mercy.

Ezekiel 46:3 Likewise the people of the land shall worship at the door of this gate before the Lord in the sabbaths and in the new moons.

Amos 8:5 saying, When will the new moon be gone, that we may sell corn? and the sabbath, that we may set forth wheat, making the ephah small, and the shekel great, and falsifying the balances by deceit?

Mark 2:23-28 The Disciples Pluck Grain on the Sabbath

(Matthew 12.1-8;Luke 6.1-5)

23 And it came to pass, that he went through the corn fields on the sabbath day; and his disciples began, as they went, to pluck the ears of corn. **24** And the Pharisees said unto him, Behold, why do they on the sabbath day that which is not lawful? **25** And he said unto them, Have ye never read what David did, when he had need, and was a hungered, he, and they that were with him? **26** How he went into the house of God in the days of Abi´athar the high priest, and did eat the showbread, which is not lawful to eat but for the priests, and gave also to them which were with him? **27** And he said unto them, The sabbath was made for man, and not man for the sabbath: **28** therefore the Son of man is Lord also of the sabbath.

<u>Luke 13:14-16, 14:3-5</u> **14** And the ruler of the synagogue answered with indignation, because that Jesus had healed on the sabbath day, and said unto the people, There are six days in which men ought to work: in them therefore come and be healed, and not on the sabbath day. **15** The Lord then answered him, and said, *Thou* hypocrite, doth not each one of you on the sabbath loose his ox or *his* ass from the stall, and lead *him* away to watering? **16** And ought not this woman, being a daughter of Abraham, whom Satan hath bound, lo, these eighteen years, be loosed from this bond on the sabbath day? *14:3-5* **3** And Jesus answering spake unto the lawyers and Pharisees, saying, Is it lawful to heal on the sabbath day? **4** And they held their peace. And he took *him,* and healed him, and let him go; **5** and answered them, saying, Which of you shall have an ass or an ox fallen into a pit, and will not straightway pull him out on the sabbath day?

John 5:8-10 8 Jesus saith unto him, Rise, take up thy bed, and walk. 9 And immediately the man was made whole, and took up his bed, and walked: and on the same day was the sabbath.

10 The Jews therefore said unto him that was cured, It is the sabbath day: it is not lawful for thee to carry *thy* bed.

The Sabbath day is Saturday, not Sunday.

SABBATICAL YEAR – *Exodus 21:2-6, 23:10, 11* 2 If thou buy a Hebrew servant, six years he shall serve: and in the seventh he shall go out free for nothing. 3 If he came in by himself, he shall go out by himself: if he were married, then his wife shall go out with him. 4 If his master have given him a wife, and she have borne him sons or daughters; the wife and her children shall be her master's, and he shall go out by himself. 5 And if the servant shall plainly say, I love my master, my wife, and my children; I will not go out free: 6 then his master shall bring him unto the judges; he shall also bring him to the door, or unto the doorpost; and his master shall bore his ear through with an awl; and he shall serve him for ever. *23:10, 11* 10 And six years thou shalt sow thy land, and shalt gather in the fruits thereof: 11 but the seventh *year* thou shalt let it rest and lie still; that the poor of thy people may eat: and what they leave the beasts of the field shall eat. In like manner thou shalt deal with thy vineyard, *and* with thy oliveyard.

Leviticus 25:1-7 **1** And the Lord spake unto Moses in mount Si´nai, saying, **2** Speak unto the children of Israel, and say unto them, When ye come into the land which I give you, then shall the land keep a sabbath unto the Lord. **3** Six years thou shalt sow thy field, and six years thou shalt prune thy vineyard, and gather in the fruit thereof; **4** but in the seventh year shall be a sabbath of rest unto the land, a sabbath for the Lord: thou shalt neither sow thy field, nor prune thy vineyard. **5** That which groweth of its own accord of thy harvest thou shalt not reap, neither gather the grapes of thy vine undressed: *for* it is a year of rest unto the land. **6** And the sabbath of the land shall be meat for you; for thee, and for thy servant, and for thy maid, and for thy hired servant, and for thy stranger that sojourneth with thee, **7** and for thy cattle, and for the beast that *are* in thy land, shall all the increase thereof be meat.

Deuteronomy 15:1-14 The Year of Release

1 At the end of *every* seven years thou shalt make a release. **2** And this *is* the manner of the release: Every creditor that lendeth *aught* unto his neighbor shall release *it*; he shall not exact *it* of his neighbor, or of his brother; because it is called the Lord's release. **3** Of a foreigner thou mayest exact *it again*: but *that* which is thine with thy brother thine hand shall release; **4** save when there shall be no poor among you; for the Lord shall greatly bless thee in the land which the Lord thy God giveth thee *for* an inheritance to possess it: **5** only if thou carefully hearken unto the voice of the Lord thy God, to observe to do all these commandments which I command thee this day. **6** For the Lord thy God blesseth thee, as he promised thee: and thou shalt lend unto many nations, but thou shalt not borrow; and thou shalt reign over many nations, but they shall not reign over thee.

Lending to the Poor

7 If there be among you a poor man of one of thy brethren within any of thy gates in thy land which the Lord thy God giveth thee, thou shalt not harden thine heart, nor shut thine hand from thy poor brother: **8** but thou shalt open thine hand wide unto him, and shalt surely lend him sufficient for his need, *in that* which he wanteth. **9** Beware that there be not a thought in thy wicked heart, saying, The seventh year, the year of release, is at hand; and thine eye be evil against thy poor brother, and thou givest him nought; and he cry unto the Lord against thee, and it be sin unto thee. **10** Thou shalt surely give him, and thine heart shall not be grieved when thou givest unto him: because that for this thing the Lord thy God shall bless thee in all thy works, and in all that thou puttest thine hand unto. **11** For the poor shall never cease out of the land: therefore I command thee, saying, Thou shalt open thine hand wide unto thy brother, to thy poor, and to thy needy, in thy land.

The Treatment of Servants

(Exodus 21.1-11)

12 *And* if thy brother, a Hebrew man, or a Hebrew woman, be sold unto thee, and serve thee six years; then in the seventh year thou shalt let him go free from thee. **13** And when thou sendest him out free from thee, thou shalt not let him go away empty: **14** thou shalt furnish him liberally out of thy flock, and out of thy floor, and out of thy winepress: *of that* wherewith the Lord thy God hath blessed thee thou shalt give unto him.

31:10, 13 **10** And Moses commanded them, saying, At the end of *every* seven years, in the solemnity of the year of release, in the feast of tabernacles, **13** and *that* their children, which have not known *any thing*, may hear, and learn to fear the Lord your God, as long as ye live in the land whither ye go over Jordan to possess it.

<u>*2 Chronicles 36:21*</u> to fulfil the word of the Lord by the mouth of Jeremiah, until the land had enjoyed her sabbaths: *for* as long as she lay desolate she kept sabbath, to fulfil threescore and ten years.

<u>*Nehemiah 10:31*</u> and *if* the people of the land bring ware or any victuals on the sabbath day to sell, *that* we would not buy it of them on the sabbath, or on the holy day: and *that* we would leave the seventh year, and the exaction of every debt.

SHEWBREAD – <u>*Exodus 25:30, 35:13, 39:36*</u> **25:30** And thou shalt set upon the table showbread before me always. **35:13** the table, and his staves, and all his vessels, and the showbread; **39:36** the table, *and* all the vessels thereof, and the showbread;

SIN OFFERING – <u>*Leviticus 4:1-35*</u> Sin Offerings

1 And the Lord spake unto Moses, saying, **2** Speak unto the children of Israel, saying, If a soul shall sin through ignorance against any of the commandments of the Lord *concerning things* which ought not to be done, and shall do against any of them: **3** if the priest that is anointed do sin according to the sin of the people; then let him bring for his sin, which he hath sinned, a young bullock without blemish unto the Lord for a sin offering. **4** And he shall bring the bullock unto the door of the tabernacle of the congregation before the Lord; and shall lay his hand upon the bullock's head, and kill the bullock before the Lord. **5** And the priest that is anointed shall take of the bullock's blood, and bring it to the tabernacle of the congregation: **6** and the priest shall dip his finger in the blood, and sprinkle of the blood seven times before the Lord, before the veil of the sanctuary. **7** And the priest shall put *some* of the blood upon the horns of the altar of sweet incense before the Lord, which *is* in the tabernacle of the congregation; and shall pour all the blood of the bullock at the bottom of the altar of the burnt offering, which *is at* the door of the tabernacle of the congregation. **8** And he shall take off from it all the fat of the bullock for the sin offering; the fat that covereth the inwards, and all the fat that *is* upon the inwards, **9** and the two kidneys, and the fat that *is* upon them, which *is* by the flanks, and the caul above the liver, with the kidneys, it shall he take away, **10** as it was taken off from the bullock of the sacrifice of peace offerings: and the priest shall burn them upon the altar of the burnt offering. **11** And the skin of the bullock, and all his flesh, with his head, and with his legs, and his inwards, and his dung, **12**

even the whole bullock shall he carry forth without the camp unto a clean place, where the ashes are poured out, and burn him on the wood with fire: where the ashes are poured out shall he be burnt.

13 And if the whole congregation of Israel sin through ignorance, and the thing be hid from the eyes of the assembly, and they have done *somewhat against* any of the commandments of the Lord *concerning things* which should not be done, and are guilty; **14** when the sin, which they have sinned against it, is known, then the congregation shall offer a young bullock for the sin, and bring him before the tabernacle of the congregation. **15** And the elders of the congregation shall lay their hands upon the head of the bullock before the Lord; and the bullock shall be killed before the Lord. **16** And the priest that is anointed shall bring of the bullock's blood to the tabernacle of the congregation: **17** and the priest shall dip his finger *in some* of the blood, and sprinkle *it* seven times before the Lord, *even* before the veil. **18** And he shall put *some* of the blood upon the horns of the altar which *is* before the Lord, that *is* in the tabernacle of the congregation, and shall pour out all the blood at the bottom of the altar of the burnt offering, which *is at* the door of the tabernacle of the congregation. **19** And he shall take all his fat from him, and burn *it* upon the altar. **20** And he shall do with the bullock as he did with the bullock for a sin offering, so shall he do with this: and the priest shall make an atonement for them, and it shall be forgiven them. **21** And he shall carry forth the bullock without the camp, and burn him as he burned the first bullock: it *is* a sin offering for the congregation.

22 When a ruler hath sinned, and done *somewhat* through ignorance *against* any of the commandments of the Lord his God *concerning things* which should not be done, and is guilty; **23** or if his sin, wherein he hath sinned, come to his knowledge; he shall bring his offering, a kid of the goats, a male without blemish: **24** and he shall lay his hand upon the head of the goat, and kill it in the place where they kill the burnt offering before the Lord: it *is* a sin offering. **25** And the priest shall take of the blood of the sin offering with his finger, and put *it* upon the horns of the altar of burnt offering, and shall pour out his blood at the bottom of the altar of burnt offering. **26** And he shall burn all his fat upon the altar, as the fat of the sacrifice of peace offerings: and the priest shall make an atonement for him as concerning his sin, and it shall be forgiven him.

27 And if any one of the common people sin through ignorance, while he doeth *somewhat against* any of the commandments of the Lord *concerning things* which ought not to be done, and be guilty; **28** or if his sin, which he hath sinned, come to his knowledge; then he shall bring his offering, a kid of the goats, a female without blemish, for his sin which he hath sinned. **29** And he shall lay his hand upon the head of the sin offering, and slay the sin offering in the place of the burnt offering. **30** And the priest shall take of the blood thereof with his finger, and put *it* upon the horns of the altar of burnt offering, and shall pour out all the blood thereof at the bottom of the altar. **31** And he shall take away all the fat thereof, as the fat is taken away from off the sacrifice of peace offerings; and the priest shall burn *it* upon the altar for a sweet savor unto the Lord; and the priest shall make an atonement for him, and it shall be forgiven him.

32 And if he bring a lamb for a sin offering, he shall bring it a female without blemish. **33** And he shall lay his hand upon the head of the sin offering, and slay it for a sin offering in the place where they kill the burnt offering. **34** And the priest shall take of the blood of the sin offering with his finger, and put *it* upon the horns of the altar of burnt offering, and shall pour out all the blood thereof at the bottom of the altar: **35** and he shall take away all the fat thereof, as the fat of the lamb is taken away from the sacrifice of the peace offerings; and the priest shall burn them upon the altar, according to the offerings made by fire unto the Lord: and the priest shall make an atonement for his sin that he hath committed, and it <u>shall be forgiven him.</u>

<u>*Numbers 6:11*</u> and the priest shall offer the one for a sin offering, and the other for a burnt offering, and make an atonement for him, for that he sinned by the dead, and shall hallow his head that same day.

SORCERY - <u>*Exodus 22:18*</u> Thou shalt not suffer a witch to live.

<u>*Leviticus 20:27*</u> A man also or woman that hath a familiar spirit, or that is a wizard, shall surely be put to death: they shall stone them with stones; their blood *shall be* upon them.

TEN COMMANDMENTS – Exodus 20:1-17 The Ten Commandments

(Deuteronomy 5.1-21)

1 And God spake all these words, saying,

2 I *am* the Lord thy God, which have brought thee out of the land of Egypt, out of the house of bondage.

3 Thou shalt have no other gods before me.

4 Thou shalt not make unto thee any graven image, or any likeness *of any thing* that *is* in heaven above, or that *is* in the earth beneath, or that *is* in the water under the earth: 5 thou shalt not bow down thyself to them, nor serve them: for I the Lord thy God *am* a jealous God, visiting the iniquity of the fathers upon the children unto the third and fourth *generation* of them that hate me; 6 and showing mercy unto thousands of them that love me, and keep my commandments.

7 Thou shalt not take the name of the Lord thy God in vain: for the Lord will not hold him guiltless that taketh his name in vain.

8 Remember the sabbath day, to keep it holy. **9** Six days shalt thou labor, and do all thy work: **10** but the seventh day *is* the sabbath of the Lord thy God: *in it* thou shalt not do any work, thou, nor thy son, nor thy daughter, thy manservant, nor thy maidservant, nor thy cattle, nor thy stranger that *is* within thy gates: **11** for *in* six days the Lord made heaven and earth, the sea, and all that in them *is*, and rested the seventh day: wherefore the Lord blessed the sabbath day, and hallowed it.

12 Honor thy father and thy mother: that thy days may be long upon the land which the Lord thy God giveth thee.

13 Thou shalt not kill.

14 Thou shalt not commit adultery.

15 Thou shalt not steal.

16 Thou shalt not bear false witness against thy neighbor.

17 Thou shalt not covet thy neighbor's house, thou shalt not covet thy neighbor's wife, nor his manservant, nor his maidservant, nor his ox, nor his ass, nor any thing that *is* thy neighbor's.

THANK OFFERINGS – *2 Chronicles 29:31* Then Hezeki´ah answered and said, Now ye have consecrated yourselves unto the Lord, come near and bring sacrifices and thank offerings into the house of the Lord. And the congregation brought in sacrifices and thank offerings; and as many as were of a free heart, burnt offerings.

TITHES – *Genesis 14:20, 28:20-22* 14:20 and blessed be the most high God,

which hath delivered thine enemies into thy hand.

And he gave him tithes of all.

28:20-22 20 And Jacob vowed a vow, saying, If God will be with me, and will keep me in this way that I go, and will give me bread to eat, and raiment to put on, 21 so that I come again to my father's house in peace; then shall the Lord be my God: 22 and this stone, which I have set *for* a pillar, shall be God's house: and of all that thou shalt give me I will surely give the tenth unto thee.

Leviticus 27:30-33 30 And all the tithe of the land, *whether* of the seed of the land, *or* of the fruit of the tree, *is* the Lord's: *it is* holy unto the Lord. 31 And if a man will at all redeem *aught* of his tithes, he shall add thereto the fifth *part* thereof. 32 And concerning the tithe of the herd, or of the flock, *even* of whatsoever passeth under the rod, the tenth shall be holy unto the Lord. 33 He shall not search whether it be good or bad, neither shall he change it: and if he change it at all, then both it and the change thereof shall be holy; it shall not be redeemed.

Deuteronomy 14:22-27 The Law of the Tithe

22 Thou shalt truly tithe all the increase of thy seed, that the field bringeth forth year by year. 23 And

thou shalt eat before the Lord thy God, in the place which he shall choose to place his name there, the tithe of thy corn, of thy wine, and of thine oil, and the firstlings of thy herds and of thy flocks; that thou mayest learn to fear the Lord thy God always. **24** And if the way be too long for thee, so that thou art not able to carry it; *or* if the place be too far from thee, which the Lord thy God shall choose to set his name there, when the Lord thy God hath blessed thee: **25** then shalt thou turn *it* into money, and bind up the money in thine hand, and shalt go unto the place which the Lord thy God shall choose: **26** and thou shalt bestow that money for whatsoever thy soul lusteth after, for oxen, or for sheep, or for wine, or for strong drink, or for whatsoever thy soul desireth: and thou shalt eat there before the Lord thy God, and thou shalt rejoice, thou, and thine household, **27** and the Levite that *is* within thy gates; thou shalt not forsake him: for he hath no part nor inheritance with thee.

2 Chronicles 31:4-12 **4** Moreover he commanded the people that dwelt in Jerusalem to give the portion of the priests and the Levites, that they might be encouraged in the law of the Lord. **5** And as soon as the commandment came abroad, the children of Israel brought in abundance the firstfruits of corn, wine, and oil, and honey, and of all the increase of the field; and the tithe of all *things* brought they in abundantly. **6** And *concerning* the children of Israel and Judah, that dwelt in the cities of Judah, they also brought in the tithe of oxen and sheep, and the tithe of holy things which were consecrated unto the Lord their God, and laid *them* by heaps. **7** In the third month they began to lay the foundation of the heaps, and finished *them* in the seventh month. **8** And when Hezeki´ah and the princes came and saw the heaps, they blessed the Lord, and his people Israel. **9** Then Hezeki´ah questioned with the priests and the Levites concerning the heaps. **10** And Azari´ah the chief priest of the house of Zadok answered him, and said, Since *the people* began to bring the offerings into the house of the Lord, we have had enough to eat, and have left plenty: for the Lord hath blessed his people; and that which is left *is* this great store.

11 Then Hezeki´ah commanded to prepare chambers in the house of the Lord; and they prepared *them*, **12** and brought in the offerings and the tithes and the dedicated *things* faithfully: over which Conani´ah the Levite *was* ruler, and Shim´e-i his brother *was* the next.

<u>Malachi 3:8-11</u> 8 Will a man rob God? Yet ye have robbed me. But ye say, Wherein have we robbed thee? In tithes and offerings. 9Ye *are* cursed with a curse: for ye have robbed me, *even* this whole nation. **10** Bring ye all the tithes into the storehouse, that there may be meat in mine house, and prove me now herewith, saith the Lord of hosts, if I will not open you the windows of heaven, and pour you out a blessing, that *there shall* not *be room* enough *to receive it.* **11** And I will rebuke the devourer for your sakes, and he shall not destroy the fruits of your ground; neither shall your vine cast her fruit before the time in the field, saith the Lord of hosts.

Matthew 23:23 Woe unto you, scribes and Pharisees, hypocrites! for ye pay tithe of mint and anise and cummin, and have omitted the weightier *matters* of the law, judgment, mercy, and faith: these ought ye to have done, and not to leave the other undone.

TITHES OF ALMS AND CHARITY –

Deuteronomy 14:28, 29, 26:12-15 **14:28** At the end of three years thou shalt bring forth all the tithe of thine increase the same year, and shalt lay *it* up within thy gates: **29** and the Levite, (because he hath no part nor inheritance with thee,) and the stranger, and the fatherless, and the widow, which *are* within thy gates, shall come, and shall eat and be satisfied; that the Lord thy God may bless thee in all the work of thine hand which thou doest. *26:12-15* **12** When thou hast made an end of tithing all the tithes of thine increase the third year, *which is* the year of tithing, and hast given *it* unto the Levite, the stranger, the fatherless, and the widow, that they may eat within thy gates, and be filled; **13** then thou shalt say before the Lord thy God, I have brought away the hallowed things out of *mine* house, and also have given them unto the Levite, and unto the stranger, to the fatherless, and to the widow, according to all thy commandments which thou hast commanded me: I have not transgressed thy commandments, neither have I forgotten *them*: **14** I have not eaten thereof in my mourning, neither have I taken away *aught* thereof for *any* unclean *use*, nor given *aught* thereof for the dead: *but* I have hearkened to the voice of the Lord my

God, *and* have done according to all that thou hast commanded me.

TITHE OF A TITHE – *Numbers 18:21, 26-28*

21 And, behold, I have given the children of Levi all the tenth in Israel for an inheritance, for their service which they serve, *even* the service of the tabernacle of the congregation. **26-28 26** Thus speak unto the Levites, and say unto them, When ye take of the children of Israel the tithes which I have given you from them for your inheritance, then ye shall offer up a heave offering of it for the Lord, *even* a tenth *part* of the tithe. **27** And *this* your heave offering shall be reckoned unto you, as though *it were* the corn of the threshingfloor, and as the fulness of the winepress. **28** Thus ye also shall offer a heave offering unto the Lord of all your tithes, which ye receive of the children of Israel; and ye shall give thereof the Lord's heave offering to Aaron the priest.

TRESPASS OFFERING – *Leviticus 5:1-19*

1 And if a soul sin, and hear the voice of swearing, and *is* a witness, whether he hath seen or known *of it*; if he do not utter *it*, then he shall bear his iniquity. **2** Or if a soul touch any unclean thing, whether *it be* a carcass of an unclean beast, or a carcass of unclean cattle, or the carcass of unclean creeping things, and *if* it be hidden from him; he also shall be unclean, and guilty. **3** Or if he touch the uncleanness of man, whatsoever uncleanness *it be* that a man shall be defiled withal, and it be hid from him; when he knoweth *of it*, then he shall be guilty. **4** Or if a soul swear, pronouncing with *his* lips to do evil, or to do good, whatsoever *it be* that a man shall pronounce with an oath, and it be hid from him; when he knoweth *of it*, then he shall be guilty in one of these. 5 And it shall be, when he shall be guilty in one of these *things*, that he shall confess that he hath sinned in that *thing*: 6 and he shall bring his trespass offering unto the Lord for his sin which he hath sinned, a female from the flock, a lamb, or a kid of the goats, for a sin offering; and the priest shall make an atonement for him concerning his sin.

7 And if he be not able to bring a lamb, then he shall bring for his trespass, which he hath committed, two turtledoves, or two young pigeons, unto the Lord; one for a sin offering, and the other for a burnt offering. 8 And he shall bring them unto the priest, who shall offer *that* which *is* for the sin offering first, and wring off his head from his neck, but shall not divide *it* asunder: 9 and he shall sprinkle of the blood of the sin offering upon the side of the altar; and the rest of the blood shall be wrung out at the bottom of the altar: it *is* a sin offering. 10 And he shall offer the second *for* a burnt offering, according to the manner: and the priest shall make an atonement for him for his sin which he hath sinned, and it shall be forgiven him.

11 But if he be not able to bring two turtledoves, or two young pigeons, then he that sinned shall bring for his offering the tenth part of an ephah of fine flour for a sin offering; he shall put no oil upon it, neither shall he put *any* frankincense thereon: for it *is* a sin offering. 12 Then shall he bring it to the priest, and the priest shall take his handful of it, *even* a memorial thereof, and burn *it* on the altar, according to the offerings made by fire unto

the Lord: it *is* a sin offering. **13** And the priest shall make an atonement for him as touching his sin that he hath sinned in one of these, and it shall be forgiven him: and *the remnant* shall be the priest's, as a meat offering.

Trespass Offerings

14 And the Lord spake unto Moses, saying, **15** If a soul commit a trespass, and sin through ignorance, in the holy things of the Lord; then he shall bring for his trespass unto the Lord a ram without blemish out of the flocks, with thy estimation by shekels of silver, after the shekel of the sanctuary, for a trespass offering: **16** and he shall make amends for the harm that he hath done in the holy thing, and shall add the fifth part thereto, and give it unto the priest: and the priest shall make an atonement for him with the ram of the trespass offering, and it shall be forgiven him.

17 And if a soul sin, and commit any of these things which are forbidden to be done by the commandments of the Lord; though he wist *it* not, yet is he guilty, and shall bear his iniquity. **18** And he shall bring a ram without blemish out of the flock, with thy estimation, for a trespass offering, unto the priest: and the priest shall make an atonement for him concerning his ignorance wherein he erred and wist *it* not, and it shall be forgiven him. **19** It *is* a trespass offering: he hath certainly trespassed against the Lord.

UNCLEAN ANIMALS – *Leviticus 11:3, 4, 9-31*

11:3 Whatsoever parteth the hoof, and is cloven-footed, *and* cheweth the cud, among the beasts, that shall ye eat. **4** Nevertheless, these shall ye not eat of them that chew the cud, or of them that divide the hoof: *as* the camel, because he cheweth the cud, but divideth not the hoof; he *is* unclean unto you. **9-31** These shall ye eat of all that *are* in the waters: whatsoever hath fins and scales in the waters, in the seas, and in the rivers, them shall ye eat. **10** And all that have not fins and scales in the seas, and in the rivers, of all that move in the waters, and of any living thing which *is* in the waters, they *shall be* an abomination unto you: **11** they shall be even an abomination unto you; ye shall not eat of their flesh, but ye shall have their carcasses in abomination. **12** Whatsoever hath no fins nor scales in the waters, that *shall be* an abomination unto you.

13 And these *are they which* ye shall have in abomination among the fowls; they shall not be eaten, they *are* an abomination: the eagle, and the ossifrage, and the osprey, **14** and the vulture, and the kite after his kind; **15** every raven after his kind; **16** and the owl, and the nighthawk, and the cuckoo, and the hawk after his kind, **17** and the little owl, and the cormorant, and the great owl, **18** and the swan, and the pelican, and the gier-eagle, **19** and the stork, the heron after her kind, and the lapwing, and the bat.

20 All fowls that creep, going upon *all* four, *shall be* an abomination unto you. **21** Yet these may ye eat of every flying creeping thing that goeth upon *all* four, which have legs above their feet, to leap withal upon the earth; **22** *even* these of them ye may eat; the locust after his kind, and the bald locust after his kind, and the beetle after his kind, and the grasshopper after his kind. **23** But all *other* flying creeping things, which have four feet, *shall be* an abomination unto you.

24 And for these ye shall be unclean: whosoever toucheth the carcass of them shall be unclean until the even. **25** And whosoever beareth *aught* of the carcass of them shall wash his clothes, and be unclean until the even. **26** *The carcasses* of every beast which divideth the hoof, and *is* not cloven-footed, nor cheweth the cud, *are* unclean unto you: every one that toucheth them shall be unclean. **27** And whatsoever goeth upon his paws, among all manner of beasts that go on *all* four, those *are* unclean unto you: whoso toucheth their carcass shall be unclean until the even. **28** And he that beareth the carcass of them shall wash his clothes, and be unclean until the even: they *are* unclean unto you.

29 These also *shall be* unclean unto you among the creeping things that creep upon the earth; the weasel, and the mouse, and the tortoise after his kind, **30** and the ferret, and the chameleon, and the lizard, and the snail, and the mole. **31** These *are* unclean to you among all that creep: whosoever doth touch them, when they be dead, shall be unclean until the even.

VOLUNTARY OFFERING – *Leviticus 7:16* But if the sacrifice of his offering *be* a vow, or a voluntary offering, it shall be eaten the same day that he offereth his sacrifice; and on the morrow also the remainder of it shall be eaten:

WATER OFFERING – *1 Samuel 7:6* And they gathered together to Mizpeh, and drew water, and poured *it* out before the Lord, and fasted on that day, and said there, We have sinned against the Lord. And Samuel judged the children of Israel in Mizpeh.

2 Samuel 23:16 And the three mighty men brake through the host of the Philistines, and drew water out of the well of Bethlehem, that *was* by the gate, and took *it*, and brought *it* to David: nevertheless he would not drink thereof, but poured it out unto the Lord

WATER OF SEPARATION – *Numbers 19:1-22*
The Purification of the Unclean

1 And the Lord spake unto Moses and unto Aaron, saying, 2 This *is* the ordinance of the law which the Lord hath commanded, saying, Speak unto the children of Israel, that they bring thee a red heifer without spot, wherein *is* no blemish, *and* upon which never came yoke. 3 And ye shall give her unto Ele-a´zar the priest, that he may bring her forth without the camp, and *one* shall slay her before his face: 4 and Ele-a´zar the priest shall take of her blood with his finger, and sprinkle of her blood directly before the tabernacle of the congregation seven times. 5 And *one* shall burn the heifer in his sight; her skin, and her flesh, and her blood, with her dung, shall he burn: 6 and the priest shall take cedar wood, and hyssop, and scarlet, and cast *it* into the midst of the burning of the heifer. 7 Then the priest shall wash his clothes, and he shall bathe his flesh in water, and afterward he shall come into the camp, and the priest shall be unclean until the even. 8 And he that burneth her shall wash his clothes in water, and

bathe his flesh in water, and shall be unclean until the even. **9** And a man *that is* clean shall gather up the ashes of the heifer, and lay *them* up without the camp in a clean place, and it shall be kept for the congregation of the children of Israel for a water of separation: it *is* a purification for sin. **10** And he that gathereth the ashes of the heifer shall wash his clothes, and be unclean until the even: and it shall be unto the children of Israel, and unto the stranger that sojourneth among them, for a statute for ever.

11 He that toucheth the dead body of any man shall be unclean seven days. **12** He shall purify himself with it on the third day, and on the seventh day he shall be clean: but if he purify not himself the third day, then the seventh day he shall not be clean. **13** Whosoever toucheth the dead body of any man that is dead, and purifieth not himself, defileth the tabernacle of the Lord; and that soul shall be cut off from Israel: because the water of separation was not sprinkled upon him, he shall be unclean; his uncleanness *is* yet upon him.

14 This *is* the law, when a man dieth in a tent: all that come into the tent, and all that *is* in the tent, shall be unclean seven days. **15** And every open vessel, which hath no covering bound upon it, *is* unclean. **16** And whosoever toucheth one that is slain with a sword in the open fields, or a dead body, or a bone of a man, or a grave, shall be unclean seven days. **17** And for an unclean *person* they shall take of the ashes of the burnt heifer of purification for sin, and running water shall be put thereto in a vessel: 18and a clean person shall take hyssop, and dip *it* in the water, and sprinkle *it* upon the tent, and upon all the vessels, and upon the persons that were there, and upon him that touched a bone, or one slain, or one dead, or a grave: 19and the clean *person* shall sprinkle upon the unclean on the third day, and on the seventh day: and on the seventh day he shall purify himself, and wash his clothes, and bathe himself in water, and shall be clean at even.

20 But the man that shall be unclean, and shall not purify himself, that soul shall be cut off from among the congregation, because he hath defiled the sanctuary of the Lord: the water of separation hath not been sprinkled upon him; he *is* unclean. **21** And it shall be a perpetual statute unto them, that he that sprinkleth the water of separation shall wash his clothes; and he that toucheth the water of separation shall be unclean until even. **22** And whatsoever the unclean *person* toucheth shall be unclean; and the soul that toucheth *it* shall be unclean until even.

WAVE OFFERING – *Exodus 29:26, 27* **26** And thou shalt take the breast of the ram of Aaron's consecration, and wave it *for* a wave offering before the Lord: and it shall be thy part. **27** And thou shalt sanctify the breast of the wave offering, and the shoulder of the heave offering, which is waved, and which is heaved up, of the ram of the consecration, *even* of *that* which *is* for Aaron, and of *that* which is for his sons:

Leviticus 23:10, 11 **10** Speak unto the children of Israel, and say unto them, When ye be come into the land which I give unto you, and shall reap the harvest thereof, then ye shall bring a sheaf of the firstfruits of your harvest unto the priest: **11** and he shall wave the sheaf before the Lord, to be accepted for you: on the morrow after the sabbath the priest shall wave it.

WHOLE BURNT OFFERING – *Deuteronomy 33:10* They shall teach Jacob thy judgments,

and Israel thy law:

they shall put incense before thee,

and whole burnt sacrifice upon thine altar.

WORSHIP – *Acts 20:7* And upon the first *day* of the week, when the disciples came together to break bread, Paul preached unto them, ready to depart on the morrow; and continued his speech until midnight.

Colossians 3:16 Let the word of Christ dwell in you richly in all wisdom; teaching and admonishing one another in psalms and hymns and spiritual songs, singing with grace in your hearts to the Lord.

1 Thessalonians 5:27 I charge you by the Lord, that this epistle be read unto all the holy brethren.

THE POINT OF SIGNIFICANCE:

Not once did you see anything that relates, mentions, implies, or suggests for lack of better terms, that we celebrate the pagan holidays (CHRISTMAS, HALLOWEEN, EASTER/ISHTAR, WORLD FAIR OPENING

DAYS, etc.) and/or observances, which are nothing more than Events in Capitalism or Nimrod and Sol Invictus worship. Imagine the Grace, Mercy, and Love from God the LORD have it we follow Exodus, Leviticus, and Deuteronomy. It would be a better feeling knowing that you are celebrating for just reasons.

SOCIAL SECURITY LAWS

CARE OF BLIND – *Leviticus 19:14* Thou shalt not curse the deaf, nor put a stumbling-block before the blind, but shalt fear thy God: I *am* the Lord.

Deuteronomy 27:18 Cursed *be* he that maketh the blind to wander out of the way:

Luke 14:13, 14 13 But when thou makest a feast, call the poor, the maimed, the lame, the blind: 14 and thou shalt be blessed; for they cannot recompense thee: for thou shalt be recompensed at the resurrection of the just.

CIVIL CODE: *BLIND* defined under 42 U.S.C. § 416i Disability; period of disability (1) (B) Blindness means central visual acuity of 20/200 or less in the better eye with the use of a correcting lens. An eye \which is accompanied by a limitation in the fields of vison such that the widest diameter of the visual field subtends an angle no greater than 20 degrees shall be considered for purposes of this paragraph as having a central visual acuity of 20/200 or less.

42 U.S.C. § 1395i-2a Hospital insurance benefits for disabled individuals who have exhausted other entitlement makes BLINDNESS eligible for hospital insurance benefits. § 1396-1 provides medical assistance through the States for the blind.

JOHN 9:25 "He answered and said, Whether he be a sinner or no, I know not: one thing I know, that, whereas I was blind, now I see."

SALE OF CHILDREN – *2 Kings 4:1-7* The Widow's Oil

1 Now there cried a certain woman of the wives of the sons of the prophets unto Eli´sha, saying, Thy servant my husband is dead; and thou knowest that thy servant did fear the Lord: and the creditor is come to take unto him my two sons to be bondmen. **2** And Eli´sha said unto her, What shall I do for thee? tell me, what hast thou in the house? And she said, Thine handmaid hath not any thing in the house, save a pot of oil. **3** Then he said, Go, borrow thee vessels abroad of all thy neighbors, *even* empty vessels; borrow not a few. **4** And when thou art come in, thou shalt shut the door upon thee and upon thy sons, and shalt pour out into all those vessels, and thou shalt set aside that which is full. **5** So she went from him, and shut the door upon her and upon her sons, who brought *the vessels* to her; and she poured out. **6** And it came to pass, when the vessels were full, that she said unto her son, Bring me yet a vessel. And he said unto her, *There is* not a vessel more. And the oil stayed. **7** Then she came and told the man of God. And he said, Go, sell the oil, and pay thy debt, and live thou and thy children of the rest.

QUESTION: Would signing a birth certificate registered to the State be selling our children into bondage with what information that there is on the matter of these bonds being sold on the stock market? Or, is the exposing, purchasing, and inundation of cartoon and commercial media, selling our children to corporations the better example? Research the material in the question to become familiar with the question being asked. This way, you'll see how this is related to LAW without getting too in depth about the topic.

DEAF - *Leviticus 19:14* Thou shalt not curse the deaf, nor put a stumbling-block before the blind, but shalt fear thy God: I *am* the Lord.

42 U.S.C. § 247b-4a observes the infant early detection of deafness, which is considered to be a communication disorder, through TECHNOLOGY and medical evaluation.

42 U.S.C. § 285m. Purpose of Institute The general purpose of the *National Institute on Deafness and Other Communication Disorders* is the conduct and support of research and training, the dissemination of health information, and other programs with respect to disorders of hearing and other communication processes, including diseases that affect hearing, balance, voice, speech, language, taste and smell.

Basically, the federal government is testing on our children and people without offering solutions that work but solutions that benefit SEVERAL DIFFERENT ORGANIZATIONS.

DEBTS - *Deuteronomy 15:1-12* The Year of Release

1 At the end of *every* seven years thou shalt make a release. **2** And this *is* the manner of the release:

Every creditor that lendeth *aught* unto his neighbor shall release *it*; he shall not exact *it* of his neighbor, or of his brother; because it is called the Lord's release. **3** Of a foreigner thou mayest exact *it again*: but *that* which is thine with thy brother thine hand shall release; **4** save when there shall be no poor among you; for the Lord shall greatly bless thee in the land which the Lord thy God giveth thee *for* an inheritance to possess it: **5** only if thou carefully hearken unto the voice of the Lord thy God, to observe to do all these commandments which I command thee this day. **6** For the Lord thy God blesseth thee, as he promised thee: and thou shalt lend unto many nations, but thou shalt not borrow; and thou shalt reign over many nations, but they shall not reign over thee.

Lending to the Poor

7 If there be among you a poor man of one of thy brethren within any of thy gates in thy land which the Lord thy God giveth thee, thou shalt not harden thine heart, nor shut thine hand from thy poor brother: **8** but thou shalt open thine hand wide unto him, and shalt surely lend him sufficient for his need, *in that* which he wanteth. **9** Beware that there be not a thought in thy wicked heart, saying, The seventh year, the year of release, is at hand; and thine eye be evil against thy poor brother, and thou givest him nought; and he cry unto the Lord against thee, and it be sin unto thee. **10** Thou shalt surely give him, and thine heart shall not be grieved when thou givest unto him: because that for this thing the Lord thy God shall bless thee in all thy works, and in all that thou puttest thine hand unto. 11 For the poor shall never cease out of the land: therefore I command thee, saying, Thou shalt open thine hand wide unto thy brother, to thy poor, and to thy needy, in thy land.

The Treatment of Servants

(Exodus 21.1-11)

12 *And* if thy brother, a Hebrew man, or a Hebrew woman, be sold unto thee, and serve thee six years; then in the seventh year thou shalt let him go free from thee.

CORPUS JURIS CIVILIS: MODERN SLAVERY (DEBT BONDAGE): Since 1933 under CANON LAW, the signing of a BIRTH CERTIFICATE in a foundling hospital (ship on the land) declares the child to be a WARD OF THE STATE creating a bond, title, insured securities and then mailed to the DEPARTMENT OF HUMAN RESOURCES, legal slavery by hospital and the State. This ensures the payment of TAXES from you, falling under their jurisdiction when civilly summoned, and with no rights whatsoever. This is done under the CESTUI QUE VIE ACT OF 1666.

Your LIVING TESTIMONY in the faith that Jesus the Christ is Lord and Redeemer (the head of household) in the form of an AFFIDAVIT is your truth in fact upon the record. Even if Biden says "they cannot be redeemed".

EMPLOYEES – *Exodus 20:10* but the seventh day *is* the sabbath of the Lord thy God: *in it* thou shalt not do any work, thou, nor thy son, nor thy daughter, thy manservant, nor thy maidservant, nor thy cattle, nor thy stranger that *is* within thy gates:

Deuteronomy 24:14, 15 **14** Thou shalt not oppress a hired servant *that is* poor and needy, *whether he be* of thy brethren, or of thy strangers that *are* in thy land within thy gates: **15** at his day thou shalt give *him* his hire, neither shall the sun go down upon it; for he *is* poor, and setteth his heart upon it: lest he cry against thee unto the Lord, and it be sin unto thee.

Malachi 3:5 And I will come near to you to judgment; and I will be a swift witness against the sorcerers, and against the adulterers, and against false swearers, and against those that oppress the hireling in *his* wages, the widow, and the fatherless, and that turn aside the stranger *from his right*, and fear not me, saith the Lord of hosts.

CIVIL PROCEDURE: You only gain SOCIAL SECURITY INCOME when working. 42 U.S.C. § 301 defines recipients of said social security income have to be of old age or disabled. Payments from the federal government are distributed to States a designated amount of funds by the Secretary of the Treasury per quarter to pay for these aged needy and medically induced individuals. EMPLOYEES can expect to collect this income after the age of 65.

HANDICAPPED – *Leviticus 19:14* Thou shalt not curse the deaf, nor put a stumbling-block before the blind, but shalt fear thy God: I *am* the Lord.

Luke 13:13, 14 13 But when thou makest a feast, call the poor, the maimed, the lame, the blind: **14** and thou shalt be blessed; for they cannot recompense thee: for thou shalt be recompensed at the resurrection of the just.

CIVIL CODE: 42 U.S.C. §1382i Medical and social services for certain handicapped persons grants a THREE YEAR PROGRAM, a Federal and State pilot program to be exact, to appropriate sums of money necessary to establish and carry out the program to provide medical and social services for CERTAIN handicapped individuals.

LAME – ***Luke 13:13, 14*** 13 But when thou makest a feast, call the poor, the maimed, the lame, the blind: **14** and thou shalt be blessed; for they cannot recompense thee: for thou shalt be recompensed at the resurrection of the just.

NON COMPOS MENTIS: Not of sound mind; insane.

LOANS – ***Exodus 22:25*** If thou lend money to *any of* my people *that is* poor by thee, thou shalt not be to him as a usurer, neither shalt thou lay upon him usury.

CIVIL PROCEDURE: Typically, in SOCIAL SECURITY there is no loan permitted to anyone out of the OASDI Trust Fund, 1. If it is below 10% of money in given trust. 2. States are federally given loans under SOCIAL SECURITY with given permissions on how to use such funds. **§ 1395ccc.**

Offset of payments to individuals to collect past-due obligations arising from breach of scholarship and loan contract breaks down an individual's obligation to pay any past due balances covered under the Federal loan insurance

ORPHANS – *Exodus 22:22, 23* Ye shall not afflict any widow, or fatherless child. 23If thou afflict them in any wise, and they cry at all unto me, I will surely hear their cry;

Deuteronomy 14:28, 29, 24:17-22, 26:12, 13 **14:28** At the end of three years thou shalt bring forth all the tithe of thine increase the same year, and shalt lay *it* up within thy gates: **29** and the Levite, (because he hath no part nor inheritance with thee,) and the stranger, and the fatherless, and the widow, which *are* within thy gates, shall come, and shall eat and be satisfied; that the Lord thy God may bless thee in all the work of thine hand which thou doest. ***24:17-22*** **17** Thou shalt not pervert the judgment of the stranger, *nor* of the fatherless; nor take a widow's raiment to pledge: **18** but thou shalt remember that thou wast a bondman in Egypt, and the Lord thy God redeemed thee thence: therefore I command thee to do this thing.

19 When thou cuttest down thine harvest in thy field, and hast forgot a sheaf in the field, thou shalt not go again to fetch it: it shall be for the stranger, for the fatherless, and for the widow: that the Lord thy God may bless thee in all the work of thine hands. **20** When thou beatest thine olive tree, thou shalt not go over the boughs again: it shall be for the stranger, for the fatherless, and for the widow. **21** When thou gatherest the grapes of thy vineyard, thou shalt not glean *it* afterward: it shall be for the stranger, for the fatherless, and for the widow. **22** And thou shalt remember that thou wast a bondman in the land of Egypt: therefore I command thee to do this thing. ***26:12, 13*** **12** When thou hast made an end of tithing all the tithes of thine increase the third year, *which is* the year of tithing, and hast given *it* unto the Levite, the stranger, the fatherless, and the widow, that they may eat within thy gates, and be filled; **13** then thou shalt say before the Lord thy God, I have brought away the hallowed things out of *mine* house, and also have given them unto the Levite, and unto the stranger, to the fatherless, and to the widow, according to all thy commandments which thou hast commanded me: I have not transgressed thy commandments, neither have I forgotten *them*.

Jeremiah 7:6, 7 **6** *if* ye oppress not the stranger, the fatherless, and the widow, and shed not innocent blood in this place, neither walk after other gods to your hurt; **7** then will I cause you to dwell in this place, in the land that I gave to your fathers, for ever and ever.

Zechariah 7:10-12 **10** and oppress not the widow, nor the fatherless, the stranger, nor the poor; and let none of you imagine evil against his brother in your heart. **11** But they refused to hearken, and pulled away the shoulder, and stopped their ears, that they should not hear. **12** Yea, they made their hearts *as* an adamant stone, lest they should hear the law, and the words which the Lord of hosts hath sent in his Spirit by the former prophets: therefore came a great wrath from the Lord of hosts.

Malachi 3:5 And I will come near to you to judgment; and I will be a swift witness against the sorcerers, and against the adulterers, and against false swearers, and against those that oppress the hireling in *his* wages, the widow, and the fatherless, and that turn aside the stranger *from his right*, and fear not me, saith the Lord of hosts.

CIVIL CODE: 42 U.S.C. § 192 **Chief of bureau; investigations and reports** "The Children's Bureau shall be under the direction for a CHIEF, to be appointed by the President, by and with the advice and consent of the Senate. The said bureau shall investigate and report to the Secretary of Health and Human Services, upon all matter pertaining to the welfare of children and child life among all classes of OUR PEOPLE, and shall especially investigate the questions of infant mortality, the birth rate, ORPHANAGE affecting children in the SEVERAL STATES AND TERRITORIES." But may never come near a HEAD OF HOUSEHOLD, a MAN OF CHRIST.

PLEDGES - *Exodus 22:26, 27* **26** If thou at all take thy neighbor's raiment to pledge, thou shalt deliver it unto him by that the sun goeth down: **27** for that *is* his covering only, it *is* his raiment for his skin: wherein shall he sleep? and it shall come to pass, when he crieth unto me, that I will hear; for I *am* gracious.

Deuteronomy 24:6, 10-13 24:6 No man shall take the nether or the upper millstone to pledge: for he taketh *a man's* life to pledge. **10-13 10** When thou dost lend thy brother any thing, thou shalt not go into his house to fetch his pledge. **11** Thou shalt stand abroad, and the man to whom thou dost lend shall bring out the pledge abroad unto thee. **12** And if the man *be* poor, thou shalt not sleep with his pledge: **13** in any case thou shalt deliver him the pledge again when the sun goeth down, that he may sleep in his own raiment, and bless thee: and it shall be righteousness unto thee before the Lord thy God.

PLEDGE IN NOAH WEBSTER 1828: In law, a gage or security real or personal, given for the repayment of money. It is of two kinds, *vadium vivum,* a LIVING PLEDGE, as when a man BORROWS money and grants an estate to be held by the pledgee, till the rents and profits shall refund the money, in which case the land or pledge is said to be LIVING; or it is *vadium mortuum,* A DEAD PLEDGE, IN OTHER WORDS A MORTGAGE.

In this case, no pledge has been honored to the Afro American who has been reclassified as dead in law through civiliter mortuus.

POOR - *Exodus 22:25-27* **25** If thou lend money to *any of* my people *that is* poor by thee, thou shalt not be to him as a usurer, neither shalt thou lay upon him usury. **26** If thou at all take thy neighbor's raiment to pledge, thou shalt deliver it unto him by that the sun goeth down: **27** for that *is* his covering only, it *is* his raiment for his skin: wherein shall he sleep? and it shall come to pass, when he crieth unto me, that I will hear; for I *am* gracious.

Leviticus 19:9, 10, 25:35-37 **9** And when ye reap the harvest of your land, thou shalt not wholly reap the corners of thy field, neither shalt thou gather the gleanings of thy harvest. **10** And thou shalt not glean thy vineyard, neither shalt thou gather *every* grape of thy vineyard; thou shalt leave them for the poor and stranger: I *am* the Lord your God. ***25:35-37* 35** And if thy brother be waxen poor, and fallen in decay with thee; then thou shalt relieve him: *yea, though he be* a stranger, or a sojourner; that he may live with thee. **36** Take thou no usury of him, or increase: but fear thy God; that thy brother may live with thee. **37** Thou shalt not give him thy money upon usury, nor lend him thy victuals for increase.

Deuteronomy 14:28, 29, 15:7-11, 24:19-22, 26:12, 13

28 At the end of three years thou shalt bring forth all the tithe of thine increase the same year, and shalt lay *it* up within thy gates: **29** and the Levite, (because he hath no part nor inheritance with thee,) and the stranger, and the fatherless, and the widow, which *are* within thy gates, shall come, and shall eat and be satisfied; that the Lord thy God may bless thee in all the work of thine hand which thou doest.

15:7-11 Lending to the Poor

7 If there be among you a poor man of one of thy brethren within any of thy gates in thy land which the Lord thy God giveth thee, thou shalt not harden thine heart, nor shut thine hand from thy poor brother: **8** but thou shalt open thine hand wide unto him, and shalt surely lend him sufficient for his need, *in that* which he wanteth. **9** Beware that there be not a thought in thy wicked heart, saying, The seventh year, the year of release, is at hand; and thine eye be evil against thy poor brother, and thou givest him nought; and he cry unto the Lord against thee, and it be sin unto thee. **10** Thou shalt surely give him, and thine heart shall not be grieved when thou givest unto him: because that for this thing the Lord thy God shall bless thee in all thy works, and in all that thou puttest thine hand unto. **11** For the poor shall never cease out of the land: therefore I command thee, saying, Thou shalt open thine hand wide unto thy brother, to thy poor, and to thy needy, in thy land.

24:19-22 **19** When thou cuttest down thine harvest in thy field, and hast forgot a sheaf in the field, thou shalt not go again to fetch it: it shall be for the stranger, for the fatherless, and for the widow: that the Lord thy God may bless thee in all the work of thine hands. **20** When thou beatest thine olive tree, thou shalt not go over the boughs again: it shall be for the stranger, for the fatherless, and for the widow. **21** When thou gatherest the grapes of thy vineyard, thou shalt not glean *it* afterward: it shall be for the stranger, for the fatherless, and for the widow. **22** And thou shalt remember that thou wast a bondman in the land of Egypt: therefore I command thee to do this thing.

26:12, 13 **12** When thou hast made an end of tithing all the tithes of thine increase the third year, *which is* the year of tithing, and hast given *it* unto the Levite, the stranger, the fatherless, and the widow, that they may eat within thy gates, and be filled; **13** then thou shalt say before the Lord thy God, I have brought away the hallowed things out of *mine* house, and also have given them unto the Levite, and unto the stranger, to the fatherless, and to the widow, according to all thy commandments which thou hast commanded me: I have not transgressed thy commandments, neither have I forgotten *them*.

Zechariah 7:10-12 10 and oppress not the widow, nor the fatherless, the stranger, nor the poor; and let none of you imagine evil against his brother in your heart. 11 But they refused to hearken, and pulled away the shoulder, and stopped their ears, that they should not hear. 12 Yea, they made their hearts *as* an adamant stone, lest they should hear the law, and the words which the Lord of hosts hath sent in his Spirit by the former prophets: therefore came a great wrath from the Lord of hosts.

Luke 3:11, 14:13, 14 3:11 He answereth and saith unto them, He that hath two coats, let him impart to him that hath none; and he that hath meat, let him do likewise.14:13, 14 13 But when thou makest a feast, call the poor, the maimed, the lame, the blind: 14 and thou shalt be blessed; for they cannot recompense thee: for thou shalt be recompensed at the resurrection of the just.

CIVIL PROCEDURE: 42 U.S.C. § 256 Notes eligibility to receive a grant through the Secretary to strengthen the effectiveness, efficiency, and coordination of services for the uninsured and underinsured for coordinated health care services. §256(2)(K) under eligibility requirements says "demonstrates the consortium's commitment to serve the community without regard to the ability of an individual or family to pay by arranging for or providing free or reduced charge care for the POOR".

SERVANTS – *Exodus 20:10* but the seventh day *is* the sabbath of the Lord thy God: *in it* thou shalt not do any work, thou, nor thy son, nor thy daughter, thy manservant, nor thy maidservant, nor thy cattle, nor thy stranger that *is* within thy gates:

Leviticus 25:39-46 **39** And if thy brother *that dwelleth* by thee be waxen poor, and be sold unto thee; thou shalt not compel him to serve as a bondservant: **40** *but* as a hired servant, *and* as a sojourner, he shall be with thee, *and* shall serve thee unto the year of jubilee: **41** and *then* shall he depart from thee, *both* he and his children with him, and shall return unto his own family, and unto the possession of his fathers shall he return. **42** For they *are* my servants, which I brought forth out of the land of Egypt: they shall not be sold as bondmen. **43** Thou shalt not rule over him with rigor; but shalt fear thy God. **44** Both thy bondmen, and thy bondmaids, which thou shalt have, *shall be* of the heathen that are round about you; of them shall ye buy bondmen and bondmaids. **45** Moreover, of the children of the strangers that do sojourn among you, of them shall ye buy, and of their families that *are* with you, which they begat in your land: and they shall be your possession. **46** And ye shall take them as an inheritance for your children after you, to inherit *them for* a possession; they shall be your bondmen for ever: but over your brethren the children of Israel, ye shall not rule one over another with rigor.

Deuteronomy 24:14, 15 **14** Thou shalt not oppress a hired servant *that is* poor and needy, *whether he be* of thy brethren, or of thy strangers that *are* in thy land within thy gates: **15** at his day thou shalt give *him* his hire, neither shall the sun go down upon it; for he *is* poor, and setteth his heart upon it: lest he cry against thee unto the Lord, and it be sin unto thee.

Ephesians 6:5-9 **5** Servants, be obedient to them that are *your* masters according to the flesh, with fear and trembling, in singleness of your heart, as unto Christ; **6** not with eyeservice, as menpleasers; but as the servants of Christ, doing the will of God from the heart; **7** with good will doing service, as to the Lord, and not to men: **8** knowing that whatsoever good thing any man doeth, the same shall he receive of the Lord, whether *he be* bond or free. **9** And, ye masters, do the same things unto them, forbearing threatening: knowing that your Master also is in heaven; neither is there respect of persons with him.

§1381 under **SUBCHAPTER XVI-SUPPLEMENTAL SECURITY INCOME FOR AGED, BLIND, OR DISABLED** establishes a national program to provide supplemental security income to individuals who have attained age 65 or are blind or disabled in appropriated sums.

FREEING OF SLAVES – *Exodus 21:2-4* **2** If thou buy a Hebrew servant, six years he shall serve: and in the seventh he shall go out free for nothing. **3** If he came in by himself, he shall go out by himself: if he were married, then his wife shall go out with him. **4** If his master have given him a wife, and she have borne him sons or daughters; the wife and her children shall be her master's, and he shall go out by himself.

Leviticus 25:40, 41, 47-55 **40** *but* as a hired servant, *and* as a sojourner, he shall be with thee, *and* shall serve thee unto the year of jubilee: **41** and *then* shall he depart from thee, *both* he and his children with him, and shall return unto his own family, and unto the possession of his fathers shall he return. *47-55* **47** And if a sojourner or stranger wax rich by thee, and thy brother *that dwelleth* by him wax poor, and sell himself unto the stranger *or* sojourner by thee, or to the stock of the stranger's family: **48** after that he is sold he may be redeemed again; one of his brethren may redeem him: **49** either his uncle, or his uncle's son, may redeem him, or *any* that is nigh of kin unto him of his family may redeem him; or if he be able, he may redeem himself. **50** And he shall reckon with him that bought him from the year that he was sold to him unto the year of jubilee: and the price of his sale shall be according unto the number of years, according to the time of a hired servant shall it be with him. **51** If *there be* yet many years *behind*, according unto them he shall give again the price of his redemption out of the money that he was bought for. **52** And if there remain but few years unto the year of jubilee, then he shall count with him, *and* according unto his years shall he give him again the price of his redemption. **53** *And* as a yearly hired servant shall he be with him: *and the other* shall not rule with rigor over him in thy sight. **54** And if he be not redeemed in these *years*, then he shall go out in the year of jubilee, *both* he, and his children with him. **55** For unto me the children of Israel *are* servants; they *are* my servants whom I brought forth out of the land of Egypt: I *am* the Lord your God.

Deuteronomy 15:12-18, 23:15, 16 The Treatment of Servants

(Exodus 21.1-11)

12 *And* if thy brother, a Hebrew man, or a Hebrew woman, be sold unto thee, and serve thee six years; then in the seventh year thou shalt let him go free from thee. **13** And when thou sendest him out free from thee, thou shalt not let him go away empty: **14** thou shalt furnish him liberally out of thy flock, and out of thy floor, and out of thy winepress: *of that* wherewith the Lord thy God hath blessed thee thou shalt give unto him. **15** And thou shalt remember that thou wast a bondman in the land of Egypt, and the Lord thy God redeemed thee: therefore I command thee this thing today. **16** And it shall be, if he say unto thee, I will not go away from thee; because he loveth thee and thine house, because he is well with thee; **17** then thou shalt take an awl, and thrust *it* through his ear unto the door, and he shall be thy servant for ever. And also unto thy maidservant thou shalt do likewise. **18** It shall not seem hard unto thee, when thou sendest him away free from thee; for he hath been worth a double hired servant *to thee*, in serving thee six years: and the Lord thy God shall bless thee in all that thou doest. (**23:15, 16**)15 Thou shalt not deliver unto his master the servant which is escaped from his master unto thee: 16he shall dwell with thee, *even* among you, in that place which he shall choose in one of thy gates, where it liketh him best: thou shalt not oppress him.

CIVIL PROCEDURE: At the age of 65 is one considered, RETIRED, which is to withdraw, retreat, from a public place into privacy. Never truly FREE.

INHERITANCE OF SLAVES - *Leviticus 25:46*
And ye shall take them as an inheritance for your children after you, to inherit *them for* a possession; they shall be your bondmen for ever: but over your brethren the children of Israel, ye shall not rule one over another with rigor.

CIVIL PROCEDURE: INHERITANCE in Title 42 U.S.C. §1382a., is considered UNEARNED INCOME but is still income and therefore taxable.

REDEMPTION OF SLAVES - *Leviticus 25:47-55*
47 And if a sojourner or stranger wax rich by thee, and thy brother *that dwelleth* by him wax poor, and sell himself unto the stranger *or* sojourner by thee, or to the stock of the stranger's family: **48** after that he is sold he may be redeemed again; one of his brethren may redeem him: **49** either his uncle, or his uncle's son, may redeem him, or *any* that is nigh of kin unto him of his family may redeem him; or if he be able, he may redeem himself. **50** And he shall reckon with him that bought him from the year that he was sold to him unto the year of jubilee: and the price of his sale shall be according unto the number of years, according to the time of a hired servant shall it be with him. **51** If *there be* yet many years *behind*, according unto them he shall give again the price of his redemption out of the money that he was bought for. **52** And if there remain but few years unto the

year of jubilee, then he shall count with him, *and* according unto his years shall he give him again the price of his redemption. **53** *And* as a yearly hired servant shall he be with him: *and the other* shall not rule with rigor over him in thy sight. **54** And if he be not redeemed in these *years*, then he shall go out in the year of jubilee, *both* he, and his children with him. **55** For unto me the children of Israel *are* servants; they *are* my servants whom I brought forth out of the land of Egypt: I *am* the Lord your God.

§1104. Unemployment Trust Fund (c) Sale or redemption of obligations Any obligations acquired by the Fund (except special obligations issued exclusively to the Fund) may be SOLD at the market price, and such special obligations may be redeemed at par plus accrued interest.

§1395i. Federal Hospital Insurance Trust Fund (e) Interest on and proceeds from sale or redemption of obligations The interest on, and the proceeds from the sale or REDEMPTION of, any obligations held in the Trust Fund shall be credited to and form a part of the Trust Fund.

§1395t. Federal Supplementary Medical Insurance Trust Fund (e) Interest on or proceeds from sale or redemption of obligations The interest on, and the proceeds from the sale or REDEMPTION of, any obligations held in the Trust Fund shall be credited to and form a part of the Trust Fund.

TREATMENT OF SLAVES – *Exodus 21:1-11, 20*
The Treatment of Servants

(Deuteronomy 15.12-18)

1 Now these *are* the judgments which thou shalt set before them. 2 If thou buy a Hebrew servant, six years he shall serve: and in the seventh he shall go out free for nothing. 3 If he came in by himself, he shall go out by himself: if he were married, then his wife shall go out with him. 4 If his master have given him a wife, and she have borne him sons or daughters; the wife and her children shall be her master's, and he shall go out by himself. 5

And if the servant shall plainly say, I love my master, my wife, and my children; I will not go out free: 6 then his master shall bring him unto the judges; he shall also bring him to the door, or unto the doorpost; and his master shall bore his ear through with an awl; and he shall serve him for ever.

7 And if a man sell his daughter to be a maidservant, she shall not go out as the menservants do. 8 If she please not her master, who hath betrothed her to himself, then shall he let her be redeemed: to sell her unto a strange nation he shall have no power, seeing he hath dealt deceitfully with her. 9 And if he have betrothed her unto his son, he shall deal with her after the manner of daughters. 10 If he take him another *wife*, her food, her raiment, and her duty of marriage, shall he not diminish. 11 And if he do not these three unto her, then shall she go out free without money.

Leviticus 25:39-46 39 And if thy brother *that dwelleth* by thee be waxen poor, and be sold unto thee; thou shalt not compel him to serve as a bondservant: 40 *but* as a hired servant, *and* as a sojourner, he shall be with thee, *and* shall serve thee unto the year of jubilee: **41** and *then* shall he depart from thee, *both* he and his children with him, and shall return unto his own family, and unto the possession of his fathers shall he return. **42** For they *are* my servants, which I brought forth out of the land of Egypt: they shall not be sold as bondmen. **43** Thou shalt not rule over him with rigor; but shalt fear thy God. **44** Both thy bondmen, and thy bondmaids, which thou shalt have, *shall be* of the heathen that are round about you; of them shall ye buy bondmen and bondmaids. **45** Moreover, of the children of the strangers that do sojourn among you, of them shall ye buy, and of their families that *are* with you, which they begat in your land: and they shall be your possession. **46** And ye shall take them as an inheritance for your children after you, to inherit *them for* a possession; they shall be your bondmen for ever: but over your brethren the children of Israel, ye shall not rule one over another with rigor.

Deuteronomy 23:15, 16 **15** Thou shalt not deliver unto his master the servant which is escaped from his master unto thee: **16** he shall dwell with thee, *even* among you, in that place which he shall choose in one of thy gates, where it liketh him best: thou shalt not oppress him.

CIVIL PROCEDURE: Under 42 U.S.C. CHAPTER 7A SOCIAL SECURITY §405 TREATMENT OF EMPLOYEES WHOSE FEDERAL EMPLOYMENT TERMINATED AFTER MAKING ELECTION INTO SOCIAL SECURITY COVERAGE BUT BEFORE

EFFECTIVE DATE OF ELECTION means that monthly payments periodically does not apply to that person entering into FERS. Under (u) **Redetermination of entitlement (ii),** the TREATMENT OF CURRENT BENEFICIARIES is contingent upon their sobriety and the recommendation of the Secretary of Health and Human Services.

STRANGERS - *Exodus 20:10* but the seventh day *is* the sabbath of the Lord thy God: *in it* thou shalt not do any work, thou, nor thy son, nor thy daughter, thy manservant, nor thy maidservant, nor thy cattle, nor thy stranger that *is* within thy gates:

Leviticus 16:29, 19:33, 34 16:29 And *this* shall be a statute for ever unto you: *that* in the seventh month, on the tenth *day* of the month, ye shall afflict your souls, and do no work at all, *whether it be* one of your own country, or a stranger that sojourneth among you: *19:33, 34 And* if a stranger sojourn with thee in your land, ye shall not vex him. 34 *But* the stranger that dwelleth with you shall be unto you as one born among you, and thou shalt love him as thyself; for ye were strangers in the land of Egypt: I *am* the Lord your God.

Deuteronomy 10:19, 14:28, 29, 24:17-22, 26:12, 13 10:19 Love ye therefore the stranger: for ye were strangers in the land of Egypt. *14:28, 29* 28 At the end of three years thou shalt bring forth all the tithe of thine increase the same year, and shalt lay *it* up within thy gates: **29** and the Levite, (because he hath no part nor inheritance with thee,) and the stranger, and the fatherless, and the widow, which *are* within thy gates, shall come, and shall eat and be satisfied; that the Lord thy God may bless thee in all the work of thine hand which thou doest. *24:17-22* **17** Thou shalt not pervert the judgment of the stranger, *nor* of the fatherless; nor take a widow's raiment to pledge: **18** but thou shalt remember that thou wast a bondman in Egypt, and the Lord thy God redeemed thee thence: therefore I command thee to do this thing.

19 When thou cuttest down thine harvest in thy field, and hast forgot a sheaf in the field, thou shalt not go again to fetch it: it shall be for the stranger, for the fatherless, and for the widow: that the Lord thy God may bless thee in all the work of thine hands. **20** When thou beatest thine olive tree, thou shalt not go over the boughs again: it shall be for the stranger, for the fatherless, and for the widow. **21** When thou gatherest the grapes of thy vineyard, thou shalt not glean *it* afterward: it shall be for the stranger, for the fatherless, and for the widow. **22** And thou shalt remember that thou wast a bondman in the land of Egypt: therefore I command thee to do this thing. *26:12, 13* **12** When thou hast made an end of tithing all the tithes of thine increase the third year, *which is* the year of tithing, and hast given *it* unto the Levite, the stranger, the fatherless, and the widow, that they may eat within thy gates, and be filled; **13** then thou shalt say before the Lord thy God, I have brought away the hallowed things out of *mine* house, and also have given them unto the Levite, and unto the stranger, to the fatherless, and to the widow, according to all thy commandments which thou hast commanded me: I have not transgressed thy commandments, neither have I forgotten *them*.

Jeremiah 7:6, 7 **6** *if* ye oppress not the stranger, the fatherless, and the widow, and shed not innocent blood in this place, neither walk after other gods to your hurt; **7** then will I cause you to dwell in this place, in the land that I gave to your fathers, for ever and ever.

Zechariah 7:10-12 **10** and oppress not the widow, nor the fatherless, the stranger, nor the poor; and let none of you imagine evil against his brother in your heart. **11** But they refused to hearken, and pulled away the shoulder, and stopped their ears, that they should not hear. **12** Yea, they made their hearts *as* an adamant stone, lest they should hear the law, and the words which the Lord of hosts hath sent in his Spirit by the former prophets: therefore came a great wrath from the Lord of hosts.

Malachi 3:5 And I will come near to you to judgment; and I will be a swift witness against the sorcerers, and against the adulterers, and against false swearers, and against those that oppress the hireling in *his* wages, the widow, and the fatherless, and that turn aside the stranger *from his right*, and fear not me, saith the Lord of hosts.

Saturday and Sunday are usually days of labor for millions of people, following not the Law of God and keeping his covenant, which has been stated numerous times.

QUESTION: Who are the only people treated as **STRANGERS** in America when it comes to neighborhoods, exposure to high paying jobs, a normal lifestyle in a coastal climate, REAL RIGHTS in law and order, called by a certain pigment representing a void, or denied or given small loans for businesses or home buying?

USURY - *Exodus 22:25* If thou lend money to *any of* my people *that is* poor by thee, thou shalt not be to him as a usurer, neither shalt thou lay upon him usury.

Deuteronomy 23:19, 20 **19** Thou shalt not lend upon usury to thy brother; usury of money, usury of victuals, usury of any thing that is lent upon usury: **20** unto a stranger thou mayest lend upon usury; but unto thy brother thou shalt not lend upon usury: that the Lord thy God may bless thee in all that thou settest thine hand to in the land whither thou goest to possess it.

CHAPTER 7–SOCIAL SECURITY is an outline of how funds are **USED** to grant benefits to the aged needy, disabled, and/or blind.

WAGES - *Leviticus 19:13* Thou shalt not defraud thy neighbor, neither rob *him*: the wages of him that is hired shall not abide with thee all night until the morning.

Deuteronomy 24:14, 15 **14** Thou shalt not oppress a hired servant *that is* poor and needy, *whether he be* of thy brethren, or of thy strangers that *are* in thy land within thy gates: **15** at his day thou shalt give *him* his hire, neither shall the sun go down upon it; for he *is* poor, and setteth his heart upon it: lest he cry against thee unto the Lord, and it be sin unto thee.

§1381a. Basic entitlement to benefits Every aged, blind, or disabled individual who is determined under part A to be eligible on the basis of his income and resources shall in accordance with and subject to the provisions of this subchapter be paid benefits by the Commissioner of Social Security.

WIDOWS - *Exodus 22:22, 23* **22** Ye shall not afflict any widow, or fatherless child. **23** If thou afflict them in any wise, and they cry at all unto me, I will surely hear their cry;

Deuteronomy 14:28, 29, 24:17-22, 25:5-10, 26:12, 13 **28** same year, and shalt lay *it* up within thy gates: **29** and the Levite, (because he hath no part nor inheritance with thee,) and the stranger, and the fatherless, and the widow, which *are* within thy gates, shall come, and shall eat and be satisfied; that the Lord thy God may bless thee in all the work of thine hand which thou doest. *24:17-22* **17** Thou shalt not pervert the judgment of the stranger, *nor* of the fatherless; nor take a widow's raiment to pledge: **18** but thou shalt remember that thou wast a bondman in Egypt, and the Lord thy God redeemed thee thence: therefore I command thee to do this thing.

19 When thou cuttest down thine harvest in thy field, and hast forgot a sheaf in the field, thou shalt not go again to fetch it: it shall be for the stranger, for the fatherless, and for the widow: that the Lord thy God may bless thee in all the work of thine hands. **20** When thou beatest thine olive tree, thou shalt not go over the boughs again: it shall be for the stranger, for the fatherless, and for the widow. **21** When thou gatherest the grapes of thy vineyard, thou shalt not glean *it* afterward: it shall be for the stranger, for the fatherless, and for the widow. **22** And thou shalt remember that thou wast a bondman in the land of Egypt: therefore I command thee to do this thing.

25:5-10 **5** If brethren dwell together, and one of them die, and have no child, the wife of the dead shall not marry without unto a stranger: her husband's brother shall go in unto her, and take her to him to wife, and perform the duty of a husband's brother unto her. **6** And it shall be, *that* the firstborn which she beareth shall succeed in the name of his brother *which is* dead, that his name be not put out of Israel. **7** And if the man like not to take his brother's wife, then let his brother's wife go up to the gate unto the elders, and say, My husband's brother refuseth to raise up unto his brother a name in Israel, he will not perform the duty of my husband's brother. **8** Then the elders of his city shall call him, and speak unto him: and *if* he stand *to it*, and say, I like not to take her; **9** then shall his brother's wife come unto him in the presence of the elders, and loose his shoe from off his foot, and spit in his face, and shall answer and say, So shall it be done unto that man that will not build up his brother's house. **10** And his name shall be called in Israel, The house of him that hath his shoe loosed.

26:12, 13 **12** When thou hast made an end of tithing all the tithes of thine increase the third year, *which is* the year of tithing, and hast given *it* unto the Levite, the stranger, the fatherless, and the widow, that they may eat within thy gates, and be filled; **13** then thou shalt say before the Lord thy God, I have brought away the hallowed things out of *mine* house, and also have given them unto the Levite, and unto the stranger, to the fatherless, and to the widow, according to all thy commandments which thou hast commanded me: I have not transgressed thy commandments, neither have I forgotten *them*.

Ruth 4:1-12 **1** Then went Boaz up to the gate, and sat him down there: and, behold, the kinsman of whom Boaz spake came by; unto whom he said, Ho, such a one! turn aside, sit down here. And he turned aside, and sat down. **2** And he took ten men of the elders of the city, and said, Sit ye down here. And they sat down. **3** And he said unto the kinsman, Na-o´mi, that is come again out of the country of Moab, selleth a parcel of land, which *was* our brother Elim´elech's: **4** and I thought to advertise thee, saying, Buy *it* before the inhabitants, and before the elders of my people. If thou wilt redeem *it*, redeem *it*: but if thou wilt not redeem *it, then* tell me, that I may know: for *there is* none to redeem *it* besides thee; and I *am* after thee. And he said, I will redeem *it*. **5** Then said Boaz, What day thou buyest the field of the hand of Na-o´mi, thou must buy *it* also of Ruth the Moabitess, the wife of the dead, to raise up the name of the dead upon his inheritance. **6** And the kinsman said, I cannot redeem *it* for myself, lest I mar mine own inheritance: redeem thou my right to thyself; for I cannot redeem *it*.

7 Now this *was the manner* in former time in Israel concerning redeeming and concerning changing, for to confirm all things; a man plucked off his shoe, and gave *it* to his neighbor: and this *was* a testimony in Israel. **8** Therefore the kinsman said unto Boaz, Buy *it* for thee. So he drew off his shoe. **9** And Boaz said unto the elders, and *unto* all the people, Ye *are* witnesses this day, that I have bought all that *was* Elim´elech's, and all that *was* Chil´i-on's and Mahlon's, of the hand of Na-o´mi. **10** Moreover Ruth the Moabitess, the wife of Mahlon, have I purchased to be my wife, to raise up the name of the dead upon his inheritance, that the name of the dead be not cut off from among his brethren, and from the gate of his place: ye *are* witnesses this day. **11** And all the people that *were* in the gate, and the elders, said, *We are* witnesses. The Lord make the woman that is come into thine house like Rachel and like Le´ah, which two did build the house of Israel: and do thou worthily in Eph´ratah, and be famous in Bethlehem: **12** and let thy house be like the house of Pharez, whom Tamar bare unto Judah, of the seed which the Lord shall give thee of this young woman.

Jeremiah 7:6-7 **6** *if* ye oppress not the stranger, the fatherless, and the widow, and shed not innocent blood in this place, neither walk after other gods to your hurt; **7** then will I cause you to dwell in this place, in the land that I gave to your fathers, for ever and ever.

Zechariah 7:10-12 **10** and oppress not the widow, nor the fatherless, the stranger, nor the poor; and let none of you imagine evil against his brother in your heart. **11** But they refused to hearken, and pulled away the shoulder, and stopped their ears, that they should not hear. **12** Yea, they made their hearts *as* an adamant stone, lest they should hear the law, and the words which the Lord of hosts hath sent in his Spirit by the former prophets: therefore came a great wrath from the Lord of hosts.

Malachi 3:5 And I will come near to you to judgment; and I will be a swift witness against the sorcerers, and against the adulterers, and against false swearers, and against those that oppress the hireling in *his* wages, the widow, and the fatherless, and that turn aside the stranger *from his right*, and fear not me, saith the Lord of hosts.

Mark 12:40 which devour widows' houses, and for a pretense make long prayers: these shall receive greater damnation.

Acts 6:1-4 **1** And in those days, when the number of the disciples was multiplied, there arose a murmuring of the Grecians against the Hebrews, because their widows were neglected in the daily ministration. **2** Then the twelve called the multitude of the disciples *unto them*, and said, It is not reason that we should leave the word of God, and serve tables. **3** Wherefore, brethren, look ye out among you seven men of honest report, full of the Holy Ghost and wisdom, whom we may appoint over this business. **4** But we will give ourselves continually to prayer, and to the ministry of the word.

1 Timothy 5:3-16 **3** Honor widows that are widows indeed. **4** But if any widow have children or nephews, let them learn first to show piety at home, and to requite their parents: for that is good and acceptable before God. **5** Now she that is a widow indeed, and desolate, trusteth in God, and continueth in supplications and prayers night and day. **6** But she that liveth in pleasure is dead while she liveth. **7** And these things give in charge, that they may be blameless. **8** But if any provide not for his own, and specially for those of his own house, he hath denied the faith, and is worse than an infidel.

9 Let not a widow be taken into the number under threescore years old, having been the wife of one man, **10** well reported of for good works; if she have brought up children, if she have lodged strangers, if she have washed the saints' feet, if she have relieved the afflicted, if she have diligently followed every good work. **11** But the younger widows refuse: for when they have begun to wax wanton against Christ, they will marry; **12** having damnation, because they have cast off their first faith. **13** And withal they learn *to be* idle, wandering about from house to house; and not only idle, but tattlers also and busybodies, speaking things which they ought not. **14** I will therefore that the younger women marry, bear children, guide the house, give none occasion to the adversary to speak reproachfully. **15** For some are already turned aside after Satan. **16** If any man or woman that believeth have widows, let them relieve them, and let not the church be charged; that it may relieve them that are widows indeed.

42 U.S.C. §402. Old-age and survivors insurance benefit payments (e) Widow's insurance benefits is a federally issued payment issued to women who apply for widow's insurance benefits based on several contingencies. The contingencies include not being married, attained age 60 or 50 and older under a disability, filed the application for widow's benefits, is entitled to benefits, along with a few more that you can reference further if the need arises.

PROTECTION OF WOMEN – *Exodus 20:10, 21:7-11*

7 but the seventh day *is* the sabbath of the Lord thy God: *in it* thou shalt not do any work, thou, nor thy son, nor thy daughter, thy manservant, nor thy maidservant, nor thy cattle, nor thy stranger that *is* within thy gates: *21:7-11* **7** And if a man sell his daughter to be a maidservant, she shall not go out as the menservants do. **8** If she please not her master, who hath betrothed her to himself, then shall he let her be redeemed: to sell her unto a strange nation he shall have no power, seeing he hath dealt deceitfully with her. **9** And if he have betrothed her unto his son, he shall deal with her after the manner of daughters. **10** If he take him another *wife*, her food, her raiment, and her duty of marriage, shall he not diminish. **11** And if he do not these three unto her, then shall she go out free without money.

Men will argue that women are given protection under the U.S. Justice System. While there may be some truth to this, men born of the dust of the Earth, through Christ redeemed, chosen by God to follow his ways and LAWS for his name sake, must choose our women carefully, through Christ be the HEAD OF HOUSEHOLD, and raise our children upright. The system will cave in at that point.

LABOR LAWS

TREATMENT OF EMPLOYEES – *Exodus 20:10, 21:2-11, 20, 26, 27* **20:10** but the seventh day *is* the sabbath of the Lord thy God: *in it* thou shalt not do any work, thou, nor thy son, nor thy daughter, thy manservant, nor thy maidservant, nor thy cattle, nor thy stranger that *is* within thy gates: **21:2-11 2** If thou buy a Hebrew servant, six years he shall serve: and in the seventh he shall go out free for nothing. **3** If he came in by himself, he shall go out by himself: if he were married, then his wife shall go out with him. **4** If his master have given him a wife, and she have borne him sons or daughters; the wife and her children shall be her master's, and he shall go out by himself. **5** And if the servant shall plainly say, I love my master, my wife, and my children; I will not go out free: **6** then his master shall bring him unto the judges; he shall also bring him to the door, or unto the doorpost; and his master shall bore his ear through with an awl; and he shall serve him for ever.

7 And if a man sell his daughter to be a maidservant, she shall not go out as the menservants do. **8** If she please not her master, who hath betrothed her to himself, then shall he let her be redeemed: to sell her unto a strange nation he shall have no power, seeing he hath dealt deceitfully with her. **9** And if he have betrothed her unto his son, he shall deal with her after the manner of daughters. **10** If he take him another *wife*, her food, her raiment, and her duty of marriage, shall he not diminish. **11** And if he do not these three unto her, then shall she go out free without money. **20** And if a man smite his servant, or his maid, with a rod, and he die under his hand; he shall be surely punished. **26** And if a man smite the eye of his servant, or the eye of his maid, that it perish; he shall let him go free for his eye's sake. **27** And if he smite out his manservant's tooth, or his maidservant's tooth; he shall let him go free for his tooth's sake.

Leviticus 25:39-55 **39** And if thy brother *that dwelleth* by thee be waxen poor, and be sold unto thee; thou shalt not compel him to serve as a bondservant: **40** *but* as a hired servant, *and* as a sojourner, he shall be with thee, *and* shall serve thee unto the year of jubilee: **41** and *then* shall he depart from thee, *both* he and his children with him, and shall return unto his own family, and unto the possession of his fathers shall he return. **42** For they *are* my servants, which I brought forth out of the land of Egypt: they shall not be sold as bondmen. **43** Thou shalt not rule over him with rigor; but shalt fear thy God. **44** Both thy bondmen, and thy bondmaids, which thou shalt have, *shall be* of the heathen that are round about you; of them shall ye buy bondmen and bondmaids. **45** Moreover, of the children of the strangers that do sojourn among you, of them shall ye buy, and of their families that *are* with you, which they begat in your land: and they shall be your possession. **46** And ye shall take them as an inheritance for your children after you, to inherit *them for* a possession; they shall be your bondmen for ever: but over your brethren the children of Israel, ye shall not rule one over another with rigor.

47 And if a sojourner or stranger wax rich by thee, and thy brother *that dwelleth* by him wax poor, and sell himself unto the stranger *or* sojourner by thee, or to the stock of the stranger's family: **48** after that he is sold he may be redeemed again; one of his brethren may redeem him: **49** either his uncle, or his uncle's son, may redeem him, or *any* that is nigh of kin unto him of his family may redeem him; or if he be able, he may redeem himself. **50** And he shall reckon with him that bought him from the year that he was sold to him unto the year of jubilee: and the price of his sale shall be according unto the number of years, according to the time of a hired servant shall it be with him. **51** If *there be* yet many years *behind*, according unto them he shall give again the price of his redemption out of the money that he was bought for. **52** And if there remain but few years unto the year of jubilee, then he shall count with him, *and* according unto his years shall he give him again the price of his redemption. **53** *And* as a yearly hired servant shall he be with him: *and the other* shall not rule with rigor over him in thy sight. **54** And if he be not redeemed in these *years*, then he shall go out in the year of jubilee, *both* he, and his children with him. **55** For unto me the children of Israel *are* servants; they *are* my servants whom I brought forth out of the land of Egypt: I *am* the Lord your God.

<u>Deuteronomy 23:15, 16, 24:14, 15</u> 15 Thou shalt not deliver unto his master the servant which is escaped from his master unto thee: **16** he shall dwell with thee, *even* among you, in that place which he shall choose in one of thy gates, where it liketh him best: thou shalt not oppress him.

24:14, 15 **14** Thou shalt not oppress a hired servant *that is* poor and needy, *whether he be* of thy brethren, or of thy strangers that *are* in thy land within thy gates: **15** at his day thou shalt give *him* his hire, neither shall the sun go down upon it; for he *is* poor, and setteth his heart upon it: lest he cry against thee unto the Lord, and it be sin unto thee.

CIVIL LAW: Let's refer to the Fair Labor Standards Act of **1938** in 29 U.S.C. § **201-219,** beginning with **§202. Congressional finding and declaration of policy (a)** The Congress finds that existence, in industries engaged in commerce or in the production of goods for commerce, of labor conditions detrimental to the maintenance of the MINIMUM standard of living necessary for HEALTH, efficiency, and GENERAL WELL-BEING of workers, along with burdening COMMERCE in any way (mostly), **(b)** It is declared to be the policy of this chapter, through the exercise by Congress of its power to regulate commerce among the several States and with FOREIGN NATIONS, to correct and as rapidly as practicable to ELIMINATE the conditions above referred to in such industries without SUBSTANTIALLY curtailing employment or earning power. Here's a bonus from 29 U.S.C. § **202 (a)(5)** That Congress further finds that the employment of persons in domestic service in households affects commerce. How do they explain the COVID s***?

FREEDOM OF SERVANTS - *Exodus 21:2-11* **2** If thou buy a Hebrew servant, six years he shall serve: and in the seventh he shall go out free for nothing. **3** If he came in by himself, he shall go out by himself: if he were married, then his wife shall go out with him. **4** If his master have given him a wife, and she have borne him sons or daughters; the wife and her children shall be her master's, and he shall go out by himself. **5** And if the servant shall plainly say, I love my master, my wife, and my children; I will not go out free: **6** then his master shall bring him unto the judges; he shall also bring him to the door, or unto the doorpost; and his master shall bore his ear through with an awl; and he shall serve him for ever.

7 And if a man sell his daughter to be a maidservant, she shall not go out as the menservants do. **8** If she please not her master, who hath betrothed her to himself, then shall he let her be redeemed: to sell her unto a strange nation he shall have no power, seeing he hath dealt deceitfully with her. **9** And if he have betrothed her unto his son, he shall deal with her after the manner of daughters. **10** If he take him another *wife*, her food, her raiment, and her duty of marriage, shall he not diminish. **11** And if he do not these three unto her, then shall she go out free without money.

Leviticus 25:39-46 **39** And if thy brother *that dwelleth* by thee be waxen poor, and be sold unto thee; thou shalt not compel him to serve as a bondservant: **40** *but* as a hired servant, *and* as a sojourner, he shall be with thee, *and* shall serve thee unto the year of jubilee: **41** and *then* shall he depart from thee, *both* he and his children with him, and shall return unto his own family, and unto the possession of his fathers shall he return. 42For they *are* my servants, which I brought forth out of the land of Egypt: they shall not be sold as bondmen. 43 Thou shalt not rule over him with rigor; but shalt fear thy God. 44 Both thy bondmen, and thy bondmaids, which thou shalt have, *shall be* of the heathen that are round about you; of them shall ye buy bondmen and bondmaids. 45 Moreover, of the children of the strangers that do sojourn among you, of them shall ye buy, and of their families that *are* with you, which they begat in your land: and they shall be your possession. 46And ye shall take them as an inheritance for your children after you, to inherit *them for* a possession; they shall be your bondmen for ever: but over your brethren the children of Israel, ye shall not rule one over another with rigor.

Deuteronomy 15:12-18, 23:15, 16 The Treatment of Servants

(Exodus 21.1-11)

The Treatment of Servants

(Exodus 21.1-11)

12 *And* if thy brother, a Hebrew man, or a Hebrew woman, be sold unto thee, and serve thee six years; then in the seventh year thou shalt let him go free from thee. 13 And when thou sendest him out free from thee, thou shalt not let him go away empty: 14 thou shalt furnish him liberally out of thy flock, and out of thy floor, and out of thy winepress: *of that* wherewith the Lord thy God hath blessed thee

thou shalt give unto him. **15** And thou shalt remember that thou wast a bondman in the land of Egypt, and the Lord thy God redeemed thee: therefore I command thee this thing today. **16** And it shall be, if he say unto thee, I will not go away from thee; because he loveth thee and thine house, because he is well with thee; **17** then thou shalt take an awl, and thrust *it* through his ear unto the door, and he shall be thy servant for ever. And also unto thy maidservant thou shalt do likewise. **18** It shall not seem hard unto thee, when thou sendest him away free from thee; for he hath been worth a double hired servant *to thee*, in serving thee six years: and the Lord thy God shall bless thee in all that thou doest.

23:15, 16 Thou shalt not deliver unto his master the servant which is escaped from his master unto thee: **16** he shall dwell with thee, *even* among you, in that place which he shall choose in one of thy gates, where it liketh him best: thou shalt not oppress him.

CIVIL CODE: FREEDOM OF SERVANTS would be to be reclassified back to our rightful titles and free from contractual obligations which increases the growth of the Serpent's programming. Sticking to their LAWS, will we continue to lay out the weapons used against the children of God and the Bride of Christ. FREEDOM OF SERVANTS would sadly be in the form of LEAVE. **Chapter 28 – FAMILY AND MEDICAL LEAVE** in 29 U.S.C. requires an ELIGIBLE EMPLOYEE to have been employed at least 12 months and at least 1,250 hours of service with such employer. **§2612** defines ENTITLEMENT TO LEAVE as up to 12 workweeks per 12 month period for the birth of child, because of foster home placement for son or daughter, caring for a loved one, qualifying exigencies of the covered active duty in the Armed Forces, or enforcement of the Emergency Family and Medical Leave Expansion Act.

REDEMPTION OF SERVANTS – *Leviticus 25:47-55*

47 And if a sojourner or stranger wax rich by thee, and thy brother *that dwelleth* by him wax poor, and sell himself unto the stranger *or* sojourner by thee, or to the stock of the stranger's family: **48** after that he is sold he may be redeemed again; one of his brethren may redeem him: **49** either his uncle, or his uncle's son, may redeem him, or *any* that is nigh of kin unto him of his family may redeem him; or if he be able, he may redeem himself. **50** And he shall reckon with him that bought him from the year that he was sold to him unto the year of jubilee: and the price of his sale shall be according unto the number of years, according to the time of a hired servant shall it be with him. **51** If *there be* yet many years *behind*, according unto them he shall give again the price of his redemption out of the money that he was bought for. **52** And if there remain but few years unto the year of jubilee, then he shall count with him, *and* according unto his years shall he give him again the price of his redemption. **53** *And* as a yearly hired servant shall he be with him: *and the other* shall not rule with rigor over him in thy sight. **54** And if he be not redeemed in these *years*, then he shall go out in the year of jubilee, *both* he, and his children with him. **55** For unto me the children of Israel *are* servants; they *are* my servants whom I brought forth out of the land of Egypt: I *am* the Lord your God.

The REDEMPTION OF SERVANTS comes through the REDEEMER. Let's refer to the LAW OF REDEMPTION. The REDEEMER, THE KINSMAN is the one, THE SETTLOR, ordained through Christ to do so. The SERVANTS in America must realize who they are, where they are from, and if they have been reclassified as BLACK, INDIAN, or "AFRICAN" AMERICANS, having no inherent rights to anything promised to 14th amendment CITIZENS. ONLY THROUGH CHRIST may Adam be redeemed from his slavery and INDENTURED servitude.

UNIONS - *Acts 19:24-29* **24** For a certain *man* named Deme´tri-us, a silversmith, which made silver shrines for Diana, brought no small gain unto the craftsmen; **25** whom he called together with the workmen of like occupation, and said, Sirs, ye know that by this craft we have our wealth. **26** Moreover ye see and hear, that not alone at Ephesus, but almost throughout all Asia, this Paul hath persuaded and turned away much people, saying that they be no gods, which are made with hands: **27** so that not only this our craft is in danger to be set at nought; but also that the temple of the great goddess Diana should be despised, and her magnificence should be destroyed, whom all Asia and the world worshippeth.

28 And when they heard *these sayings*, they were full of wrath, and cried out, saying, Great *is* Diana of the Ephesians. **29** And the whole city was filled with confusion: and having caught Gai´us and Aristar´chus, men of Macedo´nia, Paul's companions in travel, they rushed with one accord into the theater.

CIVIL CODE: 29 U.S.C. § 2503 provides TECHNICAL ASSISTANCE in developing outreach to recruiting and hiring women, tradeswomen into labor unions, receiving this technical assistance after the Secretary's selection of 50 employers or labor unions. A LAISSEZ-FAIRE style of funding based on competition.

WAGES - *Leviticus 19:13* Thou shalt not defraud thy neighbor, neither rob *him*: the wages of him that is hired shall not abide with thee all night until the morning.

Deuteronomy 24:14, 15 **14** Thou shalt not oppress a hired servant *that is* poor and needy, *whether he be* of thy brethren, or of thy strangers that *are* in thy land within thy gates: **15** at his day thou shalt give *him* his hire, neither shall the sun go down upon it; for he *is* poor, and setteth his heart upon it: lest he cry against thee unto the Lord, and it be sin unto thee.

Matthew 20:1-16 **Laborers in the Vineyard**

1 For the kingdom of heaven is like unto a man *that is* a householder, which went out early in the morning to hire laborers into his vineyard. **2** And when he had agreed with the laborers for a penny a day, he sent them into his vineyard. **3** And he went out about the third hour, and saw others standing idle in the market place, **4** and said unto them; Go ye also into the vineyard, and whatsoever is right I will give you. And they went their way. **5** Again he went out about the sixth and ninth hour, and did likewise. **6** And about the eleventh hour he went out, and found others standing idle, and saith unto them, Why stand ye here all the day idle? **7** They say unto him, Because no man hath hired us. He saith unto them, Go ye also into the vineyard; and whatsoever is right, *that* shall ye receive. **8** So when even was come, the lord of the vineyard saith unto his steward, Call the laborers, and give them *their* hire, beginning from the last unto the first. **9** And when they came that *were hired* about the eleventh hour, they received every man a penny. **10** But when the first came, they supposed that they should have received more; and they likewise received every man a penny. **11** And when they had received *it*, they murmured against the goodman of the house, **12** saying, These last have wrought *but* one hour, and thou hast made them equal unto us, which have borne the burden and heat of the day. **13** But he answered one of them, and said, Friend, I do thee no wrong: didst not thou agree with me for a penny? **14** Take *that* thine *is*, and go thy way: I will give unto this last, even as unto thee. **15** Is it not lawful for me to do what I will with mine own? Is thine eye evil, because I am good? 16 So the last shall be first, and the first last: for many be called, but few chosen.

CIVIL CODE: 29 U.S.C. §2 established the Bureau of Labor Statistics to collect, collate, report, and publish once a month full and complete statistics of the volume of and changes in employment including the WAGES PAID. **§ 216 (c)** The Secretary is authorized to supervise the payment of the unpaid minimum wages or the unpaid overtime compensation owing to any employee or employees.

§1832 Wages, supplies, and other working arrangements (a) Payment of wages Farm labor contractors, agricultural employers, and agricultural organizations, make sure you pay up to the workers when due. **§3241 (B)(b)(1) Limitations on activities that impact wages of employees** No funds provided under this subchapter shall be used to pay the wages of incumbent employees during their participation in economic development activities provided through a statewide workforce development system.

WOMEN – *Exodus 21:7-11*– **7** And if a man sell his daughter to be a maidservant, she shall not go out as the menservants do. **8** If she please not her master, who hath betrothed her to himself, then shall he let her be redeemed: to sell her unto a strange nation he shall have no power, seeing he hath dealt deceitfully with her. **9** And if he have betrothed her unto his son, he shall deal with her after the manner of daughters. **10** If he take him another *wife*, her food, her raiment, and her duty of marriage, shall he not diminish. **11** And if he do not these three unto her, then shall she go out free without money.

CIVIL CODE: 29 U.S.C. CHAPTER 2– WOMEN'S BUREAU §12 The Women's Bureau shall be in charge of a director, a woman, to be appointed by the President. **§13** The duty of the Women's Bureau is to formulate standards and policies which shall promote the welfare of wage-earning women, improve their working conditions, increase their efficiency, and advance their opportunities for profitable employment.

29 U.S.C. CHAPTER 27—WOMEN IN APPRENTICESHIP AND NONTRADITIONAL OCCUPATIONS is one of the many ways the Federal government changes the dynamic of the Nuclear Family. They're predicting a different labor market because they are creating the standards for the change in the labor markets. Chapter 27 goes into TECHNICAL ASSISTANCE and other topics that have been brushed upon so far within this document.

HUMANE LAWS

ANIMALS - *Exodus 20:8-11, 23:5, 11, 12* **8** Remember the sabbath day, to keep it holy. **9** Six days shalt thou labor, and do all thy work: **10** but the seventh day is the sabbath of the Lord thy God: in it thou shalt not do any work, thou, nor thy son, nor thy daughter, thy manservant, nor thy maidservant, nor thy cattle, nor thy stranger that is within thy gates: **11** for in six days the Lord made heaven and earth, the sea, and all that in them is, and rested the seventh day: wherefore the Lord blessed the sabbath day, and hallowed it. ***23:5, 11, 12*** **23:5** If thou see the ass of him that hateth thee lying under his burden, and wouldest forbear to help him, thou shalt surely help with him. **11** but the seventh *year* thou shalt let it rest and lie still; that the poor of thy people may eat: and what they leave the beasts of the field shall eat. In like manner thou shalt deal with thy vineyard, *and* with thy oliveyard.

12 Six days thou shalt do thy work, and on the seventh day thou shalt rest: that thine ox and thine ass may rest, and the son of thy handmaid, and the stranger, may be refreshed.

Leviticus 22:28, 25:5-7 -- **22:28** And *whether it be* cow or ewe, ye shall not kill it and her young both in one day. **25:5-7** That which groweth of its own accord of thy harvest thou shalt not reap, neither gather the grapes of thy vine undressed: *for* it is a year of rest unto the land. **6** And the sabbath of the land shall be meat for you; for thee, and for thy servant, and for thy maid, and for thy hired servant, and for thy stranger that sojourneth with thee, **7** and for thy cattle, and for the beast that *are* in thy land, shall all the increase thereof be meat.

Deuteronomy 25:4 -- Thou shalt not muzzle the ox when he treadeth out *the corn*.

CIVIL CODE: Along with organizations such as SPCA, ASPCA, PETA, and numerous animal protection agencies, 16 U.S.C. - CONSERVATION lists the large amount of protections in place for the conservation and refuge of animals displaced from the construction of real estate and roads through once before rural areas. In relation to Universe 25 and the treatment of Afro-Americans in urban areas, there is much use of the phrase "urban areas" and the word "urban" in this particular title. Interesting finds in the CONSERVATION Title include **§410ww-24 (b)** The Commission (The Dayton Aviation Heritage Commission) staff may include specialists in areas such as interpretation, historic preservation, black history and literature, aviation history and technology, and urban revitalization. **§1247(b) Secretary of Housing and Urban Development to encourage metropolitan and other urban areas; administrative and financial assistance in connection with recreation and transportation planning; administration of urban open-space program. §1277 Land acquisition (c) Curtailment of condemnation power in urban areas covered by valid and satisfactory zoning ordinances §1455 (b)(2)** The redevelopment of deteriorating and underutilized urban waterfronts and ports that are designated in the state's management program pursuant to **§1455(d)(2)(C). §1601 Renewable Resource Assessment (a)(6)** an analysis of the rural and urban forestry opportunities to mitigate the buildup of ATMOSPHERE CARBON DIOXIDE and REDUCE THE RISK OF GLOBAL CLIMATE CHANGE. Isn't that just inhumane, un-Godly, and just plain wrong? The list doesn't stop there but I do.

ASSES – *Exodus 23:5, 12* – 23:5 If thou see the ass of him that hateth thee lying under his burden, and wouldest forbear to help him, thou shalt surely help with him. **12** Six days thou shalt do thy work, and on the seventh day thou shalt rest: that thine ox and thine ass may rest, and the son of thy handmaid, and the stranger, may be refreshed.

BIRDS - *Deuteronomy 22:6, 7* **6** If a bird's nest chance to be before thee in the way in any tree, or on the ground, *whether they be* young ones, or eggs, and the dam sitting upon the young, or upon the eggs, thou shalt not take the dam with the young: **7** *but* thou shalt in any wise let the dam go, and take the young to thee; that it may be well with thee, and *that* thou mayest prolong *thy* days.

BLIND - *Leviticus 19:14* -- Thou shalt not curse the deaf, nor put a stumbling-block before the blind, but shalt fear thy God: I *am* the Lord.

Deuteronomy 27:18 -- Cursed *be* he that maketh the blind to wander out of the way:

Luke 14:12-14 -- **12** Then said he also to him that bade him, When thou makest a dinner or a supper, call not thy friends, nor thy brethren, neither thy kinsmen, nor *thy* rich neighbors; lest they also bid thee again, and a recompense be made thee. **13** But when thou makest a feast, call the poor, the maimed, the lame, the blind: **14** and thou shalt be blessed; for they cannot recompense thee: for thou shalt be recompensed at the resurrection of the just.

CIVIL CODE: The **NATIONAL EYE INSTITUTE's**, as pointed out in **42 U.S.C. §285h.**, general purpose is the conduct and support of research, training, health information dissemination, and other programs with respect to blinding eye diseases, visual disorders, mechanisms of visual function, preservation of sight, and the special health problems and requirements of the BLIND.

CATTLE - *Exodus 20:8-11* -- **8** Remember the sabbath day, to keep it holy. **9** Six days shalt thou labor, and do all thy work: **10** but the seventh day *is* the sabbath of the Lord thy God: *in it* thou shalt not do any work, thou, nor thy son, nor thy daughter, thy manservant, nor thy maidservant, nor thy cattle, nor thy stranger that *is* within thy gates: **11** for *in* six days the Lord made heaven and earth, the sea, and all that in them *is*, and rested the seventh day: wherefore the Lord blessed the sabbath day, and hallowed it.

Leviticus 25:5-7 -- **5** That which groweth of its own accord of thy harvest thou shalt not reap, neither gather the grapes of thy vine undressed: *for* it is a year of rest unto the land. **6** And the sabbath of the land shall be meat for you; for thee, and for thy servant, and for thy maid, and for thy hired servant, and for thy stranger that sojourneth with thee, **7** and for thy cattle, and for the beast that *are* in thy land, shall all the increase thereof be meat.

UNFORTUNATELY, it seems that CHATTEL AND CATTLE go hand in hand in LAW as CATTLE AND CHATTEL are both publicly traded commodities in the STOCK MARKET. 7 U.S.C. **§6a. Excessive speculation** blocks attempts to affect interstate commerce by limiting the amount of trade by one person or group. **§20. Market reports** features the STUDY OF TRADING IN CATTLE FUTURES CONTRACTS, which in (a) identifies that The Comptroller General of the United States shall conduct and complete a comprehensive study of the effect of trading in contracts for the future delivery of LIVE CATTLE on the cash market price of the live cattle.

COWS - *Leviticus 22:28* -- And *whether it be* cow or ewe, ye shall not kill it and her young both in one day.

CIVIL CODE: In 7 U.S.C. §1635d.(5), the PACKER is identified as "the person engaged in the business of buying cattle in commerce for purposes of slaughter, of manufacturing or preparing meats or meat food products from CATTLE (Cows in this instance) for sale or shipment in commerce, or of marketing meats or meat food products from cattle in an unmanufactured form acting as a wholesale broker, dealer, or distributor in commerce"., now, do you think if there were deadlines to meet in order to keep a farm from being usurped by the federal government, this "packer" would care about the LEVITICAL LAW from God? Or what about mass production? Would **Leviticus 22:28** be a factor?

DEAF - *Leviticus 19:14* -- Thou shalt not curse the deaf, nor put a stumbling-block before the blind, but shalt fear thy God: I *am* the Lord.

CIVIL CODE: There is a **National Deafness and Other Communication Disorders Program** as shown in **42 U.S.C. SUBPART 13,** which is an institute that researches treatments, early detection, but not enough emphasis on bridging a gap between the deaf and the hearing. Another organization, the Multipurpose deafness and other communication disorders center as highlighted in **42 U.S.C. §285m-**

3., specializes or is funded rather for techniques in early detection, to discover deterrents, and research.

EMPLOYEES - *Deuteronomy 24:14, 15* **- 14** Thou shalt not oppress a hired servant *that is* poor and needy, *whether he be* of thy brethren, or of thy strangers that *are* in thy land within thy gates: **15** at his day thou shalt give *him* his hire, neither shall the sun go down upon it; for he *is* poor, and setteth his heart upon it: lest he cry against thee unto the Lord, and it be sin unto thee.

Malachi 3:5 -- And I will come near to you to judgment; and I will be a swift witness against the sorcerers, and against the adulterers, and against false swearers, and against those that oppress the hireling in *his* wages, the widow, and the fatherless, and that turn aside the stranger *from his right*, and fear not me, saith the Lord of hosts.

It seems that the poor and needy are kept on their feet longer in today's job market with ever increasing costs of living all throughout America as of Fall 2023. They are the ones gone away from their families all day working while the recipients of government checks through immigration and/or welfare come in consistently. With high costs of school, a high price to all forms of achievement, the regular employee will have to work three times as hard, sacrificing their free time, sleep, family time, and time to get themselves truly together. There are countless practices of oppression to employees nationwide which go unnoticed or under the radar, for fear of retribution, the loss of their income, home, lifestyle, and much more.

If you are a victim of unfair practices at your work, I'll refer you to **29 U.S.C. §2617. Enforcement (a) Civil action by employees PICK WHAT STICKS.**

HANDICAPPED - *Leviticus 19:14* -- Thou shalt not curse the deaf, nor put a stumbling-block before the blind, but shalt fear thy God: I *am* the Lord.

Luke 14:12-14 -- **12** Then said he also to him that bade him, When thou makest a dinner or a supper, call not thy friends, nor thy brethren, neither thy kinsmen, nor *thy* rich neighbors; lest they also bid thee again, and a recompense be made thee. **13** But when thou makest a feast, call the poor, the maimed, the lame, the blind: **14** and thou shalt be blessed; for they cannot recompense thee: for thou shalt be recompensed at the resurrection of the just.

CIVIL CODE: 42 U.S.C. §4153 Standards for design, construction, and alteration of buildings; Secretary of Housing and Urban Development describes one of the many roles of The Secretary of Housing and Urban Development, referring to Title 19 CONSERVATION, as prescribing the alteration, construction, and design of residential structures subject to Chapter 51, to insure access to the handicapped into such buildings.

The States go further into the protections of the HANDICAPPED, for example MO Revisor of Statutes **Title VIII 108.470 Discrimination in granting of loans is unlawful** includes handicap in that statute. **71.365 Sidewalks to have wheelchair ramps.** Interestingly enough, you can catch corporations finding a silver lining in the hiring of a handicapped employee. In **Chapter 60** of the

Consolidated Laws of New York, Article 9, §187-a. Credit for employment of persons with disabilities, a credit is bestowed to a taxpayer against the taxes imposed by Chapter 60.

LAME - *Luke 14:12-14* -- 12 Then said he also to him that bade him, When thou makest a dinner or a supper, call not thy friends, nor thy brethren, neither thy kinsmen, nor *thy* rich neighbors; lest they also bid thee again, and a recompense be made thee. **13** But when thou makest a feast, call the poor, the maimed, the lame, the blind: **14** and thou shalt be blessed; for they cannot recompense thee: for thou shalt be recompensed at the resurrection of the just.

LAME has become a loosely used insult in today's society.

LOANS - *Exodus 22:25* -- If thou lend money to *any of* my people *that is* poor by thee, thou shalt not be to him as a usurer, neither shalt thou lay upon him usury.

***Deuteronomy 15:1, 2* -- 1** At the end of *every* seven years thou shalt make a release. **2** And this *is* the manner of the release: Every creditor that lendeth *aught* unto his neighbor shall release *it*; he shall not exact *it* of his neighbor, or of his brother; because it is called the Lord's release.

CIVIL CODE: 12 U.S.C. §1423 The Federal Home Loan Bank districts can be created and/or readjusted ranging from 12 districts to now having the authority to have less than 8. The Director of the Federal

Home Loan Bank can withhold or limit operations of mortgages, loans, and land titles in States if deemed necessary. The Federal Loan Agency has been remitted as of now but still worth researching due to the effects it may have had on the people today. Most "mortgages" are 15 years at minimum, surpassing the time span the Lord giveth thee, which is seven years that every creditor that lendeth, forgiveth the loan.

MAIMED - *Luke 14:12-14* -- **12** Then said he also to him that bade him, When thou makest a dinner or a supper, call not thy friends, nor thy brethren, neither thy kinsmen, nor *thy* rich neighbors; lest they also bid thee again, and a recompense be made thee. **13** But when thou makest a feast, call the poor, the maimed, the lame, the blind: **14** and thou shalt be blessed; for they cannot recompense thee: for thou shalt be recompensed at the resurrection of the just.

Maimed would be HANDICAPPED or DISABLED or sadly, CRIPPLED in our modern language. A majority of organizations, such as the AAPD (American Association of People with Disabilities) or the ACL (Administration for Community Living), are corporately funded, **political machines** that offer no real help to the disabled, only grouping or classifying everyone looking for help as DISABLED, filling the pockets of the organization. Each organization with disability in their name, find ways of changing the law rather than the outcomes of the lives of the maimed who need that help the most.

NEIGHBORS - *Leviticus 19:13* -- Thou shalt not defraud thy neighbor, neither rob *him*: the wages of him that is hired shall not abide with thee all night until the morning.

CIVIL CODE: NEIGHBORS all sharing the same goal of keeping the neighborhood safe, clean, and kept up in pristine condition is one idea but a HOA, homeowner's association, takes neighborly duties to a new level. Depending on who's running the 501(c)(4), a homeowner can incur fees that would be typically seen as unfair by anyone on the outside looking in. So, some HOA's run the risk of breaking the LAW, making up fees/citations that may be deemed unreasonable.

OPPRESSION - *Deuteronomy 24:14, 15* -- **14** Thou shalt not oppress a hired servant *that is* poor and needy, *whether he be* of thy brethren, or of thy strangers that *are* in thy land within thy gates: **15** at his day thou shalt give *him* his hire, neither shall the sun go down upon it; for he *is* poor, and setteth his heart upon it: lest he cry against thee unto the Lord, and it be sin unto thee.

CIVIL CODE: The Fair Minimum Wage Act of 2007 breakdown in 29 U.S.C. **§206. Minimum wage (a) Employees engaged in commerce; seamen on American vessels; agricultural employees** Every employer shall pay to each of his employees who in any workweek is engaged in commerce or in the production of goods for commerce, or is employed in an enterprise engaged in commerce or in the production of goods for commerce, wages at the following rates: (1) except as otherwise provided in this section, not less than—(A) $5.85 an hour beginning on the 60th day after May 25, 2007; (B) $6.55 an hour, beginning 12 months after that 60th day; and (C) $7.25 an hour, beginning 24 months after that 60th day.

ORPHANS - *Exodus 22:22-24* **22** Ye shall not afflict any widow, or fatherless child. **23** If thou afflict them in any wise, and they cry at all unto me, I will surely hear their cry; **24** and my wrath shall wax hot, and I will kill you with the sword; and your wives shall be widows, and your children fatherless.

Deuteronomy 10:18, 14:28, 29, 24:17-22, 25:5-10, 26:12, 13, 27:19

10:18 he doth execute the judgment of the fatherless and widow, and loveth the stranger, in giving him food and raiment. 14:28, 29 **28** same year, and shalt lay *it* up within thy gates: **29** and the Levite, (because he hath no part nor inheritance with thee,) and the stranger, and the fatherless, and the widow, which *are* within thy gates, shall come, and shall eat and be satisfied; that the Lord thy God may bless thee in all the work of thine hand which thou doest. *24:17-22* **17** Thou shalt not pervert the judgment of the stranger, *nor* of the fatherless; nor take a widow's raiment to pledge: **18** but thou shalt remember that thou wast a bondman in Egypt, and the Lord thy God redeemed thee thence: therefore I command thee to do this thing.

19 When thou cuttest down thine harvest in thy field, and hast forgot a sheaf in the field, thou shalt not go again to fetch it: it shall be for the stranger, for the fatherless, and for the widow: that the Lord thy God may bless thee in all the work of thine hands. **20** When thou beatest thine olive tree, thou shalt not go over the boughs again: it shall be for the stranger, for the fatherless, and for the widow. **21** When thou gatherest the grapes of thy vineyard, thou shalt not glean *it* afterward: it shall be for the stranger, for the fatherless, and for the widow. **22**And thou shalt remember that thou wast a bondman in the land of Egypt: therefore I command thee to do this thing.

25:5-10 **5** If brethren dwell together, and one of them die, and have no child, the wife of the dead shall not marry without unto a stranger: her husband's brother shall go in unto her, and take her to him to wife, and perform the duty of a husband's brother unto her. **6** And it shall be, *that* the firstborn which she beareth shall succeed in the name of his brother *which is* dead, that his name be not put out of Israel. **7** And if the man like not to take his brother's wife, then let his brother's wife go up to the gate unto the elders, and say, My husband's brother refuseth to raise up unto his brother a name in Israel, he will not perform the duty of my husband's brother. **8** Then the elders of his city shall call him, and speak unto him: and *if* he stand *to it*, and say, I like not to take her; **9** then shall his brother's wife come unto him in the presence of the elders, and loose his shoe from off his foot, and spit in his face, and shall answer and say, So shall it be done unto that man that will not build up his brother's house. **10** And his name shall be called in Israel, The house of him that hath his shoe loosed.

26:12, 13 **12** When thou hast made an end of tithing all the tithes of thine increase the third year, *which* *is* the year of tithing, and hast given *it* unto the Levite, the stranger, the fatherless, and the widow, that they may eat within thy gates, and be filled; **13** then thou shalt say before the Lord thy God, I have brought away the hallowed things out of *mine* house, and also have given them unto the Levite, and unto the stranger, to the fatherless, and to the widow, according to all thy commandments which thou hast commanded me: I have not transgressed thy commandments, neither have I forgotten *them*.

27:19 – Cursed be he that perverteth the judgment of the stranger, fatherless, and widow:

Jeremiah 7:6-7– **6** *if* ye oppress not the stranger, the fatherless, and the widow, and shed not innocent blood in this place, neither walk after other gods to your hurt; **7** then will I cause you to dwell in this place, in the land that I gave to your fathers, for ever and ever.

Zechariah 7:10-12 -- **10** and oppress not the widow, nor the fatherless, the stranger, nor the poor; and let none of you imagine evil against his brother in your heart. **11** But they refused to hearken, and pulled away the shoulder, and stopped their ears, that they should not hear. **12** Yea, they made their hearts *as* an adamant stone, lest they should hear the law, and the words which the Lord of hosts hath sent in his Spirit by the former prophets: therefore came a great wrath from the Lord of hosts.

Malachi 3:5 And I will come near to you to judgment; and I will be a swift witness against the sorcerers, and against the adulterers, and against false swearers, and against those that oppress the hireling in *his* wages, the widow, and the fatherless, and that turn aside the stranger *from his right*, and fear not me, saith the Lord of hosts.

FEDERAL GOVERNANCE: In the 1800's, there started SEVEN orphanages, by the 1830's 23, and around the "civil war" era (1850's and above) more than 70. The Civil War greatly expanded the need for orphanages due to the displacement of the Afro-Americans from their lands and homes and due to the large amount of IMMIGRANTS coming into the United States. False abandonment statistics increased the need for more organization. Introducing Charles Brace, founder of the New York Children's Aid Society with an idea to remold a child's character. Over the years it became The Children's Aid Society to currently just Children's Aid, dropping the "society" part, which reminds me of the Lloyd's of London and their "Society". Charles Brace is the creator of the ORPHAN TRAINS, which placed homeless children on the railways and sent them OUT WEST, where they would be CHOSEN by local selected families, which laid the groundwork for the CHILD WELFARE SYSTEM. After HITLER'S YOUTH finished with the trains, the program was discontinued in the 1930's. So ORPHANAGES began to disappear around that time just so the federal government can begin to take over in the form of PUBLIC SOCIAL SERVICES, allowing the formation of U.S. adoption policies, child protection laws, and FOSTER HOMES. FOSTER HOMES became government funded operations that aid (I just said "aid" not helped) **CHILDREN THAT HAVE LOST THEIR**

PARENTS, meaning children taken away from their homes due to nosey neighbors, domestic issues, and parents who are victims to some form of substance abuse.

OX - *Exodus 23:12* -- Six days thou shalt do thy work, and on the seventh day thou shalt rest: that thine ox and thine ass may rest, and the son of thy handmaid, and the stranger, may be refreshed.

Deuteronomy 25:4 Thou shalt not muzzle the ox when he treadeth out the corn.

PLEDGES - *Exodus 22:26, 27* **26** If thou at all take thy neighbor's raiment to pledge, thou shalt deliver it unto him by that the sun goeth down: **27** for that *is* his covering only, it *is* his raiment for his skin: wherein shall he sleep? and it shall come to pass, when he crieth unto me, that I will hear; for I *am* gracious.

Deuteronomy 24:6, 13 **24:6** No man shall take the nether or the upper millstone to pledge: for he taketh *a man's* life to pledge. **13** in any case thou shalt deliver him the pledge again when the sun goeth down, that he may sleep in his own raiment, and bless thee: and it shall be righteousness unto thee before the Lord thy God.

POOR - *Exodus 22:25-27* **25** If thou lend money to *any of* my people *that is* poor by thee, thou shalt not be to him as a usurer, neither shalt thou lay upon him usury. **26** If thou at all take thy neighbor's raiment to pledge, thou shalt deliver it unto him by that the sun goeth down: **27** for that *is* his covering only, it *is* his raiment for his skin: wherein shall he sleep? and it shall come to pass, when he crieth unto me, that I will hear; for I *am* gracious.

Leviticus 19:9, 10, 25:35-38 **9** And when ye reap the harvest of your land, thou shalt not wholly reap the corners of thy field, neither shalt thou gather the gleanings of thy harvest. **10** And thou shalt not glean thy vineyard, neither shalt thou gather *every* grape of thy vineyard; thou shalt leave them for the poor and stranger: I *am* the Lord your God. **25:35-37 35** And if thy brother be waxen poor, and fallen in decay with thee; then thou shalt relieve him: *yea, though he be* a stranger, or a sojourner; that he may live with thee. **36** Take thou no usury of him, or increase: but fear thy God; that thy brother may live with thee. **37** Thou shalt not give him thy money upon usury, nor lend him thy victuals for increase. **38** I *am* the Lord your God, which brought you forth out of the land of Egypt, to give you the land of Canaan, *and* to be your God.

Deuteronomy 15:7-11 Lending to the Poor

7 If there be among you a poor man of one of thy brethren within any of thy gates in thy land which the Lord thy God giveth thee, thou shalt not harden thine heart, nor shut thine hand from thy poor brother: **8** but thou shalt open thine hand wide unto him, and shalt surely lend him sufficient for his need, *in that* which he wanteth. **9** Beware that there be not a thought in thy wicked heart, saying, The seventh year, the year of release, is at hand; and thine eye be evil against thy poor brother, and thou givest him nought; and he cry unto the Lord against thee, and it be sin unto thee. **10** Thou shalt surely give him, and thine heart shall not be grieved when thou givest unto him: because that for this thing the Lord thy God shall bless thee in all thy works, and in all that thou puttest thine hand unto. **11** For the poor shall never cease out of the land: therefore I command thee, saying, Thou shalt open thine hand wide unto thy brother, to thy poor, and to thy needy, in thy land.

Nehemiah 5:1-13 The Payment of Interest Abolished

1 And there was a great cry of the people and of their wives against their brethren the Jews. **2** For there were that said, We, our sons, and our daughters, *are* many: therefore we take up corn *for them*, that we may eat, and live. **3** *Some* also there were that said, We have mortgaged our lands, vineyards, and houses, that we might buy corn, because of the dearth. **4** There were also that said, We have borrowed money for the king's tribute, *and that upon* our lands and vineyards. **5** Yet now our flesh *is* as the flesh of our brethren, our children as their children: and, lo, we bring into bondage our sons and our daughters to be servants, and *some* of our daughters are brought into bondage *already*: neither *is it* in our power *to redeem them*; for other men have our lands and vineyards.

6 And I was very angry when I heard their cry and these words. **7** Then I consulted with myself, and I rebuked the nobles, and the rulers, and said unto them, Ye exact usury, every one of his brother. And

I set a great assembly against them. **8** And I said unto them, We, after our ability, have redeemed our brethren the Jews, which were sold unto the heathen; and will ye even sell your brethren? or shall they be sold unto us? Then held they their peace, and found nothing *to answer.* **9** Also I said, It *is* not good that ye do: ought ye not to walk in the fear of our God because of the reproach of the heathen our enemies? **10** I likewise, *and* my brethren, and my servants, might exact of them money and corn: I pray you, let us leave off this usury. **11** Restore, I pray you, to them, even this day, their lands, their vineyards, their oliveyards, and their houses, also the hundredth *part* of the money, and of the corn, the wine, and the oil, that ye exact of them. **12** Then said they, We will restore *them,* and will require nothing of them; so will we do as thou sayest. Then I called the priests, and took an oath of them, that they should do according to this promise. **13** Also I shook my lap, and said, So God shake out every man from his house, and from his labor, that performeth not this promise, even thus be he shaken out, and emptied. And all the congregation said, Amen, and praised the Lord. And the people did according to this promise.

Zechariah 7:10-12 **10** and oppress not the widow, nor the fatherless, the stranger, nor the poor; and let none of you imagine evil against his brother in your heart. **11** But they refused to hearken, and pulled away the shoulder, and stopped their ears, that they should not hear. **12** Yea, they made their hearts *as* an adamant stone, lest they should hear the law, and the words which the Lord of hosts hath sent in his Spirit by the former prophets: therefore came a great wrath from the Lord of hosts.

Luke 3:11, 14:12-14 **3:11** He answereth and saith unto them, He that hath two coats, let him impart to him that hath none; and he that hath meat, let him do likewise. ***14:12-14*** **12** Then said he also to him that bade him, When thou makest a dinner or a supper, call not thy friends, nor thy brethren, neither thy kinsmen, nor *thy* rich neighbors; lest they also bid thee again, and a recompense be made thee. **13** But when thou makest a feast, call the poor, the maimed, the lame, the blind: **14** and thou shalt be blessed; for they cannot recompense thee: for thou shalt be recompensed at the resurrection of the just.

Galatians 2:10 -- Only *they would* that we should remember the poor; the same which I also was forward to do.

QUESTION: Are the POOR truly protected under the LAW, the civil law that is? While there are many programs for the POOR such as welfare, food stamps, WIC, unemployment insurance, discounted services, United Way, CATHOLIC CHURCH (Standard Oil Tycoons) CHARITIES, Salvation Army, Goodwill, just to name a few, these programs or the like typically run out of funding or misdirect their funds in a way to where the people who need help are put on waiting lists, sometimes to never to get the help they need at that moment. You can say that there is help but the run around recipients receive and the competitive nature, due to lack of resources, the poor encounter when seeking help from organizations I've mentioned can be even more challenging and mentally draining. With all of the food wasted daily from restaurants, grocery stores, and homes, it's also painful to see that food pantries often carry old and expired food in those pantries. Also, it can be tricky determining whether everyone's motives who drop off food are pure.

ABUSE OF SERVANTS - *Exodus 21:20* And if a man smite his servant, or his maid, with a rod, and he die under his hand; he shall be surely punished.

CIVIL CODE: ABUSE OF SERVANTS would be a charge of battery or assault, whichever jurisdiction one may be in. The ABUSE OF SERVANTS would possibly result to litigation. This isn't a modern American practice. A modern American practice would be to psychologically abuse workers. A form of this abuse would be using an employee who says "yes" frequently in return thinking he is going to receive a promotion or pay increase, to stay late, clean up messes out of his job description, do work intended for someone else, cheap pay for hard work, withhold bonuses, or work extra days because someone went couch surfing. In order to do something about this, which would happen first? You lose your job the petty way, called out for being excessively late for example, for speaking out or you lose your will to want to work for the company anyway and just find a new job because it isn't worth it?

FREEDOM OF SLAVES - *Exodus 21:1-11* 1 Now these *are* the judgments which thou shalt set before them. 2 If thou buy a Hebrew servant, six years he shall serve: and in the seventh he shall go out free for nothing. **3** If he came in by himself, he shall go out by himself: if he were married, then his wife shall go out with him. **4** If his master have given him a wife, and she have borne him sons or daughters; the wife and her children shall be her master's, and he shall go out by himself. **5** And if the servant shall plainly say, I love my master, my wife, and my children; I will not go out free: **6** then his master shall bring him unto the judges; he shall also bring him to the door, or unto the doorpost; and his master shall bore his ear through with an awl; and he shall serve him for ever.

7And if a man sell his daughter to be a maidservant, she shall not go out as the menservants do. **8** If she please not her master, who hath betrothed her to himself, then shall he let her be redeemed: to sell her unto a strange nation he shall have no power, seeing he hath dealt deceitfully with her. **9** And if he have betrothed her unto his son, he shall deal with her after the manner of daughters. **10** If he take him another *wife*, her food, her raiment, and her duty of marriage, shall he not diminish. **11**And if he do not these three unto her, then shall she go out free without money.

Deuteronomy 15:12-18 **12** *And* if thy brother, a Hebrew man, or a Hebrew woman, be sold unto thee, and serve thee six years; then in the seventh year thou shalt let him go free from thee. **13** And when thou sendest him out free from thee, thou shalt not let him go away empty: **14** thou shalt furnish him liberally out of thy flock, and out of thy floor, and out of thy winepress: *of that* wherewith the Lord thy

God hath blessed thee thou shalt give unto him. **15** And thou shalt remember that thou wast a bondman in the land of Egypt, and the Lord thy God redeemed thee: therefore I command thee this thing today. **16** And it shall be, if he say unto thee, I will not go away from thee; because he loveth thee and thine house, because he is well with thee; **17** then thou shalt take an awl, and thrust *it* through his ear unto the door, and he shall be thy servant for ever.

And also unto thy maidservant thou shalt do likewise. **18** It shall not seem hard unto thee, when thou sendest him away free from thee; for he hath been worth a double hired servant *to thee*, in serving thee six years: and the Lord thy God shall bless thee in all that thou doest. *23:15, 16* **15** Thou shalt not deliver unto his master the servant which is escaped from his master unto thee: **16** he shall dwell with thee, *even* among you, in that place which he shall choose in one of thy gates, where it liketh him best: thou shalt not oppress him.

QUICK BUILD: One must work. You have the FREEDOM to own a business, manage a business, work in a business, work for a business, or contract for a business. Follow the work-related rules, do a great job, follow God's LAWS, be a good person and you can HAVE YOUR FAMILY. The State has no power over a man in Christ running his kingdom.

TREATMENT OF SLAVES - *Exodus 20:10* but the seventh day *is* the sabbath of the Lord thy God: *in it* thou shalt not do any work, thou, nor thy son, nor thy daughter, thy manservant, nor thy maidservant, nor thy cattle, nor thy stranger that *is* within thy gates:

21:1-11 1 Now these *are* the judgments which thou shalt set before them. 2 If thou buy a Hebrew servant, six years he shall serve: and in the seventh he shall go out free for nothing. 3 If he came in by himself, he shall go out by himself: if he were married, then his wife shall go out with him. 4 If his master have given him a wife, and she have borne him sons or daughters; the wife and her children shall be her master's, and he shall go out by himself. 5 And if the servant shall plainly say, I love my master, my wife, and my children; I will not go out free: 6 then his master shall bring him unto the judges; he shall also bring him to the door, or unto the doorpost; and his master shall bore his ear through with an awl; and he shall serve him for ever.

7 And if a man sell his daughter to be a maidservant, she shall not go out as the menservants do. 8 If she please not her master, who hath betrothed her to himself, then shall he let her be redeemed: to sell her unto a strange nation he shall have no power, seeing he hath dealt deceitfully with her. 9 And if he have betrothed her unto his son, he shall deal with her after the manner of daughters. 10 If he take him another *wife*, her food, her raiment, and her duty of marriage, shall he not diminish. 11 And if he do not these three unto her, then shall she go out free without money.

23:12 Six days thou shalt do thy work, and on the seventh day thou shalt rest: that thine ox and thine ass may rest, and the son of thy handmaid, and the stranger, may be refreshed.

Leviticus 25:39-46 **39** And if thy brother *that dwelleth* by thee be waxen poor, and be sold unto thee; thou shalt not compel him to serve as a bondservant: **40** *but* as a hired servant, *and* as a sojourner, he shall be with thee, *and* shall serve thee unto the year of jubilee: **41** and *then* shall he depart from thee, *both* he and his children with him, and shall return unto his own family, and unto the possession of his fathers shall he return. **42** For they *are* my servants, which I brought forth out of the land of Egypt: they shall not be sold as bondmen. **43** Thou shalt not rule over him with rigor; but shalt fear thy God. 44Both thy bondmen, and thy bondmaids, which thou shalt have, *shall be* of the heathen that are round about you; of them shall ye buy bondmen and bondmaids. 45Moreover, of the children of the strangers that do sojourn among you, of them shall ye buy, and of their families that *are* with you, which they begat in your land: and they shall be your possession. **46** And ye shall take them as an inheritance for your children after you, to inherit *them for* a possession; they shall be your bondmen for ever: but over your brethren the children of Israel, ye shall not rule one over another with rigor.

CIVIL CODE: 20 C.F.R. (Code of Federal Regulations) Employees' Benefits is where you can find the source of information for Worker's Compensation Programs, Retirement, Employees' Compensation Appeals Board, Employment and Training Administration, Benefits Review Board, Joint Board For the Enrollment of Actuaries, and

Office of the Assistant Secretary for Veterans' Employment and Training Service.

Local Governments have provisions in place as for the treatment of workers that may have desirable benefits in some States and undesirable benefits in others, the same goes for counties and municipalities. Oxfam in 2021 named Oregon, California, New York, and Massachusetts as a few of the states with some of the best worker's rights in the country.

STRANGERS - *Leviticus 19:33, 34–* **33** And if a stranger sojourn with thee in your land, ye shall not vex him. **34** *But* the stranger that dwelleth with you shall be unto you as one born among you, and thou shalt love him as thyself; for ye were strangers in the land of Egypt: I *am* the Lord your God.

Deuteronomy 10:18 --he doth execute the judgment of the fatherless and widow, and loveth the stranger, in giving him food and raiment. *14:28, 29* **28** At the end of three years thou shalt bring forth all the tithe of thine increase the same year, and shalt lay *it* up within thy gates: **29** and the Levite, (because he hath no part nor inheritance with thee,) and the stranger, and the fatherless, and the widow, which *are* within thy gates, shall come, and shall eat and be satisfied; that the Lord thy God may bless thee in all the work of thine hand which thou doest. *24:17-22* **17** Thou shalt not pervert the judgment of the stranger, *nor* of the fatherless; nor take a widow's raiment to pledge: **18** but thou shalt remember that thou wast a bondman in Egypt, and the Lord thy God redeemed thee thence: therefore I command thee to do this thing.

19 When thou cuttest down thine harvest in thy field, and hast forgot a sheaf in the field, thou shalt not go again to fetch it: it shall be for the stranger, for the fatherless, and for the widow: that the Lord thy God may bless thee in all the work of thine hands. **20** When thou beatest thine olive tree, thou shalt not go over the boughs again: it shall be for the stranger, for the fatherless, and for the widow. **21** When thou gatherest the grapes of thy vineyard, thou shalt not glean *it* afterward: it shall be for the stranger, for the fatherless, and for the widow. **22** And thou shalt remember that thou wast a bondman in the land of Egypt: therefore I command thee to do this thing. ***26:12, 13*** **12** When thou hast made an end of tithing all the tithes of thine increase the third year, *which is* the year of tithing, and hast given *it* unto the Levite, the stranger, the fatherless, and the widow, that they may eat within thy gates, and be filled; **13** then thou shalt say before the Lord thy God, I have brought away the hallowed things out of *mine* house, and also have given them unto the Levite, and unto the stranger, to the fatherless, and to the widow, according to all thy commandments which thou hast commanded me: I have not transgressed thy commandments, neither have I forgotten *them*. **27:19** Cursed *be* he that perverteth the judgment of the stranger, fatherless, and widow:

Jeremiah 7:6, 7 -- **6** *if* ye oppress not the stranger, the fatherless, and the widow, and shed not innocent blood in this place, neither walk after other gods to your hurt; **7** then will I cause you to dwell in this place, in the land that I gave to your fathers, for ever and ever.

Zechariah 7:10-12 -- **10** and oppress not the widow, nor the fatherless, the stranger, nor the poor; and let none of you imagine evil against his brother in your heart. **11** But they refused to hearken, and pulled away the shoulder, and stopped their ears, that they should not hear. **12** Yea, they made their hearts *as* an adamant stone, lest they should hear the law, and the words which the Lord of hosts hath sent in his Spirit by the former prophets: therefore came a great wrath from the Lord of hosts.

Malachi 3:5 -- And I will come near to you to judgment; and I will be a swift witness against the sorcerers, and against the adulterers, and against false swearers, and against those that oppress the hireling in *his* wages, the widow, and the fatherless, and that turn aside the stranger *from his right*, and fear not me, saith the Lord of hosts.

CIVIL CODE: Amendment 14 of the U.S. Constitution - All persons born or naturalized in the United States and subject to the jurisdiction thereof, are citizens of the United States and of the State wherein they reside. No State shall make or enforce any law which shall abridge the privileges or immunities of citizens of the United States; nor shall any State deprive any person of life, liberty, or property, without due process of law; nor deny to ANY person within its jurisdiction the equal protection of the laws. Isn't the BLACK the stranger usually?

WIDOWS - *Exodus 22:22-24* -- **22** Ye shall not afflict any widow, or fatherless child. **23** If thou afflict them in any wise, and they cry at all unto me, I will surely hear their cry; **24** and my wrath shall wax hot, and I will kill you with the sword; and your wives shall be widows, and your children fatherless.

Deuteronomy 10:18-he doth execute the judgment of the fatherless and widow, and loveth the stranger, in giving him food and raiment. *14:28, 29* **28** At the end of three years thou shalt bring forth all the tithe of thine increase the same year, and shalt lay *it* up within thy gates: **29** and the Levite, (because he hath no part nor inheritance with thee,) and the stranger, and the fatherless, and the widow, which *are* within thy gates, shall come, and shall eat and be satisfied; that the Lord thy God may bless thee in all the work of thine hand which thou doest. *24:17-22* **17** Thou shalt not pervert the judgment of the stranger, *nor* of the fatherless; nor take a widow's raiment to pledge: **18** but thou shalt remember that thou wast a bondman in Egypt, and the Lord thy God redeemed thee thence: therefore I command thee to do this thing.

19 When thou cuttest down thine harvest in thy field, and hast forgot a sheaf in the field, thou shalt not go again to fetch it: it shall be for the stranger, for the fatherless, and for the widow: that the Lord thy God may bless thee in all the work of thine hands. **20** When thou beatest thine olive tree, thou shalt not go over the boughs again: it shall be for the stranger, for the fatherless, and for the widow. **21** When thou gatherest the grapes of thy vineyard, thou shalt not glean *it* afterward: it shall be for the stranger, for the fatherless, and for the widow. **22** And thou shalt remember that thou wast a bondman in the land of Egypt: therefore I command thee to do this thing. ***25:5-10*** **5** If brethren dwell together, and one of them die, and have no child, the wife of the dead shall not marry without unto a stranger: her husband's brother shall go in unto her, and take her to him to wife, and perform the duty of a husband's brother unto her. **6** And it shall be, *that* the firstborn which she beareth shall succeed in the name of his brother *which is* dead, that his name be not put out of Israel. **7** And if the man like not to take his brother's wife, then let his brother's wife go up to the gate unto the elders, and say, My husband's brother refuseth to raise up unto his brother a name in Israel, he will not perform the duty of my husband's brother. **8** Then the elders of his city shall call him, and speak unto him: and *if* he stand *to it*, and say, I like not to take her; **9** then shall his brother's wife come unto him in the presence of the elders, and loose his shoe from off his foot, and spit in his face, and shall answer and say, So shall it be done unto that man that will not build up his brother's house. **10** And his name shall be called in Israel, The house of him that hath his shoe loosed ***26:12, 13*** **12** When thou hast made an end of tithing all the tithes of thine increase the third year, *which is* the year of tithing, and hast given *it* unto the Levite, the stranger, the fatherless, and the widow, that they may eat within thy gates, and be filled; **13** then thou shalt say before the Lord thy God, I have brought away the hallowed things out of *mine* house, and also have given them unto the Levite, and unto the stranger, to the fatherless, and to the widow, according to all thy commandments which thou hast commanded me: I have not transgressed thy commandments, neither have I forgotten *them*. *27:19* Cursed *be* he that perverteth the judgment of the stranger, fatherless, and widow:

Ruth 4:1-12 -- 1 Then went Boaz up to the gate, and sat him down there: and, behold, the kinsman of whom Boaz spake came by; unto whom he said, Ho, such a one! turn aside, sit down here. And he turned aside, and sat down. 2 And he took ten men of the elders of the city, and said, Sit ye down here. And they sat down. 3 And he said unto the kinsman, Na-o´mi, that is come again out of the country of Moab, selleth a parcel of land, which *was* our brother Elim´elech's: 4 and I thought to advertise thee, saying, Buy *it* before the inhabitants, and before the elders of my people. If thou wilt redeem *it*, redeem *it*: but if thou wilt not redeem *it*, *then* tell me, that I may know: for *there is* none to redeem *it* besides thee; and I *am* after thee. And he said, I will redeem *it*. 5 Then said Boaz, What day thou buyest the field of the hand of Na-o´mi, thou must buy *it* also of Ruth the Moabitess, the wife of the dead, to raise up the name of the dead upon his inheritance. 6 And the kinsman said, I cannot redeem *it* for myself, lest I mar mine own inheritance: redeem thou my right to thyself; for I cannot redeem *it*.

7 Now this *was the manner* in former time in Israel concerning redeeming and concerning changing, for to confirm all things; a man plucked off his shoe, and gave *it* to his neighbor: and this *was* a testimony in Israel. 8 Therefore the kinsman said unto Boaz,

Buy *it* for thee. So he drew off his shoe. **9** And Boaz said unto the elders, and *unto* all the people, Ye *are* witnesses this day, that I have bought all that *was* Elim´elech's, and all that *was* Chil´i-on's and Mahlon's, of the hand of Na-o´mi. **10** Moreover Ruth the Moabitess, the wife of Mahlon, have I purchased to be my wife, to raise up the name of the dead upon his inheritance, that the name of the dead be not cut off from among his brethren, and from the gate of his place: ye *are* witnesses this day. **11** And all the people that *were* in the gate, and the elders, said, *We are* witnesses. The Lord make the woman that is come into thine house like Rachel and like Le´ah, which two did build the house of Israel: and do thou worthily in Eph´ratah, and be famous in Bethlehem: **12** and let thy house be like the house of Pharez, whom Tamar bare unto Judah, of the seed which the Lord shall give thee of this young woman.

Jeremiah 7:6, 7 -- **6** *if* ye oppress not the stranger, the fatherless, and the widow, and shed not innocent blood in this place, neither walk after other gods to your hurt; **7** then will I cause you to dwell in this place, in the land that I gave to your fathers, for ever and ever.

Zechariah 7:10-12 -- **10** and oppress not the widow, nor the fatherless, the stranger, nor the poor; and let none of you imagine evil against his brother in your heart. **11** But they refused to hearken, and pulled away the shoulder, and stopped their ears, that they should not hear. **12** Yea, they made their hearts *as* an adamant stone, lest they should hear the law, and the words which the Lord of hosts hath sent in his Spirit by the former prophets: therefore came a great wrath from the Lord of hosts.

Malachi 3:5 -- And I will come near to you to judgment; and I will be a swift witness against the sorcerers, and against the adulterers, and against false swearers, and against those that oppress the hireling in *his* wages, the widow, and the fatherless, and that turn aside the stranger *from his right*, and fear not me, saith the Lord of hosts.

Mark 12:38-40 Jesus Denounces the Scribes

(Matthew 23.1-36;Luke 11.37-54;20.45-47)

38 And he said unto them in his doctrine, Beware of the scribes, which love to go in long clothing, and *love* salutations in the market places, **39** and the chief seats in the synagogues, and the uppermost rooms at feasts: **40** which devour widows' houses, and for a pretense make long prayers: these shall receive greater damnation.

Acts 6:1-3 **1** And in those days, when the number of the disciples was multiplied, there arose a murmuring of the Grecians against the Hebrews, because their widows were neglected in the daily ministration. **2** Then the twelve called the multitude of the disciples *unto them*, and said, It is not reason that we should leave the word of God, and serve tables. **3** Wherefore, brethren, look ye out among you seven men of honest report, full of the Holy Ghost and wisdom, whom we may appoint over this business.

1 Timothy 5:16 If any man or woman that believeth have widows, let them relieve them, and let not the church be charged; that it may relieve them that are widows indeed.

CIVIL CODE: According to **5 U.S.C. §8442 Rights of a widow or widower,** the WIDOW receives or is entitled to an ***annuity*** which is calculated, the amount paid to WIDOW is regulated by The Office, along with several other factors which increase or take away from the WIDOW's annuities.

WILD ANIMALS - ***Exodus 23:11*** but the seventh *year* thou shalt let it rest and lie still; that the poor of thy people may eat: and what they leave the beasts of the field shall eat. In like manner thou shalt deal with thy vineyard, *and* with thy oliveyard.

Leviticus 23:5-7 **5** That which groweth of its own accord of thy harvest thou shalt not reap, neither gather the grapes of thy vine undressed: *for* it is a year of rest unto the land. **6** And the sabbath of the land shall be meat for you; for thee, and for thy servant, and for thy maid, and for thy hired servant, and for thy stranger that sojourneth with thee, **7** and for thy cattle, and for the beast that *are* in thy land, shall all the increase thereof be meat.

CIVIL CODE: The Animal Welfare Act (1966) is enforced by the United States Department of Agriculture and regulates the usage of animals for research, sale, testing, transportation, and public display.

16 U.S.C. CONSERVATION covers the endangered and protection of wild animal breeds while promoting commerce.

36 C.F.R. §327.11 – Control of animals. (g) Wild or exotic pets and animals or any pets displaying vicious or aggressive behavior or otherwise posing a threat to public safety or deemed a public nuisance, are prohibited from project lands and waters unless authorized by the District Commander, and are subject to removal in accordance with Federal, state, and local laws.

Local Governments also have their own particular viewpoints on when hunting season may or may not be. You may be unable to have a certain breed of animal domesticated. You may be unable to stop the bear rummaging through your trash without the approval of your local government. In essence, check with your local laws before befriending that elusive endangered squirrel you've mistaken for squirrels that you always see.

TORTS

ASSAULT – *Exodus 21:18, 19* **18** And if men strive together, and one smite another with a stone, or with *his* fist, and he die not, but keepeth *his* bed: **19** if he rise again, and walk abroad upon his staff, then shall he that smote *him* be quit: only he shall pay *for* the loss of his time, and shall cause *him* to be thoroughly healed.

TORT LAW: ASSAULT, in COMMON LAW, is an intentional or transferrable TORT with general or specific intent of harmful or offensive contact with another. In an assault, it does not need to involve the unwanted physical contact but the ANTICIPATION of such contact. A threat is just as bad as the overt act itself in law. TORTS are determined by the intent, act, result, and causation.

COMPENSATION – *Exodus 21:18, 19, 32, 35, 36, 22:7-15*
18 And if men strive together, and one smite another with a stone, or with *his* fist, and he die not, but keepeth *his* bed: **19** if he rise again, and walk abroad upon his staff, then shall he that smote *him* be quit: only he shall pay *for* the loss of his time, and shall cause *him* to be thoroughly healed. **32** If the ox shall push a manservant or a maidservant; he shall give unto their master thirty shekels of silver, and the ox shall be stoned. **35, 36** And if one man's ox hurt another's that he die; then they shall sell the live ox, and divide the money of it; and the dead *ox* also they shall divide. **36** Or if it be known that the ox hath used to push in time past, and his owner hath not kept him in; he shall surely pay ox for ox; and the dead shall be his own. ***22:7-15***
7 If a man shall deliver unto his neighbor money or stuff to keep, and it be stolen out of the man's house; if the thief be found, let him pay double. **8** If the thief be not found, then the master of the house shall be brought unto the judges, *to see* whether he have put his hand unto his neighbor's goods.

9 For all manner of trespass, *whether it be* for ox, for ass, for sheep, for raiment, *or* for any manner of lost thing, which *another* challengeth to be his, the cause of both parties shall come before the judges; *and* whom the judges shall condemn, he shall pay double unto his neighbor.

10 If a man deliver unto his neighbor an ass, or an ox, or a sheep, or any beast, to keep; and it die, or be hurt, or driven away, no man seeing *it*: **11** *then* shall an oath of the Lord be between them both, that he hath not put his hand unto his neighbor's goods; and the owner of it shall accept *thereof*, and he shall not make *it* good. **12** And if it be stolen from him, he shall make restitution unto the owner thereof. **13** If it be torn in pieces, *then* let him bring it *for* witness, *and* he shall not make good that which was torn.

14 And if a man borrow *aught* of his neighbor, and it be hurt, or die, the owner thereof *being* not with it, he shall surely make *it* good. **15** *But* if the owner thereof *be* with it, he shall not make *it* good: if it *be* a hired *thing*, it came for his hire.

CIVIL COMPENSATION: In ASSAULT, the claimant could be awarded **nominal damage**, in which no harm was applied, **compensatory damages**, the claimant gets back what he had before the assault, **injunction**, stopping repeated behavior, or **aggravated damages**, if someone's dignity is in question.

DAMAGE BY ANIMALS – *Exodus 21:32* If the ox shall push a manservant or a maidservant; he shall give unto their master thirty shekels of silver, and the ox shall be stoned.

CIVIL CODE: The action of any DAMAGE BY ANIMALS will result in lawsuits, if not solved by that pet's owner, the pet owner's insurance company, and/or the park management, depending on your jurisdictional procedures. If hurt or a neighbor, legally animal attacks can fall under

PERSONAL INJURY, which is covered in **TORTS - COMPENSATION - CIVIL COMPENSATION.**

DAMAGE BY FIRE - *Exodus 22:6* If fire break out, and catch in thorns, so that the stacks of corn, or the standing corn, or the field, be consumed *therewith;* he that kindled the fire shall surely make restitution.

TORT LAW: The same as Biblically when you are to make right by restitution, an ULTRAHAZARDOUS ACTIVITY in COMMON LAW of TORTS, a person or TORTFEASOR engaged in such activity that can be inherently hazardous, such as fire, explosives, is strictly liable for the injuries sustained to that person. Fires aren't always one's fault entirely. Vicarious liability, which is a secondary liability, stemming from *respondeat superior,* the responsibility of the superior for the acts of their subordinate, or in other words, places the responsibility of the damage to the supervisor in charge of the day to day activities.

INJURY TO ANIMALS - *Exodus 21:33-36* **33** And if a man shall open a pit, or if a man shall dig a pit, and not cover it, and an ox or an ass fall therein; **34** the owner of the pit shall make *it* good, *and* give money unto the owner of them; and the dead *beast* shall be his.

35 And if one man's ox hurt another's that he die; then they shall sell the live ox, and divide the money of it; and the dead *ox* also they shall divide. **36** Or if it be known that the ox hath used to push in time past, and his owner hath not kept him in; he shall surely pay ox for ox; and the dead shall be his own.

Leviticus 24:18-21 **18** And he that killeth a beast shall make it good; beast for beast. **19** And if a man cause a blemish in his neighbor; as he hath done, so shall it be done to him; **20** breach for breach, eye for eye, tooth for tooth: as he hath caused a blemish in a man, so shall it be done to him *again*. **21** And he that killeth a beast, he shall restore it: and he that killeth a man, he shall be put to death.

TORT LAW: INJURY TO ANIMALS would be classified as an **INTENTIONAL TORT**, sort of as a form of **ASSAULT** or **BATTERY**, which again, are categorically different, also depending on the nature of the case. Some lawyers or scholars may argue the legal obligation being the **DUTY OF CARE**, holding an individual to uphold a standard of reasonable care to avoid careless acts that could foreseeably harm others, and be seen as negligent.

LOSS OF BORROWED PROPERTY – ***Exodus 22:14, 15*** **14** And if a man borrow *aught* of his neighbor, and it be hurt, or die, the owner thereof *being* not with it, he shall surely make *it* good. **15** *But* if the owner thereof *be* with it, he shall not make *it* good: if it *be* a hired *thing*, it came for his hire.

TORT LAW: LOSS OF BORROWED PROPERTY is classified as a **NEGLIGENT TORT**; the defendant **BREACHED** a duty owed. The defendant owed a duty to the plaintiff. The defendant has **STRICT LIABILITY** to return what is due to the plaintiff.

PERSONAL INJURY – ***Leviticus 24:19, 20*** **19** And if a man cause a blemish in his neighbor; as he hath done, so shall it be done to him; **20** breach for breach, eye for eye, tooth for tooth: as he hath caused a blemish in a man, so shall it be done to him *again*.

TORT LAW: ANOTHER NEGLIGENT TORT, PERSONAL INJURY can happen if the defendant breached their duty and the plaintiff can prove due to the defendant's breach of duty his injuries were sustained. PERSONAL INJURIES may be intentional. BATTERY and ASSAULT are examples of an INTENTIONAL TORT in PERSONAL INJURY. According to the CRS Reports from Congress, another INTENTIONAL TORT can be an INTENTIONAL INFLICTION OF EMOTIONAL DISTRESS (IIED), when a tortfeasor engages in extreme conduct causing another person severe mental anguish. Defamation, an INTENTIONAL TORT, can be injurious to a person's reputation.

RIGHTS OF STRANGERS – *Exodus 12:49* **One law shall be to him that is homeborn, and unto the stranger that sojourneth among you.**

You have reached the end of **THE LAW OF THE LAND, LAWS OF THE BIBLE**

THANK YOU FOR READING THIS, NOW STRENGTHEN YOUR RELATIONSHIP WITH GOD THE LORD BY FOLLOWING THE LAWS, STATUES, AND COMMANDMENTS, KEEPING HIS COVENANT.

BE WELL.

Kevin James

kevinjameslaw.wordpress.com

LAW OF THE LAND, LAWS OF THE BIBLE

www.ingramcontent.com/pod-product-compliance
Lightning Source LLC
Chambersburg PA
CBHW050047230526
45470CB00004B/1428